THE AMERICAN AUTOMOBILE INDUSTRY

THE EVOLUTION OF AMERICAN BUSINESS: INDUSTRIES, INSTITUTIONS, AND ENTREPRENEURS

THE AMERICAN AUTOMOBILE INDUSTRY

JOHN B. RAE

Twayne Publishers

THE AMERICAN AUTOMOBILE INDUSTRY

THE EVOLUTION OF AMERICAN BUSINESS:
INDUSTRIES, INSTITUTIONS, AND ENTREPRENEURS

Copyright © 1984 by G. K. Hall & Company
All Rights Reserved
Published by Twayne Publishers
A Division of G. K. Hall & Company
70 Lincoln Street
Boston, Massachusetts 02111

Book production by Marne B. Sultz
Book design by Barbara Anderson

Typeset in 10 point Times Roman
with Univers display type
by Compset, Inc., Beverly, Massachusetts

Printed on permanent/durable
acid-free paper and bound in
the United States of America

Library of Congress Cataloging in Publication Data

Rae, John Bell, 1911-
   The American automobile industry.

   (The Evolution of American business : industries,
institutions, and entrepreneurs)
   Bibliography: p. 189
   Includes index.
   1. Automobile industry and trade—United States—
History. I. Title. II. Series: Evolution of American
business.
HD9710.U52R297   1984   338.4′76292′0973   84-6744
ISBN 0-8057-9803-X (Hardcover)
ISBN 0-8057-9808-0 (Paperback)

CONTENTS

PREFACE

This book is the product of some thirty years of studying the history of that very interesting phenomenon, the motor vehicle industry of the United States, with side trips into its counterparts in the United Kingdom and Japan. It has been a rewarding enterprise in terms of enjoyment and satisfaction, with some occasional unexpected consequences. I have been considered an antique car enthusiast, which I am not, and I have been consulted on the purchase of current cars, which I am no better qualified to advise on than any other layman. My interest has been in the growth and organization of the industry: its leadership, the evolution of its methods for manufacturing and marketing motor vehicles, and its responses to changing conditions.

I have attempted to provide here a concise history of the industry with emphasis on what I judge to be the most important features of its story and its most significant contributions to the development of the motor vehicle worldwide. The features of the story include the lapses as well as the successes. The major contributions, as will appear in the text, are the technique of mass production and marketing and the organization of large-scale business enterprise. Personalities have played a large part in the development of the industry as entrepreneurs and organizers, salesmen, and technicians. The principal figures are identified in the book, with my estimate of their roles in the automobile industry. In addition, there is an obvious continuous thread running through the history of the industry, namely, the trend to concentration and oligopoly that became noticeable as early as the first decade of the twentieth century. This trend appeared first in the United States, but it has been duplicated in virtually every motor vehicle producing country.

The history of the American motor vehicle industry falls into four primary stages. First, there is the period of origin and growth, which is covered in chapters 2 through 5 (chapter 1 is a preliminary view of the origin and introduction of the self-propelled highway vehicle). Then there is the era, approximately from 1920 to 1960, when the United States industry dominated the world automotive scene. Chapters 6 through 9 treat this era, including the response of the industry to the depression years of the 1930s, its performance in World War II, and the emergence of the UAW. Third is the effect on the industry of problems such as government regulation, foreign competition, and the need for energy conservation. These are the subject matter of chapters 10 through 12. The two concluding chapters describe the international operations of the American motor vehicle industry and give an analysis of its position as it entered the decade of the 1980s.

In studying the motor vehicle industry over this span of years I have accumulated a far greater debt for advice and assistance than I can possibly acknowledge. My research has been supported at various times by the American Philosophical Society, the Earhart Foundation, the Motor Vehicle Manufacturers Association, the National Science Foundation, Nissan Motor Corporation in U.S.A., the Sloan Research Fund of the School of Industrial Management at the Massachusetts Institute of Technology, and the Social Science Research Council.

The list of people who have helped me is now far too long to be included here. Whether I tried to enumerate them all or to be selective, I should undoubtedly leave out some who ought to be included. Readers who may be interested are referred to the introductions and prefaces to my previous works on the motor vehicle industry. For this volume I want to express my gratitude to my daughter Helen for patiently typing my drafts and to Mrs. Barbara Graham of Harvey Mudd College, who typed the final copy equally patiently. Some of the early chapters were typed by Mrs. Diane Sanchez, also of Harvey Mudd College. I am as usual indebted to my wife, Florence, for working with me on compiling the index.

JOHN B. RAE

Harvey Mudd College

CHARTS AND TABLES

CHRONOLOGY

1893   First Duryea car runs in Springfield, Massachusetts.

1895   Selden patent issued.

1896   Henry Ford's first car runs in Detroit.

1897   Regular commercial production of motor vehicles begun by Motor Carriage Department of Columbia Bicycle Co. in Hartford, Connecticut and Winton Motor Carriage Company of Cleveland, Ohio.

1899   Olds Motor Works established.

1901   Curved-dash Oldsmobile introduced.

1903   Ford Motor Company founded. Selden patent suit begun.

1908   Model T Ford introduced. W. C. Durant organizes General Motors Company. Cadillac demonstration of interchangeability at Brooklands test track, London.

1910   General Motors crisis. Bankers trust assumes control.

1911   Selden patent suit decided: valid but not infringed.

1912   Electric starter introduced by Cadillac.

1913   Moving assembly line production begun by Ford Motor Company.

1914   Ford Motor Company institutes Five-Dollar Day.

1915   Agreement for cross-licensing of patents adopted.

1916   Durant resumes control of General Motors with Du Pont support.

1921   Federal Highway Act passed, providing for primary national routes. Durant dropped from General Motors.

1923   Alfred P. Sloan becomes president of General Motors.

1925   Chrysler Corporation created from Maxwell Motor Company.

<u>**1927**</u>   Model T Ford discontinued.

1935   United Automobile Workers organized.

1937   General Motors accepts UAW as bargaining agent.

1941   Nonmilitary production of motor vehicles suspended.

1945   Civilian production resumes. Henry Ford II becomes president of Ford Motor Company.

1946   Kaiser-Frazer Corporation begins motor vehicle production.

1953   Kaiser-Frazer takes over Willys-Overland.

1954   Hudson and Nash merge as American Motors. Packard and Studebaker merge as Studebaker-Packard.

1955   Dealers Day in Court Act passed.

1956   Ford Motor Company stock put on public sale. Interstate Highway Act passed.

1964   Studebaker terminates motor vehicle production.

1965   Motor Vehicle Air Pollution Control Act passed.

1966   National Traffic and Highway Safety Act passed.

1973–1974   October–March, Arab oil embargo.

1977   American Motors agreement with Renault.

1978   Volkswagen begins manufacturing in the United States.

1979   Second gasoline crisis; consumers turned to small cars.

1980   Chrysler threatened with bankruptcy; $1.5 billion loan guaranteed by United States and Canadian governments.

CHAPTER ONE
Prelude

It has been called "this quintessential American industry," and it seems certain that if a poll were taken to determine what people regarded as the most typically American industry, the automobile industry would easily lead the field. A century ago it would have been steel, or railroads, or oil, and in the next century it may be something else, but for the twentieth century it would be difficult to challenge the primacy of motor vehicle manufacturing. Yet, as with railroads and steel, the automobile industry, also described as being "as representative of twentieth century America as commerce was of the Phoenicians," did not originate in the United States. (Both quotations are from the *New York Times Magazine,* 14 September 1980.)

The motor vehicle came into history in response to a need felt through centuries, indeed millennia: to find an efficient and economical way of travel by road. Road systems have existed since the beginning of civilization, some of them impressive. The Roman roads are well known; they provided Western Europe with its only adequate highway system for centuries after the fall of Rome itself. The Royal Road of ancient Persia could be called the first known express highway, and the Inca Empire had a well-engineered road network (for animal and foot traffic only; the Incas had no wheeled vehicles). The growth of commerce and industry produced a revival of highway building in Western Europe in the eighteenth and early nineteenth centuries, and this was reflected in an era of turnpike construction in the United States, running into the 1830s.

There was no lack of knowledge about how to build good roads, or of engineering skill to do it. The difficulty was in the vehicles. As long as animal power was the only way to move carriages and wagons, movement by road was slow and expensive. At the beginning of the nineteenth century the cost of moving goods thirty miles inland by road in the United States was as great as the cost of carrying the same goods across the Atlantic. Later, when the

1

United States government began to grant land to aid in the construction of railroads, the outer limits within which the railroads could select land were initially set as fifteen sections, or fifteen miles, on either side of the line, because this was regarded as the economical limit of wagon transportation.

Movement by water was cheaper and faster than movement by road, for both freight and passengers, and it was used in preference to land transport whenever possible. The superiority of water transportation led to extensive river improvement and canal building in Western Europe in the eighteenth and early nineteenth centuries, contemporary with the surge in highway construction. Again this activity was duplicated in the United States, climaxed by the completion of the Erie Canal in 1825, an event that reduced the cost of shipping freight between New York City and Buffalo by ninety percent. But navigable rivers are not found everywhere, and canals have definite limits to where they can be economically located. The United States had magnificent interior waterways in the Great Lakes and the Mississippi River system, but it also had vast overland distances that the lakes and the rivers could not serve. Moreover, the Appalachian barrier separated these waterways from the Atlantic seaboard, and since the expansion of the country was moving from east to west, the problem of transportation by land remained.

Then came the railroad. As a means of carrying freight and passengers it was so superior to earlier methods of land transportation that roads went into a decline until close to the end of the nineteenth century, both in the United States and Europe. Highway traffic was mainly short-distance so that maintenance of roads was left largely in the hands of local authorities; only in France was there a national highway system of good quality roads. Yet movement by road remained important; it was almost always the beginning and the end of rail or water trips, and rail lines (including interurbans, street railways, and rapid transit systems) could not serve all transportation needs. Above all, they could not provide individualized mobility. People who had to depend on rail transport could not travel at their own convenience. They were subject to fixed schedules, to long stopovers between scheduled trains, and, as accounts of travel in the late nineteenth and early twentieth centuries testify, to uncooperative ticket agents and surly train crews. There was room, therefore, for a technology of road transportation which would permit free movement of people and goods.

Early Self-Propelled Road Vehicles

A self-propelled vehicle was predicted by Roger Bacon and thought of by Leonardo da Vinci, but, according to extant records, the first to construct one was a French artillery officer, Nicholas Joseph Cugnot. He built and ran a three-wheeled, steam-powered vehicle in 1769, with the idea that it could be used to pull cannon. His engine was ingeniously designed for such an early stage in the use of steam power, but the vehicle proved to be slow and awkward, and Cugnot's idea went no farther. In 1801 the Englishman Richard Trevithick built a steam locomotive intended for road use, but it proved too heavy for the roads of the time. Four years later Oliver Evans, an American whose genius has never been fully appreciated, ran a steam-driven contraption in Philadelphia called the *Orukter Amphibolos* (digger that works both ways). It was actually a dredge for use in Philadelphia harbor, but Evans put it on wheels and drove it through the streets to demonstrate that steam propulsion was practical. He also submitted a proposal to the directors of the Philadelphia and Lancaster Turnpike for the use of "steam waggons" on their highway, accompanied by calculations of the savings in time and cost over horse-drawn vehicles. Unfortunately the directors missed their chance for immortality by rejecting the proposal.

The subsequent development of steam locomotion produced some interesting British experiments with steam omnibuses during the middle decades of the nineteenth century. They were clumsy vehicles, given to shooting out soot and sparks and occasionally to boiler explosions, but in these respects they were no worse than the railway locomotives and steamboats of the same period. Some of them maintained regular schedules for a few years. They never realized their full potential or had a chance to create an industry, because they were driven off the roads by the enmity of stage coach operators and later the railways, who with considerable prescience saw in self-propelled road vehicles a potential threat to their then lucrative passenger traffic. The railway companies were the primary influence behind the Locomotives on Highways Act of 1867, which required self-propelled vehicles on a public highway to be limited to four miles an hour and to be preceded by a man on foot carrying a red flag. This law remained in effect until 1896. Herbert Austin, one of the great British automotive pioneers, later claimed that the Red Flag law had no effect on the growth of the British automobile industry because there were no self-propelled vehicles capable of going over four miles an hour before the 1890s. The claim may be valid as far as gasoline-powered cars are concerned, but the Red Flag law must have had an adverse effect on the development of steam automobiles. The omnibus experiments do not appear to have been imitated in other countries. In the United States Sylvester Roper of Roxbury, Massachusetts, built ten experimental steam cars between 1859 and 1895, but never carried his work into commercial production.

There was also a place in the nineteenth-century economy for a power plant with less bulk and cost than a steam engine, for small industrial establishments that did not need the high power output at which a steam engine runs most efficiently. Such a power plant would be adaptable for a road vehicle. A number of experiments were made with internal combustion, without success until a Belgian named Etienne Lenoir produced a two-cycle motor using coal gas as fuel. He put it on a vehicle, which he drove in Paris in 1862, but then it was abandoned. A number of Lenoir engines were used as stationary power plants, but they proved to be noisy and inefficient. A Viennese named Siegfried Markus has been credited with building and operating one or more motor vehicles in the mid-1870s. It is claimed that his work was stopped because neighbors complained of the noise, but there is no clear proof that Markus actually did build an operable vehicle. If he did, it was a number of years later.

The noisiness of these early internal combustion engines was finally solved in 1878, when a German business man named Nicholas Otto produced a gas engine using the now familiar four-stroke cycle. The four-cycle theory had been described some years earlier by a French engineer, Beau de Rochas, but he never went from theory to practice.

The "silent Otto" was highly successful as a stationary power plant, but an engine using coal gas for fuel had obvious limitations as a power plant for a vehicle. However, by this time petroleum was becoming plentiful and offered a solution. An American, George Brayton, exhibited a two-cycle engine at the Centennial Exhibition in Philadelphia in 1876. It was used briefly on a street railway in Rhode Island, and to some extent as a stationary engine. However, the gasoline automobile was not to be an American invention. That distinction very definitely goes to Germany. Karl Benz, who had experience with railway locomotives, and Gottlieb Daimler, who had been a mechanic with the firm of Otto and Langen, both produced workable gasoline vehicles in 1885 and continued to do so—as well as spending the rest of their lives in a bitter dispute about which one did it first.

In spite of their priority, neither Daimler nor Benz made cars in any significant numbers for many years; indeed their companies did not get into large scale production until they were merged in 1925 after both their founders had died. Daimler's great contribution was to recognize that an internal combustion engine for a motor vehicle had to operate at high speed, at least 1,000 rpm, and set out to design and build such an engine. Benz introduced spark ignition. The first genuine automobile industry grew up in France, where Armand Peugeot in 1889 and the woodworking concern of Panhard and Levassor in 1890 began to build motor vehicles commercially, using the Daimler engine under license. They also coined the term "automobile." France's good roads and lack of restrictive legislation contributed much to giving the country this lead in founding a new industry.

The American Highway Revival

In the last third of the nineteenth century inland transportation in the United States was dominated by the railroads. With limited exceptions, travel over any considerable distance and movement of freight in any substantial quantity either went by rail or not at all. There was still heavy water traffic on the Great Lakes and a considerable amount of coastwise shipping, but these were of value only to limited areas. Railroad competition had ended the great days of Mississippi steamboating, and only a few canals remained in operation. For the most part communities or individuals without ready access to rail transportation were virtually isolated. Hamlin Garland's *Son of the Middle Border* has a poignant description of the terrible loneliness of farm life in remote areas, especially for the women.

Better roads would help to alleviate this situation, but there were stronger pressures at work. The story of the Grangers, the Farmers' Alliances, and the Populists is a familiar one in American history. The railroad companies had great power, and they were accused of using it arbitrarily and inequitably. The political attempts at regulation before the twentieth century were ineffective, largely because they dealt with surface manifestations rather than seeking the heart of the problem, and they are not part of the background of the automobile industry in any case. Another way to weaken the power of the railroads was to encourage alternative methods of transportation, and for this reason there was growing agitation for improved "farm-to-market" roads. This agitation had some results, but little before the turn of the century. Roads might be improved, but transportation over them with horse-drawn vehicles was still slow and cumbersome.

A more potent force in improving roads and in other ways helping to usher in the era of the automobile was the sudden popularity of the bicycle in the 1880s and 1890s. The bicycle craze began when J. F. Starley invented the "safety bicycle"—the modern bicycle, in place of the high-wheeled velocipede—in Coventry, England, in 1885. Even before that bicycling had been growing in popularity. In 1878 Albert A. Pope began to manufacture bicycles in Hartford, Connecticut, with the trade name of Columbia, and two years later a League of American Wheelmen was organized. Thousands of Americans of both sexes and all ages poured out on to their country's highways and discovered that those highways left much to be desired. The cyclists provided the greatest driving force behind the Good Roads movement until the motorists took over in the early years of the twentieth century.

The bicycle set the stage for the automobile in a more direct way through the development of many techniques that were transferred to motor vehicle manufacture. Bicycle makers learned to use tubular steel framing, wire wheels, ball and roller bearings, the differential axle, and variable speed transmissions. Perhaps most important of all, the bicycle was responsible for the invention of the pneumatic tire by Dr. J. B. Dunlop in 1888. The relationship is vividly illustrated in the bicycle makers who became prominent in automobile manufacturing: Pope, Winton, Rambler, Peerless, Thomas, Pierce in the United States; Morris, Rover (Starley's company), Humber, Hillman in the United Kingdom; Opel in Germany. Hiram Percy Maxim, one of the pioneers of American automobile manufacturing, put it this way:

> It has been the habit to give the gasoline engine all the credit for bringing the automobile—in my opinion this is the wrong explanation. We could have built steam vehicles in 1880, or indeed in 1870, but we did not. We waited until 1895.
>
> The reason why we did not build road vehicles before this, in my opinion, was because the bicycle had not yet come in numbers and had not directed men's minds to the possibilities of independent long distance travel over the ordinary highway. We thought the railroad was good enough. The bicycle created a new demand which it was beyond the ability of the railroad to supply. Then it came about that the bicycles could not satisfy the demand which it had created. A mechanically-propelled vehicle was wanted instead of a foot-propelled one, and we know now that the automobile was the answer. (Maxim, 4)

Background for the American Automobile

Maxim's explanation is sound as far as it goes, but it does not go far enough. There had to be factors in the economic and social condition of the United States to account for the introduction of the motor vehicle at a particular period of time—specifically the 1890s—and for the course that the American automobile industry took once it had been established. The same consideration applies to Europe. The technology was available. Experiments with horseless carriages were going on throughout the western world, but in each country the economic and social conditions were sufficiently different to give its automobile industry a distinctive character of its own.

For the United States the last third of the nineteenth century was a period of rapid industrial growth and physical expansion. In that time the nation grew to be the world's leading industrial producer. Population rose from just over thirty million at the start of the Civil War until it was pressing the 100 million mark by the end of the century. At the time of the Civil War the area between the Missouri River and the Sierra Nevada was largely unsettled; after the census of 1890 the Census Bureau was able to report that there was no longer any unbroken frontier line. In the same period this area was spanned by four railroad lines going all the way to the Pacific and penetrated by several others.

The economic expansion was occasionally interrupted, with major depressions in 1873 and 1893, but it always recovered after a year or two and invariably increased in scale. When the twentieth century arrived the United States was a wealthy country, with an overall standard of living higher than was to be found anywhere else. Some groups and some areas did not share in this prosperity, but that is true of any society. In general, the United States offered a large, steadily expanding market, with wealth and income well enough distributed so that an unusually high proportion of the population represented potential customers for an entrepreneur with an attractive idea.

Americans have customarily been regarded as a mobile people—restless might be a more accurate term. Whether they were actually more mobile by nature than anyone else or whether, with an almost empty continent before them, they simply had more opportunity is an open question. The Westward Movement is a basic theme in American history. Achieving greater mobility has been a stimulus to invention, an important economic problem, and a recurrent political issue from the time of Albert Gallatin's Report on Roads and Canals in 1804 through the internal improvements controversies of the pre–Civil War period to the question of support for railroad expansion and later of railroad regulation, and eventually to the agitation for highway improvement. The list of American inventions and innovations in transportation is a long one. It includes the steamboat, plus ingenious adaptations to the special conditions of the Mississippi and its tributaries; the Conestoga wagon and the Concord coach, both representing a maximum of efficiency for horse-drawn road transport; innumerable improvements in railroading, such as sleeping cars, swivel trucks, refrigerator cars, air brakes, and automatic couplers. Not included, interestingly in view of what was to happen, were the internal combustion engine or a mechanically-propelled road vehicle (Evans's *Orukter* cannot be counted because it was a one-shot operation with no visible influence on subsequent developments).

But American technology has progressed as much by adapting and improving the ideas of others as it has by original invention. As far as the horseless carriage was concerned, the United States was ready for it, economically, socially, and technologically, as the end of the century approached, so that it made no difference where it was actually invented. By the latter part of the 1890s the country was stable and prosperous and its future outlook was promising. The depression of 1893 had come to an end, and the defeat of William Jennings Bryan assured a predominantly middle-class, business-oriented society of a stable currency. At the same time, the long price deflation that followed the Civil War halted and an upswing began, partly because of an expansion in the currency base resulting from new gold discoveries in South Africa and the Yukon.

The description of American society as basically middle class applies even though about two thirds of the population of the United States still lived on farms or in small towns. Nearly all Americans accepted the prevalent middle-class outlook and values, which stressed individual self-reliance and private enterprise. Agrarian discontent became a powerful political force, and in this same period organized labor grew in strength, but neither movement displayed any appreciable desire for revolutionary change in the American political or economic structure. They simply wanted reforms within the existing system, and the two major reforms that ushered in the last decade of the century, the Interstate Commerce Act of 1887 and the Sherman Antitrust Act of 1890, owed more to pressure from small-scale, middle-class business men than from farm or labor groups. Neither was effective at the time, but the same middle-class spirit of reform would later create progressivism and stimulate legal action on control of trusts and interstate commerce, in expectation of influencing American society in the direction of greater democracy and individual opportunity.

The causes of discontent had subsided by the last half of the 1890s. Prices were rising and the economy was flourishing. The national mood was optimistic, reinforced by the easy victory in the Spanish-American War, admittedly against pathetically weak opposition. People were talking again about "Manifest Destiny." This atmosphere was not really necessary to reinforce the general American willingness to accept new technologies, but it undoubtedly helped to strengthen a belief that great new opportunities were opening up— and the novelty called the horseless carriage was one of them.

Among the limited accomplishments of the agitation to improve rural roads was the Federal government's 1893 creation of an Office of Road Inquiry, the precursor of the present Federal Highway Administration, in the Department of Agriculture. Then, as now, urban transportation also had its problems and needs. The big metropolises were spreading out, with the aid of commuter railroads, interurbans, and trolley lines, but they still had to have a heavy volume of road traffic. In the large cities there were complaints about street congestion caused by slow-moving carts and wagons, to say nothing of the pollution caused by the many horses needed to pull those vehicles. Small cities were less able to use rail transport because of the heavy capital investment required, but they also had their traffic problems. Improving road and street surfaces was one way to expedite movement and to reduce the cost of haulage; the first stretch of concrete pavement in the United States was laid in Bellefontaine, Ohio, in 1893.

To repeat, conditions were ripe for an innovation in highway transportation, and there was little doubt about what it would be. Horseless carriages were beginning to appear on American roads in small numbers. Most, especially the gasoline-powered variety, were crude and inefficient, and their production scarcely qualified as an industry (the census of 1900 put motor vehicle manufacturing under "Miscellaneous Manufactures") but they were greeted with what now looks like prophetic optimism. Thomas A. Edison states confidently in 1895 that it was only a question of time before all the carriages and trucks in every large city would be motor-driven. *Scientific American* was less sanguine. It saw a place for motor vehicles, but warned its readers that the horse would never be dethroned and that the horseless vehicle would never have anything but a secondary place. Most Americans fell somewhere between these two positions but generally hoped that Edison was right.

The realization of these hopes rested with perhaps a dozen individuals who were sufficiently intrigued by the potentialities of the horseless carriage to venture into design and production. The shape that the American automobile industry would take depended, first, on their ability to design and build operable vehicles so as to convince the public that the motor car really had a future. Still more, the shape of the industry would be determined by these individuals' concepts for use of the automobile. Would it be a luxury item, or something to be used for sport—most of the publicity given to motor carriages at this time came from racing—or did it have wider prospects?

CHAPTER TWO
The Origins

The first workable gasoline-powered road vehicles were built in Germany in 1885 by Karl Benz and Gottlieb Daimler, and commercial manufacture of motor vehicles was well established in France in the mid-1890s, when the horseless carriage was still an experimental curiosity in the United States. Britain in 1897 witnessed an ambitious but unsuccessful attempt to create an automotive monopoly through control of patents, an effort made just a year after the repeal of the Locomotives on Highways Act, or "Red Flag Law."

At that time (1897) rudiments of an American automobile industry were faintly discernible; what little had been done is well described as wrestling with mechanical problems already solved in Europe. There was, in fact, an astonishing and unaccountable gap in the transmission of technical knowledge. As late as 1895, when Hiram Percy Maxim undertook to build a self-propelled road vehicle, he knew nothing of the progress already made in Europe. He was an 1892 graduate of M.I.T. and he knew about the Otto four-cycle gas engine, but he did not know if gasoline could be exploded in a cylinder and had to find out by experimenting in the yard of the American Projectile Company in Lynn, Massachusetts, using empty shell cases and a small quantity of gasoline (he was aware that it would explode; his problem was whether it could be exploded under controlled conditions). The progress made in Europe was known in the United States—at least by a few. A handful of wealthy Americans imported European automobiles, and William Steinway, the piano manufacturer, actually secured a license about 1890 to build Daimler engines in the United States. This venture did not succeed, but Steinway was for a time the American distributor for Daimler cars.

11

The American Pioneers

Charles and Frank Duryea, two brothers with mechanical skill and experience in repairing bicycles, built the first successful American gasoline automobile in Springfield, Massachusetts, in 1893, based on ideas they had got from descriptions of Benz's car in *Scientific American.* They then attempted to go into production with backing from a group of Springfield businessmen and built thirteen cars in the next five years. They received some favorable publicity when one of their cars won a race sponsored by the *Chicago Times Herald* in 1895, a fifty-five mile run through icy streets that only one other entrant, a Benz, finished; and another came in first in the London-Brighton road rally that celebrated the repeal of Britain's Red Flag Law. However, the company was dissolved when the Duryeas quarreled over the matter of credit for the first car. (Their sister, Mrs. Atina Duryea Nielson, told the author that Charles had the original idea but "younger brother" Frank was responsible for building a vehicle that would run.)

Next came Elwood Haynes, an engineer who as superintendent of the Indiana Natural Gas and Oil Company had to do a good deal of traveling by road and decided that it would be easier with a mechanically-powered vehicle. He

The Duryea Car, 1893.
Courtesy of the Motor Vehicle Manufacturers Association

built his first car in Kokomo, Indiana, in 1894, with the help of two brothers, Edgar and Elmer Apperson, who operated a machine shop in Kokomo. Haynes and the Appersons succeeded four years later in achieving commercial production of an automobile called the Haynes-Apperson, but they later separated in a dispute over credit for the 1894 car (a chronic problem among automotive pioneers) and formed their own companies, which survived into the 1920s but were never large-scale producers. After Haynes came Maxim, whose experiments with shell cases and gasoline convinced him that a gasoline driven vehicle would work. It is an interesting example of the transfer of technology that Maxim's knowledge of and experience with explosives led him to the gasoline engine, and some years later his experience with gasoline engines led to his invention of the Maxim silencer for firearms, using the principle of the automobile engine muffler. In 1895 he installed a gasoline engine on a tricycle (he said that was all he could afford) and tested the vehicle on the roads of eastern Massachusetts. The first thing he learned was that he had to have a clutch to disengage the engine from the driving wheels; on his initial test he had to run off the road into a plowed field to stop.

Three more experimental gasoline cars appeared in 1896, built, in order, by Charles Brady King and Henry Ford in Detroit, and Alexander Winton in Cleveland. King was an engineer who had got the idea of a mechanical road vehicle from a two-cycle gas engine exhibited at the Chicago's World's Fair in 1893. He later went into business making, among other things, gasoline engines for motorboats. He was acquainted with Henry Ford, and he and his assistant, Oliver E. Barthel, gave Ford advice and help in building his first car. King later became superintendent of the Northern Motor Car Company, but his interest subsequently turned to aircraft engines and he ceased to be active in the automobile industry.

Henry Ford at this time was an obscure figure, chief engineer of the Detroit Illuminating Company (now Detroit Edison) and some years away from being a successful automobile manufacturer. Like the Duryeas, he had got his ideas about a motor vehicle from articles about European cars in technical magazines. This 1896 car was called a "quadricycle" because of its light weight (500 pounds), which may indicate that Henry Ford was already thinking of a low-priced car. However, it is impossible to know what Ford had in mind in those early days. His own memory was notoriously and even conveniently inaccurate. He later claimed to have built his first car in 1892, which would have given him priority over the Duryea brothers, but there is no evidence to support this claim.

Alexander Winton was a Scottish engineer who became a successful bicycle manufacturer in Cleveland, Ohio. As the builder of the sixth American gasoline automobile he had no claim to originality of invention, but as the owner of a prosperous bicycle business he was in a stronger position than any of his predecessors to undertake commercial production. He was, for a few years, the leading producer of gasoline automobiles in the United States.

Founding the Industry

There was no lack of technical skill in the United States, but technical skill by itself has never been enough to insure success in the manufacture and sale of motor vehicles. What can be called the Henry Ford myth has left behind a widespread belief that the American automobile industry was created by un-tutored geniuses working on the proverbial shoestring. Ford may have been a genius, but in mechanical matters he was hardly an untutored one. He was a trained machinist and at one time was a member of the American Society of Mechanical Engineers. Even with this background it took him seven years from the completion of his first car in 1896 before he could meet the conditions for successful production. Some capital was necessary, perhaps not much in those early days, but enough to get the enterprise going until—if all went well—there was sufficient sales volume to make it self-supporting, and this took management skill. It was usually helpful to have an established industrial base that could not only supply capital but manufacturing facilities, manage-ment, and skilled labor. Virtually all the pioneer American automobile manu-facturers had technical training or business experience, frequently both, and usually were already in a business that could turn to motor vehicles fairly read-ily. They were makers of bicycles, horse-drawn carriages and wagons, or sta-tionary gas engines, or operators of machine shops, or metal fabricators. Eu-rope had the same experience.

Common to automotive entrepreneurs in both the United States and Western Europe was the problem of deciding what to build. In the 1890s the time ap-peared ripe for a self-propelled highway vehicle, but it was unclear what the most desirable means of propulsion was going to be. The choice lay among electricity, steam, and the internal combustion engine, and a good many con-temporary observers would have rated them in that order. The electric auto-mobile was silent and odorless, required no transmission, and could be driven by a woman as easily as a man. It was and still is ideal for short, limited-speed runs, and at the turn of the century was popular with society ladies for driving about town. Electric cars appeared early. The first recorded American-built model was designed by William Morrison in Des Moines, Iowa, in 1891, and driven in Chicago a year later, but Morrison does not appear to have gone any farther. Within the next few years, however, electric automobiles were produced by a considerable number of manufacturers. A steam car likewise required no gear shifting, had plenty of power, and after the introduction of the flash boiler could be started easily in one or two minutes. By comparison a gasoline engine had to be cranked to start it, an arduous and sometimes dangerous task; it was noisy and emitted a disagreeable exhaust; and it had to have an elaborate transmission mechanism because of the high speed at which the engine had to operate.

There were of course countervailing factors. As early as 1895 Thomas A. Edison pointed out the limitations of the electric automobile—its inability to go far or fast without draining the battery—and predicted that the future of the motor vehicle lay in some form of naphtha engine. The steam automobile was a formidable competitor; in fact, Ransom E. Olds and Henry Ford considered steam power at first. However, the high pressures needed for a steam engine small enough to put in an automobile made for difficult and expensive maintenance, and eventually the gasoline powered car proved the winner, but the outcome was far from obvious at the beginning.

The year 1897 can be accepted as the year when an American automobile industry actually came into existence. It was in fact celebrated as such fifty years later by the city of Hartford, Connecticut, which made a reasonably well-founded claim to be the industry's birthplace. In 1897 the Pope Manufacturing Company of Hartford began to produce motor vehicles, both electric and gasoline-powered. At that time Pope was the largest manufacturer of bicycles in the United States, and his career provides a good and fairly typical example of how most automobile companies actually came into existence. Colonel Albert A. Pope, also distinguished as a forceful promoter of the Good Roads movement, was a manufacturer in Boston who became interested in bicycles in 1877. He bought an abandoned sewing machine factory in Hartford to use for making bicycles under the name "Columbia" and in a little over ten years had a large-scale organization, with its own plant for making tires and steel tubing as well as finished bicycles. Consequently, when the firm undertook to build motor vehicles, it was well equipped to do so in terms of manufacturing facilities, financial resources, and managerial and technical talent.

The Pope organization's attention was drawn to Hiram P. Maxim's experiments in 1895 by Henry Souther, the head of its research division and, like Maxim, a graduate of M.I.T., with the result that Maxim was brought to Hartford as chief engineer of a Motor Carriage Department. This department built some 500 electric and forty gasoline cars in the two years from 1897 to 1899. Maxim would have preferred it the other way round, but his superiors had no faith in the future of the internal combustion engine. George M. Day, general manager of the Pope Manufacturing Company, told Maxim, "You cannot get people to sit over an explosion." In contrast to the innovations of the French, American automobile design lingered at the buggy-with-an-engine stage, and the engine was usually located under the seat.

Nevertheless, Pope's output went well beyond what any other would-be American motor vehicle manufacturer was managing at that time. If the horseless carriage was going to take hold, Pope appeared to be in a commanding position, but the company's ascendancy lasted just two years. This was the era of the trusts, and Colonel Pope and his associates were swept up in the fever. The story is too complicated to be given in full detail, but these are the essentials. In 1898 a group of financiers who had been involved in electric traction promotion, including William C. Whitney, P. A. B. Widener, Anthony N. Brady, and Thomas F. Ryan, became interested in an organization called the Electric Vehicle Company, which operated a dozen electric cabs in New York City. These were built by Morris and Salom of Philadelphia, who had made their first electric car, the "Electrobat," in 1894. They sold their company to Isaac L. Rice, the founder of the Electric Storage Battery Company (Exide) and the Electric Boat Company. These cabs performed well in a severe blizzard in New York, running on the sidewalks when the streets were blocked, and the traction magnates were allured by the prospect of founding a giant concern to operate electric cabs in all major cities, and possibly monopolizing the entire electric automobile industry. To this end they acquired and greatly expanded the Electric Vehicle Company, which in turn acquired the Pope Motor Carriage Department in 1899. Day became president of the Electric Vehicle Company, which then absorbed several other makers of electric automobiles. Along the way it also became the owner of the Selden patent on gasoline automobiles, but that part of the story has to be told later.

Colonel Pope accepted this arrangement because he himself was heavily involved in forming a combination of bicycle producers known as the American Bicycle Company—less flatteringly as the "Bicycle Trust"—composed of forty-five companies and capitalized at $40 million. Both these operations failed. The American Bicycle Company was formed just as the bicycle boom came to an end, and the "Bicycle Trust" promptly collapsed. The Electric Vehicle Company had a somewhat longer illness. The performance of electric cabs in the New York blizzard proved to be a short-term advantage. In normal operation they were to be clumsy and costly vehicles. After each run a cab had to have its battery replaced, and since each battery weighed a ton, this was a time-consuming and complicated operation.

By the start of the twentieth century it was obvious that in pinning its hopes on electric automobiles the Electric Vehicle Company had backed the wrong horse. It tried to turn to gasoline cars, but it was reduced to exploiting the

Selden patent, and, as will be seen, it failed at that too. In the panic of 1907 the Electric Vehicle Company went into receivership. It was reorganized as the Columbia Motor Car Company, which vanished into Benjamin Briscoe's short-lived combine, the United States Motor Company, in 1910.

The other automotive landmark of 1897 was the founding of the Winton Motor Carriage Company in Cleveland, Ohio. Winton, as stated, experimented with motor vehicles and ran a gasoline car in 1896, the sixth American-built gasoline-driven vehicle. Formation of the company followed, and on 24 March 1898 Winton sold a car to Robert Allison of Port Carbon, Pennsylvania, which he claimed as the first sale of an American gasoline car built on a regular production basis rather than as an experimental model. The price was $1,000 and the profit $400. Later in 1898 Winton advertised his product by driving one of his cars from Cleveland to New York. He followed the approximate route of the Thomas E. Dewey Thruway, but Winton characterized the roads he found as "outrageous." However, his feat brought a reward in the form of an investment of $5,000 by Professor Irving Metcalf of Oberlin College—an unusual occurrence in itself. Not many college professors in 1898 can have had $5,000 to invest in such a speculative venture.

Like Henry Ford, Winton drove his own cars in races: both men believed that it was good advertising. In a short time the Winton company became the country's leading producer of gasoline automobiles—not that that made it large-scale. After five years of operation it was making six cars a day. It stayed in business some twenty-five years, and it might have gone on to greatness but for Winton's lack of interest in, or real talent for, day-to-day management. He liked to experiment with new mechanical ideas, but once he had them working he wanted to move on to something else, and no one like Ford's James S. Couzens appeared in the Winton organization.

Pope and Winton were the start of the American automotive industry. In the next few years builders of horseless carriages proliferated, and vanished almost as fast. The Motor Vehicle Manufacturers Association lists some 3,200 names of motor vehicles produced by about 1,900 firms in the United States since 1893, and there were undoubtedly others that left no trace. At the beginning it was easy to enter the industry. All that was required was some mechanical skill and a building where the vehicle could be assembled from parts made elsewhere. The cars were sold for cash—this is still the rule in the American automobile industry—and the parts bought on credit, so that if production could be achieved and if buyers could be found, the operation could finance itself. These were big "ifs." The system carried no guarantee and in fact it failed far more often than it worked. The rate of attrition in the automobile industry has always been high, but it does not seem to have deterred prospective entrants. In 1899 there were already thirty producers of motor vehicles in the United States, practically all of them miniscule. They were divided among New England, the Middle Atlantic states, and the Middle West.

A few of the aspiring producers who followed on the heels of Pope and Winton made some contribution to the future growth of the industry. The list might begin with Thomas L. Jeffery, who as maker of the Rambler bicycle had been Pope's major rival. He sold out to the American Bicycle Company and began to build Rambler cars at an abandoned bicycle factory in Kenosha, Wisconsin, in 1901. His company later became Nash, which in turn was one of the components of American Motors. Little is known about Jeffery. He was evidently a capable business man; he got out of the bicycle business ahead of its collapse, and he got into the automobile industry and stayed in it until he was ready to leave.

In 1901 George N. Pierce began building cars in Buffalo, New York. He had been a manufacturer of bird cages, then spokes for bicycle wheels, and finally complete bicycles before he turned to motor carriages. Pierce eventually produced the Pierce-Arrow, one of the best known of American luxury cars, distinguished by having its headlights mounted on the front mudguards. The Peerless Motor Car Company of Cleveland, Ohio, began to manufacture automobiles in 1900. Its progression had been from washing machines to bicycles to cars. The Peerless was another luxury vehicle which failed to survive the 1929 crisis.

Other once-familiar names to appear at this time were Moon, made in St. Louis, and Franklin, built in Syracuse, New York, and for many years the only well-known American car to have an air-cooled engine. More important, and more illustrative of the development of the industry, were two important ventures into steam automobile production. The Stanley twins, Francis E. and Freelan O., were Maine Yankees of considerable technical talent who tinkered with a number of things before they began making steam automobiles in Newton, Massachusetts in 1897. They sold their business and patents to a corporation called the Automobile Company of America, capitalized at $2,500,000 and headed by Amzi L. Barber, a manufacturer of asphalt—an early evidence of interlocking between motor vehicles and highway development—and John Brisben Walker, publisher of *Cosmopolitan* magazine.

Barber and Walker separated soon afterward. Walker took the name Mobile Company of America and built steamers in Tarrytown, New York, for a few years. Barber adopted the name Locomobile and located in Bridgeport, Connecticut. This company had a somewhat longer run because it changed from steam to gasoline cars in 1902, a step taken under the direction of Barber's son-in-law, Samuel T. Davis, Jr., who became president of Locomobile at this time. Davis was a graduate of Rensselaer Polytechnic Institute and evidently a capable administrator. In conjunction with Andrew L. Riker, a talented automotive engineer, Davis made the Locomobile a prominent luxury car until, like others of its kind, it became a casualty of the Great Depression.

Meanwhile the Stanleys returned in 1901 with new patents and reopened their Newton factory. The Stanley Steamer became the best known of American steam automobiles, but despite its reputation it was never a major factor in the motor vehicle market. The Stanleys were eccentrics; they seem to have built cars chiefly for their own enjoyment rather than for profit. They refused to advertise or make any other effort to market their product; anyone who wanted to buy a Stanley Steamer had to take the initiative. They never made more than a few hundred cars a year, and when Francis was killed in an automobile accident in 1918, Freelan lost interest and let the company go out of business.

The most promising prospect for the steam automobile to become an effective competitor in the growing motor vehicle market came from the White family of Cleveland, Ohio, owners of the White Sewing Machine Company. Three brothers, Windsor, Rollin, and Walter, started experimenting with steam cars in 1899, using the sewing machine plant, and produced their first car two years later. Rollin, who was an engineer, was the designer; when the automobile part of the business became the White Motor Company, Walter, who was an attorney, handled the management. The Whites were the first in the United States to use a flash boiler, invented by Leon Serpollet in France in 1899, and in general represented the most advanced steam automobile technology for their time. Nevertheless, in 1910 the company abandoned steam and switched to gasoline cars, and a few years later it chose to concentrate on commercial vehicles exclusively.

Why did the steam automobile die? It had attractive features: no transmission, no need to keep the engine running when the vehicle was stopped, and high horsepower. The steam car still has its ardent partisans, and with the advent of problems of air pollution and oil shortage, there has been agitation to revive it on the ground that a steam engine emits less pollutant and burns less oil. However, the steam car also had, and has, its handicaps. To make a steam engine small enough to be practical in an automobile, high pressures are necessary (600 psi or more) and this means high cost in construction and a degree of skill in maintenance not likely to be found in the local service station. Moreover, a steam engine has a lower thermal efficiency than an internal combustion engine of comparable capacity. It was never possible to build steam automobiles as cheaply as gasoline cars, and once the gasoline engine had been refined beyond its initial crudity, the outcome of the competition was certain.

In the United States at the beginning of the twentieth century, the gasoline automobile was favored by the ready availability and low cost of gasoline, but in Western Europe, which had no domestic sources of petroleum, the same thing happened. Steam cars gave way to the internal combustion engine just as rapidly as in the United States.

The demise of the steam automobile was therefore a matter of straightforward economics. There was some belief that buyers turned away from them because they were afraid of boiler explosions, but this seems doubtful. There is no record of a steam automobile blowing up; any such event would have been well publicized by the makers of gasoline and electric cars. A long-range factor militating against the steam automobile in the United States in its competition with the internal combustion engine, apart from the latter's inherently superior thermal efficiency, was the question of supplying the steam car with suitable boiler water. There was no problem in New England when the motor vehicle first appeared, because there were villages every few miles, each with a horse trough in its central square containing soft water fit for boiler use. However, these conditions did not apply in many other parts of the country, especially in the West, as the railroads had already discovered. There were wide areas where they had to haul in their boiler water, and this situation would certainly have been a handicap to the use of steam automobiles.

CHAPTER THREE
The Industry Takes Form

A very small proportion of the total starts in automobile manufacturing did not come to dead ends. In the first decade of the twentieth century a number of firms emerged and survived to form the basic structure of the American automobile industry as it would exist for the next fifty years. The names arouse nostalgic memories among automobile enthusiasts—Ford, Buick, Maxwell, Olds, Reo, Cadillac, Hudson, Packard, Studebaker, Overland, Marmon.

Of these, the Olds Motor Works for a time appeared to have the most likely prospect of becoming the leader of the American automobile industry. It was founded in 1899 by Ransom Eli Olds, already a successful manufacturer of stationary gasoline engines, with financial backing to the tune of $200,000 from Samuel L. Smith and his son Frederic, Michigan business men with whom Olds had previously been associated. As mentioned in chapter 2, Olds had earlier experimented with steam propulsion for a road vehicle and in 1893 sold the second of his steamers to a British firm, the Francis Times Company, for use in India. Olds later said that this car was lost in a shipwreck. His business operations had been conducted in Lansing, Michigan, but the Motor Works was located in Detroit until it burned down in 1901. The only thing saved from the fire was the prototype of the one-cylinder, curved-dash buggy that became immortal as the "Merry Oldsmobile." It was formerly thought that this fire was a landmark event in Olds history because it forced the company to concentrate on this one model, but it is now established that Olds intended to do that anyway. The immediate result of the fire was to move the Olds Motor Works to Lansing when a Lansing business group put up $4,800 to buy a fifty two-acre former fairground as a site for a new factory. A more important consequence was that much of the manufacturing had to be contracted out and this process involving three firms that would later come to play major roles in the automobile industry: Leland and Faulconer, machine tool builders, who made the engines for the Oldsmobile; John and Horace Dodge, machinists, who made the transmissions; and Benjamin and Frank Briscoe, sheet metal fabricators, who built the bodies.

The buggy was a striking success. By 1904 annual production had risen to the phenomenal level of 5,000—then Olds left the company and the "Merry Oldsmobile" was discontinued. There was evidently a dispute between him and the Smiths. It has been assumed that Olds wanted to continue turning out his buggy while they thought that the market lay with heavy touring cars, and that because the Smiths controlled the company they shortsightedly threw away the opportunity to pioneer in the quantity production of low-priced cars. This is an oversimplified explanation. If this was the cause of the dispute, then the Smiths were right. Given the roads and streets of the period, cars had to be substantial and sturdy. The curved-dash buggy, although attractive, was too light: it would shake itself to pieces in a fairly short time. Olds himself returned to the motor vehicle industry with a new company to which he gave his initials "REO"; and it is noteworthy that he made no effort to build a counterpart to the "Merry Oldsmobile."

The Olds Motor Works had another important role in the formation of the American automobile industry. It was a training ground for individuals who worked there for a time and then went out to found their own companies. There was Jonathan D. Maxwell, who left Olds in 1904 to join with the brothers Benjamin and Frank Briscoe to form the Maxwell-Briscoe Motor Car Company, which later became Maxwell and eventually Chrysler. The Briscoes were sheet metal manufacturers of Detroit who had become major suppliers of automobile radiators. They were unusual among automotive pioneers in that they had banking connections with the House of Morgan and had Morgan assistance in launching Maxwell-Briscoe. Although the organizers were Detroit men, they started production in the former factory of the Mobile Company in Tarrytown, New York. Robert C. Hupp was another Olds engineer who established his own company (1908), the maker of the Hupmobile, but he left the Hupp firm, or was pushed out, three years later. The company itself remained small-scale.

Maxwell and Hupp had had other experience with automobiles before they went to Olds, but Roy D. Chapin, future secretary of commerce in the Hoover administration, and Howard E. Coffin, one of the greatest of the early American automotive engineers, got their automotive start in the Olds Motor Works. They left together in 1905 about the time of the Olds-Smith dispute, but there is no direct evidence that Olds's departure had anything to do with theirs. Bas-

William C. Durant
(1860–1947)

Ransom Eli Olds
(1864–1950)

ically they wanted to go into business for themselves. Needing financial support, they first joined forces with E. R. Thomas, maker of the "Thomas Flyer" in Buffalo, New York, to produce a car called the Thomas-Detroit. A year later Thomas sold his interest to Hugh Chalmers and the car and the company became Chalmers-Detroit. Chalmers was an aggressive promoter and salesman who for a few years seemed on the edge of becoming a leading figure in the automobile industry, but he never got beyond the edge. He and Edward Jordan, who became the producer of the Jordan car in Cleveland, had a common business background that they shared with Thomas J. Watson, the founder of IBM, and Alvan Macauley, later president of Packard. They had all been outstanding salesmen for the National Cash Register Company and had all incurred the displeasure of NCR's autocratic president, John Patterson, and been fired.

One of Chapin's feats while he was still with the Olds Motor Works was to drive a curved-dash Oldsmobile from Detroit to New York in 1901 to display it at the New York Automobile Show, these shows having become an important medium for advertising and selling cars. He went from Detroit through Ontario to Buffalo and then followed the route Winton had taken three years before, finding the roads still unsatisfactory. In upstate New York Chapin used the towpath of the Erie Canal for 150 miles because it was better built than the roads in the area. His trip took seven days, and he had practically to rebuild the car en route. Edgar and Elmer Apperson also required a week to drive a Haynes-Apperson from Kokomo to New York in the same year. These journeys dramatized the poor condition of American roads at the time—in 1900, outside of cities, there were less than 200 miles of hard-surfaced highway in the entire United States—but they also demonstrated that even with poor roads, long journeys by motor vehicle were now practical, although just barely so. This point was illustrated still more forcibly in 1903, when three trips were made by car from San Francisco to New York: the first by a Vermont doctor and his chauffeur, in a Winton in sixty-three days, the second and third by a Packard and an Oldsmobile sent to match the feat for advertising purposes, in fifty-three and sixty-five days respectively.

The arrangement with Thomas and Chalmers did not satisfy Chapin and Coffin, and in 1908 they formed their own company to build a car of Coffin's design. The company was called the Hudson Motor Car Company and the car the Hudson, because the venture was started with an investment of $90,000 from J. L. Hudson, owner of Detroit's biggest department store. It was manifestly not feasible to follow the customary practice of naming the car for its designer. Chapin's business skill and Coffin's engineering talent made Hudson a profitable operation; it continues as a part of American Motors.

Studebaker had a distinctive origin. When the horseless carriage appeared on the scene, the Studebaker Brothers Manufacturing Company of South Bend, Indiana, was the largest manufacturer of horse-drawn vehicles in the world. The management wisely decided that this new mode of highway transportation should be looked into and did some experimenting at the turn of the century. However, Studebaker's main effort at first went into marketing cars made by others, beginning in 1904 with the Garford Manufacturing Company of Elyria, Ohio, a former maker of bicycle parts. Under this arrangement Garford built the engine and chassis, while Studebaker added the body and sold the vehicle under the name Studebaker Garford. Four years later Studebaker sought additional productive capacity through a similar arrangement with the Everitt-Metzger-Flanders Company, just formed to make a car called EMF. Basically it was a combination of three small automobile firms in Detroit, Northern, Wayne, and Deluxe, and some parts manufacturers. Walter Flanders had been Ford's plant superintendent and was one of the earliest of a long line of Ford executives to have difficulties with the head of the firm and leave. B. F. Everitt and William Metzger were Detroit businessmen who became fascinated with the automobile industry and moved in and out of it for a quarter of a century with admirable persistence and not much success.

This system did not work well. Studebaker had the sales outlets, but men whose experience was in selling carriages and wagons, and who were still doing it, were not necessarily the best qualified salesmen of motor vehicles. There was friction between the companies, until it was resolved by consolidating the whole enterprise as the Studebaker Corporation in 1910, with financial support from the House of Morgan. Studebaker, as a large and long-established firm, had access to the New York money market.

Other carriage and wagon builders converted to automobile manufacturing at the beginning of the twentieth century and some lasted a respectable length of time: Auburn, Dort, Elcar, Cole, Velie. The only one other than Studebaker to become a major factor in the industry was Overland, which started making cars in Indianapolis in 1906. The company became part of John North Willys's automotive empire and will be discussed in that context in chapter 5.

Four important future participants in the American motor vehicle industry also made their appearance in the early years of the twentieth century: Ford, Buick, Cadillac, and Maxwell-Briscoe. In 1899 Henry Ford secured backing to go into production from a syndicate of Detroit businessmen headed by a lumber dealer named William A. Murphy. They organized the Detroit Automobile Company with Ford as superintendent, but this effort was a failure, for reasons that remain obscure. Ford had no experience in industrial production and he seems to have been undecided about what to produce. After a year the

Detroit Automobile Company was dissolved and replaced by the Henry Ford Company, still with Murphy's backing.

Then came the first of the numerous disagreements with business associates that marked Henry Ford's career. He was building and driving racing cars to gain publicity for himself and the company, and Murphy became convinced that Ford was so absorbed in this activity that he was neglecting the production of marketable automobiles. Ford on his part claimed that Murphy and his associates would not let him design cars according to his ideas. At any rate Ford was dismissed and Henry M. Leland of Leland and Faulconer was asked to take over in 1902. Besides making engines for Oldsmobiles, Leland and Faulconer built gasoline engines for motorboats.

Leland reorganized the concern as the Cadillac Motor Car Company, naming both the firm and its product for the founder of Detroit, Antoine de la Mothe Cadillac. Ford found another backer not long afterward in Alexander Malcomson, a Detroit coal dealer, and they established the present Ford Motor Company on 10 June 1903. The rise of Henry Ford and the Ford Motor Company is the theme of the next chapter.

The Buick Motor Car Company, also organized in 1903, was named for David Dunbar Buick, who had sold a plumbing supply business in Detroit to devote his attention to gasoline engines and then to motor vehicles. He evidently had technical talent, because his "valve-in-head" motor became a distinguishing feature of the Buick car, but he was totally unable to get into production. When he had spent all his own money he got support from the Briscoes, but they soon became discouraged and sold this interest to James H. Whiting, a wagon manufacturer of Flint, Michigan. Whiting became discouraged in his turn and in 1904 sold control of the Buick Motor Car Company to another Flint businessman, William Crapo "Billy" Durant, a dynamic personality who had made a fortune as co-owner of the Durant-Dort Carriage Company. He became the founder of General Motors, and his story and Buick's will be further developed in chapter 5.

The Briscoes tried again after their unhappy association with Buick, this time in partnership with Jonathan D. Maxwell, who, as previously mentioned, had served at the Olds Motor Works and before that had been a mechanic at the Apperson machine shop. As stated before, Maxwell-Briscoe began operations in the former Mobile Company plant in Tarrytown, New York. It was very well equipped, and also the Briscoes had connections with the House of Morgan through their sheet metal business, so that the location near New York City gave encouragement to some Morgan partners to raise $250,000 of the company's $500,000 capital.

Of the remaining important automobile companies to be founded in this period, the beginning of Reo has been described. For a time this second Olds venture was successful; by 1908 the Reo was one of the four leading sellers, along with Ford, Buick, and Maxwell-Briscoe. It lost that position but held up moderately well until the 1930s, when the company gave up passenger car production and became exclusively a truck manufacturer. Ransom E. Olds might have had Henry Ford's place in automotive history. He had the talent, but he lacked Ford's drive and his single-minded absorption in building a car for the mass market.

Packard and Marmon were both examples of automobiles that originated in a parent firm. With Packard, it was the Packard Electric Company of Warren, Ohio. James Ward Packard became interested in motor vehicles in the 1890s and would undoubtedly have entered the automobile industry even if he had not bought a Winton that proved defective. When he complained, Winton allegedly told him to build a better car himself if he could and Packard accepted the challenge. At any rate he began production in 1900. Soon afterward the Packard Motor Car Company attracted the attention of Henry B. Joy, son of the railroad magnate, James F. Joy, and a successful businessman in his own right. Joy bought control of the company, moved it to Detroit, which was his home, and expanded it with backing from his financial associates in Michigan. Packard himself remained in Warren and ceased to have an active role in the management of the company. Its early growth has to be attributed to Joy.

The Marmon car came from the firm of Nordyke and Marmon, manufacturers of flour milling machinery in Indianapolis. Howard C. Marmon built an automobile for his own use in 1903 and the firm began commercial production a year later. The Marmon experience was unusual in that a separate company for the automobile part of the business was not organized until 1926; the firm was content to build a limited number of high quality vehicles. In fact, Marmon cars were the American equivalent of the Rolls-Royce. They were another victim of the Great Depression.

In addition, the Pope organization returned to the automobile business on an ambitious scale. Some motor vehicles were being made in American Bicycle Company plants, Waverley electrics in Indianapolis and steam trucks at what had been the H. A. Lozier and Company bicycle factory in Toledo, Ohio. Albert A. Pope organized this part of the business as the International Motor Car Company (this was one of several early automobile makers to use the ambitious title "International") and converted the Lozier plant to gasoline cars. Lozier himself, like so many bicycle makers, then went into the automobile business on his own.

When the Bicycle Trust disintegrated, the International Motor Car Company was reconstituted as the Pope Motor Car Company in 1903, certainly a landmark year in the founding of the American automobile industry. The new company had an impressive line of four models, built at four different locations: Pope-Toledo, the luxury car, at the former Lozier factory; Pope-Hartford, the medium-priced model, at the original Columbia bicycle plant in Hartford, which meant that the new Pope organization and the Electric Vehicle Company were now manufacturing automobiles in competition with each other in adjoining plants that had originally both been part of the Pope Manufacturing Company; the Pope-Tribune, designed as a low-priced offering, at another former bicycle factory in Hagerstown, Maryland; and the Waverley electric in Indianapolis.

It looks as if Albert A. Pope was anticipating what William C. Durant intended for General Motors and what Alfred P. Sloan later defined as "a car for every purse and every purpose." If so, Colonel Pope had already lost his opportunity. The Pope organization had had a promising lead as a motor vehicle manufacturer, but it lost managerial and technical talent when Day, Maxim, and others went to the Electric Vehicle Company, and the failure of the Bicycle Trust weakened Pope financially. In addition, Hartford, Hagerstown, and even Indianapolis had geographical limitations as centers of automobile manufacturing in comparison with the Great Lakes cities. If the Pope-Tribune was meant for a mass market, it should have been produced in Toledo, not in Hagerstown. Finally, in 1903 there were new and vigorous competitors on the scene who had not existed when the Pope organization began to build automobiles in 1897. The Pope Motor Car Company could not weather the panic of 1907 and was liquidated in 1913.

To sum up, in the first ten years of the twentieth century the American automobile industry consisted of an astounding assortment of hundreds of firms of which a limited number had achieved some stability. It was a classic example of a free market. Entry into the industry was easy and cheap, competition was unrestricted, and there were no legislative restrictions on what could be built and sold. Sources of capital ranged from J. P. Morgan and Co. to strictly local and personal resources. Where there was a parent company, like White Sewing Machine or Studebaker, it helped with financial support and factory space as well as with managerial and technical skill. The automobile firms that started on their own were mainly financed in their formative years by their dealers and dealers' banks through the system of selling cars strictly for cash. The dealers' purchases and costs had to be financed until the vehicles were sold, and this was done by countless local banks. Sometimes the system worked; more often it did not. When it did, the manufacturer could then build up capital by plowing back profits. The Ford Motor Company was by far the most successful practitioner of this technique. It was in fact by this method that Ford raised the funds to become the innovator of one of the great distinctive American contributions to the motor vehicle industry: mass production for a mass market.

Concentration in Detroit

In 1910 the structure of the American automobile industry was still forming, although it was possible to see that the larger firms were gaining an increasingly advantageous position. One fact, however, was already obvious: Detroit was the center of motor vehicle manufacturing. Various explanations have been offered for the concentration of the automobile industry in Detroit and all undoubtedly contributed, but no one of them is sufficient in itself. Detroit is well located for water transport of bulk materials like coal and ore, but it is no better located than other Great Lakes ports and its automobile factories were not direct consumers of iron ore until the Ford Motor Company installed a steel mill at its River Rouge plant in 1920. The Michigan hardwood forests are credited with promoting a substantial carriage industry that provided a base for automobile manufacturing. This was so, but the carriage industry was by no means restricted to Michigan; it flourished in Indiana and Ohio as well.

One theory holds that Detroit at the turn of the century was a city of small shops, so that it did not have its managerial and technical talent and its financial resources already committed to a single large industry, like steel in Pittsburgh and oil in Cleveland. The idea is plausible, except that both Pittsburgh and especially Cleveland produced a number of important motor vehicle firms. Nor was financial support the explanation. It used to be believed that Middle Western bankers were more sympathetic to this new industry than Easterners but there is no evidence to support this theory. Maxwell-Briscoe started in Tarrytown because it could get support in New York and was turned down in Detroit, and Studebaker had Morgan backing. Actually, where banks were concerned, the fundamental support for the automobile industry came from the thousands of local banks that financed the dealers. The producers lived, if they lived, on the cash payments from their dealers.

The real explanation comes down to people, to the fortuitous circumstance that a remarkable group of automobile entrepreneurs appeared simultaneously in the Detroit area. Until 1905 there were more automobile factories in Indianapolis than in Detroit, but Indianapolis did not have leadership comparable to Ford, Durant, Joy, Leland, Briscoe, Chapin, Coffin, Dodge, and Olds (although Olds was now located in Lansing, his automotive career began in Detroit), and even lesser figures like Everitt and Metzger. Together they made Detroit the principal center of motor vehicle production in the nation and eventually in the world, and once the concentration was established it grew on itself. Detroit came to exercise a magnetic attraction on everyone, individual or organization, who wished to be involved in the manufacturing of motor vehicles.

CHAPTER FOUR

The American Contribution: Mass Production

With motor vehicles, as with much of modern technology, the original invention was made in Europe and was then applied in the United States in novel ways and on an expanded scale. The great American contributions were, first, the concept of the automobile as an item of mass consumption and from that to the creation of the technique of mass production; and second, the development of a system of industrial organization for managing the large enterprises that the mass market for motor vehicles required.

The concept of a mass market for automobiles was distinctively American. In its early days the horseless carriage was seen as a "rich man's toy" and this attitude prevailed in Europe for many years. Even in the United States Woodrow Wilson, while he was president of Princeton University, deplored the motor car as an encouragement of socialism because he thought it incited the poor to envy the rich. Actually, all it has ever incited among the poor throughout the world has been a desire to own one.

American manufacturers started with some built-in advantages. The United States offered a larger domestic market than any European producer could command, and its higher standard of living made proportionally more Americans potential purchasers of a car. At any rate American automobile men were unmistakably the pioneers in making the motor vehicle an article of general consumption and use.

Seeking the Low-Priced Car

The development of mass production and the mass market in the automobile industry is inseparably and properly identified with Henry Ford. Yet Ford was

neither the only one nor the first to see the vast potential in successfully producing what he termed "a car for the great multitude." Olds was the first to
try, but he, as we have seen, failed or was unable to follow through. He had
imitators: Alanson Brush, who designed the motors for the early Cadillacs,
brought out a lightweight "Runabout" that enjoyed a brief popularity. His
backer was Frank Briscoe, brother of Benjamin. None of these attempts lasted
long, because they were proceeding in the wrong way. Olds, Brush, and the
others set out to build a low-priced car by existing methods, and this could be
done only by flimsy construction. The Olds buggy was too delicate. The
Brush Runabout used wood extensively to achieve light weight and low cost,
and it became characterized as "wooden body, wooden axles, wooden wheels,
wooden run."

Henry Ford found the correct formula, which was to design a car suited to
the needs of the mass market first and then devise a method of manufacturing
it cheaply. This was not a solution that Henry Ford worked out logically; it is
doubtful that he ever worked anything out logically. Ford was a skilled mechanic and held the position of chief engineer for the Detroit Illuminating
Company when he began to experiment with horseless carriages, but his technique was based on cut-and-try and his decisions were intuitive rather than
reasoned.

The story of Henry Ford has been told repeatedly and in elaborate detail, so
that it need only be summarized here. He grew up on a farm in Dearborn,
Michigan, but left early to follow his strong mechanical bent in nearby Detroit.
He began to experiment with a motor vehicle some time in the early 1890s
and, as has already been told, ran his first car in Detroit in 1896. Then after
two failures at commercial production, he founded the Ford Motor Company
in 1903. His support came from a Detroit coal dealer named Alexander Malcomson, the brothers John and Horace Dodge, and several others. Of the original capitalization of $100,000 only $28,000 was actually paid in, most of it
by Malcomson. The Dodges contributed materials and their machine shop was
to build the engines for the Ford cars. Malcomson's bookkeeper, James S.
Couzens, who put in $1,000 at the start, became Ford's brilliant business man-
ager and eventually United States senator from Michigan. Ford himself had
learned enough from his previous experiences to stipulate that he should have
a quarter of the company's stock, equal to Malcomson's share, for his designs
and services.

Ford appears to have contemplated a popular-priced car early in his automotive career and even to have had some grasp of how to go about it. He said
when the Ford Motor Company was founded, "The way to make automobiles
is to make one automobile just like another automobile, to make them come

from the factory just alike—just like one pin is like another pin when it comes from a pin factory." When he made this statement in 1903 his company was a long way from being able to put it into effect, but Ford kept this objective in sight. In 1905 he and Malcomson quarreled over what to produce. The issue was similar to the split between Olds and the Smiths, but Ford had a stronger position in his company. The Dodges supported him, so that he was able to force Malcomson out and assume complete control. The company was still making several models and doing reasonably well, but it concentrated increasingly on realizing its founder's dream.

These years when he was working to achieve his dream show Henry Ford at his best. He was open to new ideas (as long as he did not have to give someone else credit for them), and he was innovative. For example, the Ford Motor Company was the first American automobile manufacturer to use vanadium steel, which had the advantage of combining strength with lightness. Ford also gathered about him a group of highly talented assistants. Couzens handled the business affairs of the company and with Norval Hawkins organized the Ford dealer network. On the technical side were men like C. H. (for Childe Harold) Wills, metallurgist and designer; Charles E. Sorensen ("Cast-iron Charlie"), who would become general manager of the Ford Motor Company and set a record of forty years service before he was fired; and William S. Knudsen, who established the regional assembly plants—another Ford innovation that cut transportation costs by reducing the need to ship complete cars over long distances.

There were faint signs of future weakness also. None of these men had a title or a clearly defined position in the company, because Henry Ford continued to think of it as a small shop where everyone knew everyone else and there was no need for formal organization. He believed that each employee should find what he could do best and do it. This brand of anarchy was never applied on the plant floor, but it made for confusion and rivalry in management, and Ford seems to have considered that desirable. The talented group held together reasonably well through the attainment of mass production, but by 1920 all except Sorensen had gone—Knudsen to General Motors, where he played a key role in ending the Ford ascendancy.

However, these problems were all under the surface during Ford's creative period. The first important step toward his goal was the Model N of 1906, a car that clearly anticipated the Model T of two years later. The Model N was popular enough to put Ford among the four leading American producers, with a total output of over 8,000 units in 1906 and over 6,000 in the depression year of 1907. It is worth pointing out that the "Big Three" of later years was already foreshadowed in the top four. Reo fell behind and eventually dropped out, but Ford went on to greatness, Buick was the nucleus of General Motors, and Maxwell-Briscoe, after several corporate reincarnations, became Chrysler.

The Model T, "Tin Lizzie," was put on the market in 1908, the answer to Ford's quest for the car for the mass market and the most famous automobile ever built. It was sturdily constructed to withstand hard use, mounted high to negotiate the rutted country roads of the day, and easy to operate and maintain. Owners could do much of their own maintenance and repair work. It had a simple four-cylinder, 20 h.p. engine and a planetary transmission giving two speeds forward and one in reverse. Shifting gears, reversing, and braking were all done by foot pedals operating through bands on the transmission drums, so that a confused driver could always stop the car by pushing any two pedals. Like all motor vehicles of that era, the engine was started with a crank handle—the electric starter did not come until 1912 and was never standard equipment on the Model T. This technique demanded care. The crank handle on any car could kick back unexpectedly and broken arms and jaws were not uncommon. A unique feature of the Model T was a magneto built into the flywheel, which provided current for the electrical systems once the engine was started. In later years when the Model T was equipped with electric lights, this had the disadvantage that the lights dimmed when the car slowed down, but there was not much night driving in those days anyway.

"Tin Lizzie" was an immediate and spectacular success. Over ten thousand were sold in its first year and eighteen thousand in its second, making Ford easily the leading manufacturer of automobiles in the country, in fact in the world. Total United States production of motor vehicles for these years is shown in table 14-1. The success of the Model T was so great that Henry Ford decided to abandon all other Ford models and concentrate his company's resources exclusively on the production of Model T's. This was a critical decision and a bold one. The rapidly mounting demand for the car appeared to justify the risk, but the market for motor vehicles was still new and untested: a change in public taste would have been disastrous. However, it turned out that Ford had made the right choice; Model T sales continued to rise geometrically.

The achievement had two major flaws from Ford's point of view, both stemming from the existing techniques of production. Each car was assembled in place, with parts and components brought to the chassis and put on by a work gang, and even with some specialization in the allocation of work and greater efficiency in the placement of tools it was not possible either to keep up with the demand for Model T's or to reduce the production cost so that the car could be sold for much less than $1,000. Henry Ford firmly believed that a much greater market would open up if the selling price could be brought below $600.

He obviously had the car that the mass market wanted; his problem was to find a way to manufacture it cheaply and in large quantity.

The Moving Assembly Line

To appreciate the true nature of the Ford achievement it is necessary to understand mass production, both what it is and what it is not. It is frequently equated with quantity production and generally with cheap production, but neither is correct. Quantity production can be attained by handicraft methods if necessary, by adding more workers and more of the kind of machines already in use. This will increase output, but it will not reduce costs; it is more likely to raise them. Similarly, if cheapness is the sole objective, any system of production will do, but there is a vital difference between making cheap goods and making quality goods at low cost. The latter is the objective of mass production.

True mass production requires the integration of five components: precision, standardization, interchangeability, synchronization, and continuity. All these existed in the industrial world before the automobile came on the scene; the first known successful application of interchangeability is Johannes Gutenberg's use of movable type in the fifteenth century. (This is what Gutenberg really invented. The flatbed press that he used for printing goes back to the ancient world.) Industrialization had also familiarized the world with large-scale, low-cost production through mechanization, but not until the twentieth century had the world known such production of anything as complicated as a motor vehicle.

These components of mass production were known and used in the American industrial system well before 1900. Standardization and interchangeability go back to the early nineteenth century, to the Harper's Ferry and Springfield arsenals and people like Eli Whitney and Samuel Colt. Continuous flow production was demonstrated even earlier, by Oliver Evans's grist mill in Newport, Delaware, in 1787. The conveyor was also familiar; in fact, Henry Ford later claimed that he got the idea of the assembly line from a disassembly line—the conveyors used in meat packing plants—which may or may not be so. Within the automobile industry itself technical standardization was promoted by the Association of Licensed Automobile Manufacturers (ALAM) until it dissolved in 1911, by which time standardization had been taken up by the Society of Automotive Engineers (SAE). In 1908, the year that the Model T appeared, the Cadillac Motor Car Company gave a striking demonstration of precision, standardization, and interchangeability. Three Cadillacs were dismantled at the Brooklands track of the British Royal Automobile Club, the parts scrambled, and ninety of them removed at random by officials of the club. These were replaced from the stock of the Cadillac distributor in London, and his mechanics reassembled the three cars, which then ran perfectly in a 500-mile test. This feat won for Cadillac the British Dewar Trophy.

Cadillac was awarded the same trophy four years later for one of the most important American contributions to automotive technology, the electric starter. The risks of cranking an automobile by hand were well known and were a serious handicap to widespread use of cars, but until 1912 there was no satisfactory alternative. The electric starter was a joint achievement of the Cadillac engineering staff and Charles F. Kettering, then head of the Dayton Engineering Laboratories Company (Delco). The major difficulty was to design a starting motor that would be powerful enough to turn the engine over without being excessively bulky and heavy. This was the problem that Kettering solved by utilizing the same concept that he had applied some years earlier in designing the electric cash register for the National Cash Register Company, namely, the motor could be kept small because it was not required to deliver a constant power output but only to provide an occasional surge.

It was appropriate that these awards should go to Cadillac. The company's founder and head, Henry M. Leland, was a rigorous precisionist, trained in the machine tool firm of Brown and Sharpe in Providence, Rhode Island, where vernier calipers and micrometers were major items of production. Leland had already made a profound impression on young Alfred P. Sloan, Jr., who as head of the Hyatt Roller Bearing Company did business with Cadillac. When complaints were made about his bearings Sloan went to see Leland and was told, "Young man, Cadillacs are made to run, not just to sell. You must grind your bearings accurately. Even though you make thousands, the first and last should be precisely alike."

Thus all the pieces necessary to the solution of Henry Ford's problem were in existence and well known when his company faced the question of how to increase the output and at the same time lower the unit cost of Model T cars. What was needed was for someone to put these pieces together into an integrated technique of production. Here we encounter an historical oddity. Probably no industrial process has ever been studied more intensively, at the time and ever since, than the introduction of assembly line production by the Ford Motor Company, and yet it is still impossible to identify positively the originator of the idea or precisely what stimulated it. Opinion leans to Clarence Avery, who had joined the company after being Edsel Ford's high-school manual arts teacher, but the evidence is inconclusive. Charles E. Sorensen said simply that the moving assembly line came about because a large number of people in the company were concentrating on the problem of how to improve production, and this is probably as satisfactory an explanation as can be found.

After much experimentation the moving assembly line came to fruition in 1913. It was the first tested with magnetos, and when this experiment succeeded the system was gradually extended until it was applied to the entire car. In August of that year chassis were pulled through the plant with rope and windlass while Ford and his aides calculated the optimum speed and proper height for the assembly line and the synchronization of subassemblies and parts supplies. There is an obvious debt here to the time-and-motion study techniques that were being vigorously propounded in those days by Frederick W. Taylor and others. Henry Ford himself was certainly not a student of scientific management, but its ideas were so much in the industrial climate at the time that he and his lieutenants could hardly have avoided being aware of them.

The key elements of this system were first, moving the work to the worker instead of vice versa; and second, having each worker perform a single operation, requiring as little skill as could be devised. In short, the concept of assembly-line production was basically simple (once it had been demonstrated), but the execution was not. It required elaborate planning, complex and expensive tooling, and exact synchronization of the movement of materials through the plant and along main and subsidiary assembly lines. These first Ford assembly lines were in fact crude by later standards. They could turn out only a rigorously uniform product, exemplified for the Model T by the statement, possibly apocryphal, that is attributed to Henry Ford: "The customer can have it any color he wants as long as he wants it black."

It was still a revolution in methods of production and was immediately recognized as such. The adoption of the moving assembly line was the second of the fundamental decisions that put Ford at the top of the automotive world, the first being the decision to make only Model T's. In both cases the responsibility rested squarely on Henry Ford. There have been questions, justifiable enough, about who deserved credit for the design of the Model T or the concept of the moving assembly line, but the final choice had to be Henry Ford's. He was president and majority stockholder of the Ford Motor Company. With the assembly line in particular, if the savings in unit cost or the expected volume of sales had failed to materialize, total disaster for Ford and his company would have been unavoidable.

As it was, the results astonished the world. Sales of Model T's rose from approximately 78,000 in 1911–12, the last full fiscal year before assembly-line operations began, to 248,000 in 1913–14, the first year of complete assembly-line production (the fiscal year was 1 October–30 September). Meanwhile the selling price of the touring car declined from $600 in 1912 to $490 in 1914. Both trends continued, with a minor interruption during World War I. In fact, by 1920 three fifths of all the motor vehicles in the United States and half of all those in the world were Model T Fords.

This feat attracted worldwide attention to the Ford Motor Company, greatly magnified when on 5 January 1914 the company announced a basic wage rate of five dollars a day, roughly twice the prevailing rate in Detroit at the time. Eager job seekers descended on the Ford plant in thousands and a few days after the announcement the crowds had to be dispersed with firehoses. As with virtually everything else Henry Ford did, the motivations for the five-dollar day have been exhaustively examined without any satisfactory conclusion being reached. Ford had a way of rationalizing his actions after the event, or having them rationalized for him, and it is seldom possible to pinpoint what really motivated him at the time. The five-dollar day has been attributed to a wish to share the company's enormous profits with its work force, to raise wages so as to create a market for Ford cars, to forestall possible I.W.W. activity, to reduce labor turnover, or simply to give order to the company's wage structure. One feature of the five-dollar day that has been overlooked is that half of it was regarded by the company as wages, which put the Ford Motor Company at about the top of the current prevailing wage level in Detroit. The other half was considered to be a distribution of profits, a privilege rather than a right, so that in Henry Ford's eyes conditions could properly be imposed requiring a worker to be "worthy" of this share in the company's profits.

In this respect the five-dollar day was an example of the "welfare capitalism" that was coming into favor at that time. It has been claimed that the idea came from Couzens rather than Ford. Some Ford executives, and to some extent Henry Ford himself, were genuinely concerned about the welfare of the work force, and this action on wages was accompanied by the creation of a Sociological Department whose function was to be of assistance to the work force. Under Dean Samuel N. Marquis, the Episcopal clergyman who was its first head, and John R. Lee, who succeeded him, this department seems to have been genuinely helpful, especially to newly arrived immigrant workers. Later its staff came to be regarded as "snoopers" for management. The five-dollar wage was hedged with qualifications in practice, and the Sociological Department was short-lived, but it was all magnificent publicity for the Ford Motor Company, and Henry Ford always had an acute sense for publicity.

The Ford production methods were promptly imitated by the company's major competitors—they had no alternative if they wanted to survive. In fact, although no one could have anticipated it at the time, Ford had made oligopoly in the motor vehicle industry ultimately inevitable. In the long run there was no way in which a small firm whose output did not justify the mass production technique could remain competitive, even in the limited market of high-priced luxury cars. Ford could build Lincolns and General Motors Cadillacs with the great advantage of being able to spread their overhead costs over a broader base. Other industries also adopted the assembly-line technique: washing machines, electric refrigerators, agricultural implements, for instance.

Organization was another matter. The monolithic structure of the Ford Motor Company was satisfactory for a time, while the company was doing nothing but making Model T's as rapidly as possible. Henry Ford wanted to build a highly integrated vertical organization, with complete control of its raw materials and parts supplies. He even bought the Detroit, Toledo and Ironton Railroad, a profitable operation for a time because it controlled the Ford Motor Company's traffic and was therefore able to negotiate favorable interchange agreements with the Eastern trunk lines whose tracks it intersected, and when the great new River Rouge plant was built it contained its own steel mill.

But Henry Ford never understood that while the informal organization he began with might work well enough in a small shop, it was not right for a concern that had become the world's biggest manufacturer of motor vehicles. The flaws in the Ford style of management did not show while the company was establishing its supremacy in production, but the Ford Motor Company would not be the one to demonstrate how a giant automobile firm should be organized.

The Selden Patent Case

While the Ford Motor Company was climbing from nowhere to the top of the automotive world, it was engaged in a lawsuit that profoundly affected the entire industry. The Selden patent was taken out in 1895 by George B. Selden, a patent attorney of Rochester, New York, and claimed to cover any road vehicle using an internal combustion engine. Selden had seen a Brayton oil engine at the Centennial Exposition in 1876, and was impressed by the possibility of using it for a road vehicle. This was a two-cycle engine which had some success as a stationary power plant and was tested on a street railway in Rhode Island. Selden filed his application in 1877 and in the ordinary course of things would have received his patent two years later, at a time when a patent on a self-propelled road vehicle would have been nothing more than a curiosity. However, the law as it then stood permitted a two-year extension if the application was amended before the patent was issued, and Selden managed to keep his application pending for sixteen years. The patent was finally issued in 1895

(U.S. Patent no. 549,160), just when it was beginning to have some potential value. If it had been issued in 1879, it would have expired in 1896.

Selden's motives have never been clearly established. He undoubtedly wanted to delay the issue of the patent until it had some value, but he also tried to develop his idea and get support for it. At one point he had a prospect of $5,000 from a Rochester businessman but frightened him off by predicting that some day there would be more motor-driven than horse-drawn vehicles on the streets of Rochester. He made some efforts to build engines, without success. He never made a vehicle conforming to the patent specifications before the Ford case began. Then, just four years after the patent was issued, Selden sold it to the Electric Vehicle Company for $10,000 and a fifth of whatever royalties were collected.

In 1900 the Electric Vehicle Company sued the Winton Motor Carriage Company, then the country's chief producer of gasoline automobiles, for infringement of the Selden patent, but the case never reached a conclusion. The leading firms in the industry were all small and had no desire for expensive litigation, and the floundering Electric Vehicle Company was in no better position. Consequently, an agreement was reached to form an Association of Licensed Motor Vehicle Manufacturers (ALAM) to administer the patent. A five-member executive committee, with the Electric Vehicle Company as a permanent member, was to have the power to issue licenses, with a royalty of 1 ¼ percent of the catalog price of each car manufactured, later reduced to 0.8 percent. One fifth of the royalties was to go to Selden, two fifths to the Electric Vehicle Company, and two fifths to the ALAM. The industry was split on the issue, with some important producers like Reo and Maxwell-Briscoe refusing to acknowledge the validity of the patent.

This was the situation when the Ford Motor Company was founded. Henry Ford inquired about getting a license and was told that he would have to wait until he had demonstrated that he could build cars that met the ALAM standards. The association professed to be protecting the public from fly-by-night producers who left their buyers with orphan cars, but its policy was also designed to discourage any newcomer from entering the industry. It would not issue a license until the prospective entrant showed that he could manufacture motor vehicles that met the Association's standards, yet if the patent was valid, no newcomer could legally build a motor vehicle until after he had been granted a license. Ironically, George B. Selden was caught in this impasse and refused the right to build cars under his own patent. He finally got financial backing in 1905 to produce cars in Rochester, applied to the ALAM for a license, and was rejected on the same grounds as Ford. A year later his company bought a Buffalo concern that did have a license, so there actually was a Selden car on the market until 1914.

Henry Ford responded differently. He disapproved of patents anyway, and the snub from the ALAM angered him so that he decided to fight. He was encouraged in this course by his Philadelphia distributor, John Wanamaker. The legal battle was well publicized, as the contestants fought in advertisements as well as in court. The ALAM ran warnings, "Don't buy a lawsuit with your car," to which Ford replied by guaranteeing to bond every buyer of a Ford car against any legal liability. The United States district court where the suit was filed (Southern District of New York) ruled in favor of the ALAM in 1909, and most of the companies that had sided with Ford deserted, but he persisted and in 1911 the Circuit Court of Appeals held that the Selden patent applied only to vehicles using the Brayton engine and that therefore it was "valid but not infringed."

It was an historic victory for Henry Ford. The Selden case provided enormous favorable publicity for the Ford Motor Company, because in the public eye Ford was cast as David fighting the monopolistic Goliath. It was an inexact picture, as such pictures frequently are. By 1909 the Model T was well on its way and by the time the case was finally resolved, David was considerably bigger than Goliath. Nor was Goliath in any real sense a monopoly, because the members of the ALAM competed with each other. If the decision had gone the other way, the Ford Motor Company was well able to pay whatever penalties might have been incurred; it would have been inconvenienced, but it was in no danger of being put out of business.

The Selden case had more effect on the automobile industry as a whole than it did on the Ford Motor Company. It was obvious that no one except the lawyers would benefit if automobile companies were constantly in court over patent claims, so in 1915 the National Automobile Chamber of Commerce, now the Motor Vehicle Manufacturers Association, was formed for the primary purpose of administering a cross-licensing agreement. The Ford Motor Company did not join, because Henry Ford was not an organization man. However, since he disapproved of patents, his company's abstention made no difference to the cross-licensing system. The Ford Motor Company licensed its patents freely and helped itself to those in the cross-licensing pool. The system worked. There has been no other major patent suit since in the American automobile industry. A further important consequence was that the United States patent laws were revised to prevent repetition of Selden's delaying technique.

CHAPTER FIVE

The American Contribution: Industrial Organization

The American automobile was born during the era of the great "trusts," so that it was undoubtedly inevitable that the idea of forming combinations of motor vehicle firms, even moving toward a possible automobile trust, should emerge early in the history of the industry. Actually it appeared first in Great Britain, where a promoter named Harry J. Lawson organized the British Motor Syndicate as early as 1897 with the object of monopolizing the British motor car industry through control of patents. Two years later Lawson and an even more flamboyant American promoter and confidence man named Edward J. Pennington formed the Anglo-American Rapid Vehicle Company with a capitalization of $75 million and a claim to control over two hundred automotive patents. Their announced intention was to merge the principal American and British automobile companies. The capitalization was of course absurd for the automobile industry as it existed in 1899, and the scheme quickly evaporated.

The organizers of the Electric Vehicle Company had monopoly in view; in fact they were dubbed the "Lead-Cab Trust." They were better businessmen than Lawson or Pennington, but unfortunately for them their very considerable experience in the world of finance gave them no understanding of the manufacture and sale of motor vehicles.

The Early Combinations

The first at least partially successful steps toward combination in the American automobile industry were taken by two men with records of previous achievement in business and at least as much experience in the industry as anyone had

43

in the first decade of the twentieth century. Benjamin Briscoe has already been mentioned as a Detroit sheet metal manufacturer who had the foresight to begin making automobile radiators and then joined with Jonathan Maxwell in 1903 to form the Maxwell-Briscoe Motor Car Company. William Crapo Durant came from a wealthy family in Flint, Michigan. He left school at the age of sixteen to work for himself and had a successful career as a salesman. He made a fortune with the Durant-Dort Carriage Company in Flint and then in 1904 bought control of the floundering Buick Motor Car Company. Durant could be a good manager when he chose to concentrate on it, and before long he had made the Buick car one of the leading sellers, while Buick himself disappeared into obscurity.

Early in 1908 Durant and Briscoe attempted to form a combination of their own companies, Buick and Maxwell-Briscoe, with the other two leading producers, Ford and Reo. This proposal originated with Briscoe. Both wanted to see greater stability and security in a highly volatile industry, where a mass of small firms was struggling to survive and new entrants were constantly appearing, usually to disappear again shortly but in the meantime unsettling the market for the more established companies. Briscoe had somewhat more experience in the automotive industry than Durant and, more important, an association with J. P. Morgan and Company. He seems to have believed that a combination of the leading producers would squeeze out the marginal companies and establish a position of price leadership. Durant on his part hoped to create a large organization making a variety of models—so that a bad year for one would not mean disaster—and controlling its own parts suppliers.

Nothing came of the scheme. Henry Ford asked $3 million in cash (which in those days meant in gold) for the Ford Motor Company, whereupon R. E. Olds demanded as much for Reo, and this was farther than the House of Morgan was prepared to go. Ford's position in this negotiation remains obscure. There seems to be no good reason why he should have wanted to sell a company that was doing very well with the Model N and just putting the Model T on the market. The Selden case was in progress and might go against him, and it is barely possible that Henry Ford saw enough uncertainty in his future to be willing to consider an attractive offer. It is much more likely that he set a figure he knew could not be met because he never seriously intended to sell the Ford Motor Company.

Durant and Briscoe tried again with a proposed International Motor Company based on Buick and Maxwell-Briscoe, but this attempt failed when J. P. Morgan and Company withdrew as one of the underwriters because it suspected Durant of planning to use the merger to speculate in Buick stock. The two promoters then separated to form their own combinations. Durant's came first. It was incorporated in New Jersey on 16 September 1908 and was named the General Motors Company. It began with a nominal capital of $2,000 raised in its first year to $60 million.

With Buick as the base, Durant put together a sprawling structure in the next two years. It had three other good passenger car builders (Cadillac, Oldsmobile, and Oakland, later Pontiac), but only Buick and Cadillac were effective money-makers at the time. Others in the collection were the Cartercar, which had a friction drive that in theory gave an almost unlimited choice of gear ratios but in practice wore out rapidly, and the Elmore, which had a two-cycle engine. Durant took them on the ground that the friction drive or the two-cycle engine might represent the future of the automobile. It was a reasonable enough position in 1909, except that the H-slot transmission had by then been adopted by every one except Henry Ford, and the four-cycle engine had been universally accepted as superior in the technology of the time. Both companies became a total loss. There was also an assortment of parts manufacturers, some good, like the Champion Ignition Company (spark plugs), and others worthless. The worst acquisition was a concern called the Heany Lamp Company, which claimed to have a patent on a new type of incandescent lamp and for which Durant paid $7 million. Then the patent was found to be fraudulent. All these concerns, good and bad, were acquired with General Motors stock except Cadillac, for which Durant had to pay $4 million in cash. He again tried for the Ford Motor Company, but Ford now quoted a price of $8 million cash and this was well beyond Durant's resources, as Ford undoubtedly knew. The whole General Motors structure was flimsy and disorganized. It was put together solely on the basis of what could be acquired, with an astonishing disregard of both technological and financial merit, and it rested mainly on the earnings of Buick and Cadillac. Not surprisingly, it collapsed in 1910, and General Motors came close to dying in infancy. That it survived was due to the efforts of Henry M. Leland, who put the reputation and resources of Cadillac behind an effort to preserve the company, and a banking syndicate led by James J. Storrow of Lee, Higginson and Company of Boston.

The syndicate has been harshly criticized for the severity of the terms it imposed. General Motors was made a loan of $15 million at 6 percent, of which it actually netted only $12.5 million, and the syndicate took six million shares of GM stock as an additional commission. Durant had to resign as president, although he remained on the board of directors. Yet something can be said for the bankers. Strange as it may sound three quarters of a century later, General Motors in 1910 was a poor risk. It was a ramshackle structure without

Charles W. Nash
(1864–1948)

Courtesy of the Motor Vehicle Manufacturers Association

Walter P. Chrysler
(1875–1940)

Courtesy of the Motor Vehicle Manufacturers Association

order or system in its management and dependent almost entirely on the earnings of Buick. Storrow was no grasping money grabber. He was a public-spirited citizen whose memory still lives in Boston, and he devoted himself wholeheartedly to the rehabilitation of General Motors—not just its finances but its administrative structure and its technical performance as well, including the creation of a research department.

Storrow's greatest contribution to General Motors was unquestionably to bring Charles W. Nash and Walter Chrysler into the company. Nash's life story reads like a Horatio Alger novel: an orphan, he ran away at the age of twelve from the farmer to whom he had been bound out, worked for some years as a migrant farm laborer, and eventually attracted the attention of Durant's partner, J. Dallas Dort. He was taken into the Durant-Dort carriage factory and rose to become general manager in 1908. The company's business then was to make bodies for Buick. When Durant was pushed out of General Motors he recommended Nash to Storrow as the man to take charge of Buick. The division was in difficulties, earnings having declined in 1910 because Durant had stripped the company of cash in order to buy control of Cadillac. With the help of an upswing in the automobile market, Nash made Buick financially healthy again and as a result was made president of General Motors in 1912.

Since Nash lacked an engineering background, he needed technical help when he became president of the Buick Motor Car Company. For this purpose Storrow, who was a director of the American Locomotive Company, recruited Walter P. Chrysler, a self-taught engineer who had become manager of the American Locomotive works in Pittsburgh. Chrysler's experience was with locomotives, but he had become fascinated by motor vehicles, so much so that he accepted a salary reduction from $12,000 to $6,000 a year for the opportunity of getting into the automobile industry. (He made it up very rapidly.) When Nash became president of General Motors, Chrysler succeeded him as president of Buick.

When the banker's stock-voting trust expired at the end of 1915, General Motors was solvent. Most of its indebtedness had been paid off, its stock represented tangible assets, and the vehicle models that it had kept in production were selling well. The price paid for this achievement was a drastic pruning of unprofitable operations (Oldsmobile narrowly escaped elimination), curtailment of expenses, and suspension of dividends on common stock. This last may have been necessary, but it proved unfortunate for the Storrow-Nash regime, because it opened the way for the return of Billy Durant.

Durant was in no way abashed by his downfall. He promptly organized a new company to build a low-priced car designed by a Swiss-French engineer named Louis Chevrolet, who had been a racing driver for Buick. The Chevrolet 490 (named for its planned selling price) was a great success, whereupon Durant raised the company's capitalization from $20 to $80 million and proceeded to offer five shares of Chevrolet stock for one of General Motors. At the same time a substantial Du Pont interest was being built in General Motors. This was initiated by Du Pont's treasurer, John J. Raskob, who was seeking promising investments for the high profits that his company and its stockholders were making under the stimulus of World War I. He developed an interest in General Motors, became associated with Durant, and succeeded in enlisting the support of Pierre S. du Pont.

Thus when the bankers' trust expired at the end of 1915, Durant and the Du Ponts together controlled General Motors, and Durant again became president. He and the Du Ponts were not allies in the sense that they had any formal agreement about the management of General Motors; it was just that Raskob and Pierre du Pont admired Durant and saw him as the type of dynamic leader they believed General Motors needed. Storrow and Nash, rather than face the return of Durant, left to establish the Nash Motor Car Company by buying the Thomas L. Jeffery Company in Kenosha, Wisconsin. Its founder was now dead and his successors had replaced the Rambler name with Jeffery. Storrow and Nash wanted to take Walter Chrysler with them, but Durant kept him as president of Buick by offering him a salary of $500,000 a year.

While Durant was going through these gyrations with General Motors, his erstwhile associate Benjamin Briscoe was attempting a similar scheme of his own. It emerged in 1910 as the United States Motor Company, built around Maxwell-Briscoe. The principal backer was Anthony N. Brady, one of the financiers who had been involved in the Electric Vehicle Company; indeed, one of the companies included in United States Motor was the Columbia Motor Car Company, formed when the Electric Vehicle Company went bankrupt in 1907 and was reorganized. (This makes the Electric Vehicle Company a remote ancestor of the Chrysler Corporation and could give Chrysler a claim to be the oldest rather than the youngest of the current surviving American automobile manufacturers.)

Briscoe may have been a better manager than Durant, but the United States Motor Company was a hopeless prospect from the start. It contained only one sound company, Maxwell-Briscoe; the remainder consisted of an assortment of small-scale and mostly unsuccessful motor vehicle manufacturers, like Columbia and the Brush Runabout Company. In September 1912 the United States Motor Company went into receivership. The banking house of Eugene Meyer and Company organized a committee to find out what could be salvaged, and a decision was reached to bring in Walter E. Flanders to reorganize the company. Flanders, as previously described, had been Ford's plant manager and then one of the founders of EMF, which was taken over by Studebaker. He was not happy with Studebaker and early in 1912 left to found his own company. The Meyer group bought the company in order to get Flanders, besides paying him a million dollars in cash and two and three quarters million in stock of the successor to United States Motor.

The Flanders reorganization emerged as the Maxwell Motor Company, the Maxwell name being preserved because it was well known and was considered to have sales value. Both Briscoe and Maxwell resigned when the receivership occurred. Briscoe was less fortunate than Durant. He tried other automobile ventures, but none achieved any prominence or lasted long.

The only other combination of any consequence was put together a few years later by John North Willys. Willys was a salesman who had built up a dealership for selling several makes of bicycles and automobiles in Elmira, New York; the exclusive franchise dealership, restricted to one make of car, still lay in the future. He became involved with two small Indianapolis producers, Overland and Marion, and when the panic of 1907 arrived found that he could not get deliveries of cars on which he had already made deposits. A trip to Indianapolis disclosed that the Overland Company was short of cash and about to shut down. Willys took vigorous measures, including persuading the creditors to take stock instead of cash, and in 1908 the revival of the economy found the Overland Company hard pressed to fill its orders. Willys took over the Marion company and then moved the entire operation to Toledo, Ohio, where the depression had put the Toledo plant of the Pope Motor Company on the market. He then reorganized the enterprise as the Willys-Overland Company and saw its output rise from 4,000 cars in 1909 to 18,000 in 1910.

This was the beginning of Willys's expansion. He bought into the Garford Automobile Company of Elyria, Ohio, which had made cars for Studebaker, and the Gramm Motor Truck Company of Lima. His intention was to develop a Willys-Overland line of trucks, but this arrangement soon broke down. Willys retained the Garford factory and used it to produce the automobile that became the Willys-Knight, using the sleeve-valve engine designed by Charles Y. Knight in 1905. It was quieter than contemporary poppet-valve engines and it enjoyed some popularity in Europe, but Willys was the only American motor vehicle manufacturer to show a strong interest in it.

In the next few years he acquired control of the Fisk Rubber Company of Chicopee, Massachusetts, the New Process Gear Company of Syracuse, New York, the Electric Auto-Lite Company of Toledo, and the Duesenberg Motors Company of Elizabeth, New Jersey. He tried to effect a merger of Willys-Overland, Hudson, Chalmers, and Electric Auto-Lite, but this plan fell through. During World War I Willys became president of the Curtiss Aeroplane and Motor Company, with government approval in the hope that he could stimulate production. However, Willys provided no integrated organization for this assortment of companies. He created a Willys Corporation in 1917, but it was simply a holding company with stock interest in the various members of the group. The only unifying factor was Willys himself.

General Motors: Durant to Sloan

When Billy Durant resumed control of General Motors, he simply picked up the pursuit of his dream of a great automotive combine with a variety of product lines and its own sources of parts and components. For a time he appeared to be moving toward this end boldly but with basically good judgment. The anomalous situation which had resulted in the Chevrolet Motor Car Company controlling General Motors was tidied up by organizing a new General Motors Corporation in 1918 which became the owner of both Chevrolet and the General Motors Company by exchanges of stock. It also acquired another Durant creation, the United Motors Corporation, formed in 1916 as a combination of parts manufacturers.

Two of these units have particular importance. One was Delco, whose acquisition brought Charles F. Kettering into the General Motors orbit. The other was the Hyatt Roller Bearing Company of Harrison, New Jersey, whose president was an M.I.T. graduate named Alfred P. Sloan, Jr. Sloan had taken over the management of this company some years before from its founder, John Wesley Hyatt, a brilliant inventor but an indifferent businessman, and had given its tapered roller bearing a commanding position in the automobile market—presumably after he had taken Henry Leland's advice about accuracy. In his autobiography, *Adventures of a White Collar Man,* he tells how he was at first disposed to reject Durant's proposal rather than give up his company's independence, but when he thought it over he realized that Hyatt had become too big to be independent. It needed an assured market the size of General Motors or Ford, and so Sloan decided to go along with Durant. When the parent company absorbed United Motors in 1918, Sloan became a vice-president of General Motors.

The expansion of General Motors in the second Durant regime started off more soundly than during his first. United Motors was a combination of good companies that had something to offer the organization. In the boom that followed World War I Durant added Fisher Body, the leading manufacturer of automobile bodies, and formed the General Motors Acceptance Corporation to handle the increasingly complex operation of financing automobile sales. He also bought, on his own, a company making electric refrigerators (he got it for $100,000) and sold it at cost to General Motors. When his fellow directors asked why a manufacturer of motor vehicles should make electric refrigerators, Durant airily replied that both cars and refrigerators were boxes containing motors. The success of the Frigidaire vindicated Durant's judgment. All these steps occurred in 1919.

He did not do as well with a venture into tractor manufacturing, taken in the face of vigorous opposition from Walter Chrysler. Yet this was an excusable error of judgment on Durant's part. The Ford Motor Company seemed to be doing well with its Fordson tractor (begun in 1916) and Willys had just added the Moline Plow Company to his conglomeration, so that the agricultural implements and motor vehicle industries appeared to be moving together. International Harvester was, and remains, a major truck manufacturer. However, Chrysler was right. Ford is the only automobile manufacturer ever to have had any success with tractors, and it has withdrawn from the field twice.

This incident and the Frigidaire episode illustrate the weakness in the General Motors structure—Durant himself. He tried to run the entire organization, and he too frequently acted on impulse. Worse still, he became increasingly involved in the stock market—he reputedly had seventy brokerage accounts, so that he was giving General Motors only part of his attention. Chrysler, not a markedly patient person, found himself frustrated by Durant's interference in the affairs of Buick without Chrysler's knowledge, and he was repeatedly irked by being called from Flint to Detroit on company matters and then left to cool his heels in Durant's outer office while Billy was on the telephone with his brokers. The Samson tractor fiasco was too much for him. Buick was responsible for half of General Motors' earnings and as far as Chrysler was concerned, the money he was bringing in was being squandered. Early in 1920 he quit.

Sloan, a highly methodical individual, was equally disturbed by the lack of organization and order in General Motors. Shortly after Chrysler left he worked out the administrative plan that he subsequently applied and submitted it to Durant, who approved it and then simply set it aside. When the depression of 1920–21 struck, car sales fell precipitously and Sloan felt that General Motors should cut prices and expenses, including the completion of the General Motors Center in Detroit. Durant would not, and in the matter of the Center Raskob seems to have encouraged him to continue the work. Sloan, much distressed, took a leave of absence and a trip to Europe to consider his position, and he had actually decided to resign when word reached him that the Durant regime was over.

The sharp decline in the economy and the accompanying drop in stock prices that occurred in 1920 caught Durant hopelessly overextended, and to make matters worse, he gambled on a brief slump—hence he rejected Sloan's advice to lower prices and reduce expenses. As depressions go, this was a short one, but just a little too long to save Durant. His affairs were so entangled that he did not know himself what his obligations were. As reports of Durant's predicament started to leak out, the Du Ponts took alarm. The business decline was affecting General Motors' financial position adversely, and the company and Durant were so closely identified that if Durant went bankrupt he might very well pull General Motors down with him. So the Du Pont Company stepped in to bail Billy out by purchasing his two and a half million shares of General Motors, on condition that he withdraw completely from the organization. When this operation was completed, Du Pont held a 23 percent interest in General Motors.

Pierre S. du Pont took Durant's place as president principally as a step to restore investor confidence. Since he had little experience with the automobile industry, he left the actual running of the company to Sloan as executive vice-president, including the implementing of Sloan's plan of reorganization. In 1923, when General Motors was safely stable again, Du Pont stepped out and Sloan took his place.

The essence of Sloan's plan for reorganization was to bring order and effective control into the sprawling structure of General Motors without sacrificing the advantages that decentralization offered in flexibility and encouraging initiative at all levels of management. To this end the assorted companies that constituted General Motors were converted into autonomous divisions, with overall policymaking and control exercised through the president by an executive committee and a financial committee. There were also central agencies for research, advertising, product planning, and so on; they were to have an advisory relationship with the divisions. Sloan's former college associate, Irenée du Pont, introduced an almost identical organization plan at Du Pont, at this same time, and in view of the close Du Pont relationship with General Motors, it was a natural assumption that the two plans had a common origin. Actually they did not. The similarity was a unique coincidence; in fact, each adopted this organization structure for opposite reasons. General Motors wanted to pull a chaotic structure together, whereas Du Pont was seeking to diversify from being a centralized manufacturer of explosives.

Sloan remained a president of General Motors until 1937, when he became chairman of the board. By that time General Motors had become the largest privately owned manufacturing enterprise in the world. Before his death Sloan had the satisfaction of seeing his management system become a model for large organizations, and in particular of seeing it adopted by Ford and Chrysler.

Willys, Maxwell, and Ford

The combination of managerial skill and adequate financing that General Motors found was unusual in the American automobile industry of this immediate postwar period. There were well-managed companies—Hudson, Nash, and Packard can be cited as examples—but they were well below the General Motors scale of operation, to say nothing of Ford. The other attempted combinations continued to flounder. The Willys Corporation expanded further in the boom that immediately followed the war, raising its capitalization to $50 million, but it disintegrated during the panic of 1920. An attempt by Walter Chrysler to reorganize the corporation failed, and receivership followed late in 1921. The Willys Corporation had to be liquidated. Rivalry between Chrysler and Willys probably contributed to this unsatisfactory result, but Willys managed to salvage something from the wreckage. In the time that Chrysler gave him by staving off the receivership, Willys managed to raise enough money from Toledo businessmen to keep control of Willys-Overland.

In the meantime Chrysler had planned a six-cylinder car that he thought might help to resuscitate the Willys Corporation. It was to be built at the former Duesenberg aircraft engine plant in Elizabeth, New Jersey, and was to bear Chrysler's name. When his efforts to save the Willys Corporation failed, he tried to buy the plant for Maxwell-Chalmers, another victim of the depression that Chrysler was trying to save. However, he was outbid by his old boss Billy Durant, who had rebounded from his 1921 disaster to form another ambitious and speculative structure called Durant Motors. It was probably just as well for Chrysler. The car that was to have been the Chrysler emerged as the Flint, and it turned out to be just another automobile.

Maxwell was of course the relic of Benjamin Briscoe's attempt to duplicate General Motors. For some years the company did well. It leased the Chalmers Motor Company in 1917 and had plans for expansion when the war ended, but then signs of trouble appeared. Walter Flanders resigned in 1914. His talents lay in production and apparently stopped there. He was killed in a highway accident in 1923 after a brief term with the Rickenbacker Motor Car Company, an organization founded in Detroit in 1921 to capitalize on the prestige of Eddie Rickenbacker, the country's leading ace of World War I. The president was Flanders's old associate B. F. Everitt. The company produced a high-priced car and also undertook large-scale but unsuccessful body-building, which Everitt had been engaged in. The losses in this part of the operation absorbed the working capital and the Rickenbacker Motor Company went out of business in 1927.

The Maxwell Motor Car Company was just as highly capitalized as its predecessor, United States Motor, and its cars had an indifferent mechanical reputation (Flanders's previous effort, the EMF, was nicknamed "Every Mechanical Fault"). Chalmers had a high reputation as a salesman, but at that stage of the automobile industry salesmanship was not enough, if indeed it ever has been. The supersalesmen of that era who became automotive entrepreneurs—Durant, Willys, Chalmers—all failed as organizers. Durant and Willys had some early success in stimulating production at Buick and Overland but then they got badly entangled when they moved to large-scale operations. Alfred P. Sloan observed that in those early days selling the cars was not especially difficult; the major problem was to produce them, not just in sufficient numbers but with adequate reliability.

When the crisis came in 1920 Maxwell-Chalmers was heavily in debt. Chrysler's help was invoked by a banking syndicate, recourse to which had become standard procedure for ailing automobile companies. This one was headed by the Chase Securities Company, which had also been involved with Willys. The syndicate gave Chrysler the support he needed: $4 million to tide the company over and another $15 million to put a redesigned and mechanically sound Maxwell on the market at a selling price of $995, which gave a profit of $5 per car. Both Maxwell and Chalmers went through receivership and were combined into a new Maxwell Motor Corporation with a capital of $40 million. In 1923, when he was fully clear of his Willys obligations, Chrysler became president.

The Ford situation was different. The Ford Motor Company continued to dominate the automotive world. In 1922 it was even able to expand by acquiring the Lincoln Motor Car Company, a step that represented a break with the policy followed since 1908 of concentrating on a single model. Lincoln had been founded in 1917 by Henry Leland and his son Wilfred to build Liberty aircraft engines; Leland senior had wanted to do it at Cadillac, but when Durant showed no interest he left General Motors at the age of seventy four to embark on what he saw as a patriotic duty. After the war the Lelands converted to the production of a luxury car, named for the president who was Henry Leland's great hero and for whom he had cast his first vote in 1864 as a young man of twenty one.

Like many other firms, Lincoln was caught short of working capital in the 1920 depression, but what threw it into receivership was a tax bill for $4.5 million that failed to allow for depreciation the company was legally entitled to and should have been only $500,000. By the time the ponderous mecha-

Courtesy of the Motor Vehicle Manufacturers Association

Alfred P. Sloan, Jr.
(1875–1966)

Courtesy of the Henry Ford Museum, The Edison Institute

Henry Ford
(1863–1947)

nism of government acknowledged the error, it was too late. The Ford Motor Company bought Lincoln for $8 million, to the accompaniment of panegyrics in the press about Henry Ford's generosity in coming to the rescue of an old friend. Whatever his motive, it was not generosity. Leland was hardly an old friend. He was the man who twenty years before had taken over when the backers of the Henry Ford Company had given up on Ford and had converted it into the Cadillac Motor Car Company. At the receiver's sale the judge raised the price for Lincoln from Ford's original bid of $5 million to $8 million; if anyone was being generous, it was clearly the judge.

The most convincing explanation of the Lincoln purchase is that Edsel Ford instigated it. He was now officially president of the Ford Motor Company, although his father kept all effective power firmly in his own hands. Edsel, along with other Ford officials, was trying vainly to persuade his father that the Model T had had its day, and he appears to have seen in the Lincoln an opportunity to give the company a foothold in a different market.

There was a verbal agreement between Ford and the Lelands that they later claimed assured them that they would be left in full charge of the Lincoln company. Instead, the plant was taken over by Sorensen and other Ford men, who proceeded to run it as they saw fit and ignore the Lelands completely. This could simply have been a normal exhibition of Sorensen's carefully culti- vated abrasiveness and discourtesy, but Henry Ford made no effort to inter- vene—which was also normal. The Lelands also claimed that their stockhold- ers as well as their creditors were to have been paid off and unsuccessfully took Ford to court.

This dispute was the least of the legal problems that Henry Ford encoun- tered. In a libel suit against the *Chicago Tribune* in 1916—because the news- paper called Ford's pacifist views seditious—he won a nominal judgment, but the case is now remembered only for his usually misquoted assertion, "His- tory is more or less bunk." Another legal entanglement was more serious for the Ford Motor Company. Ford had made enormous profits on the Model T, but in 1916 it ceased to pay extra dividends and limited the stockholders to its regular dividend of 5 percent monthly on the company's authorized capital of $2 million. The Dodge brothers thereupon brought suit in behalf of the minor- ity stockholders to compel distribution of three fourths of the company's sur- plus of $60 million.

Ford was accumulating the surplus for expansion, in particular the construc- tion of the giant River Rouge plant, and he argued that this use of the compa- ny's earnings enabled it to create employment, pay higher wages, and lower prices. He believed his stockholders were being sufficiently reimbursed be- cause they had already received more in dividends than they had invested—

one of the points that came up in the testimony was whether he had called them parasites or not. Thus the Dodge case raised interesting issues regarding the proper use of corporate earnings.

Ford lost and promptly decided to get rid of his minority stockholders. He was particularly annoyed with the Dodges because, as he saw it, they were using their Ford profits to produce a competing car. He achieved his end by threatening to leave the Ford Motor Company and build a new and cheaper car in a company called Henry Ford and Son, which had been formed in 1916 to build Fordson tractors. He had used a similar threat—or ruse—against Malcomson. Whether he meant it seriously or not, it worked. He was able to buy out the other stockholders for just over $100 million. Couzens, who had left the company in 1915, was able to bargain for $1,000 a share more than the other stockholders and got $29 million, a good return on an initial investment of $1,000 sixteen years before.

The timing of this step was hardly optimal in terms of careful fiscal planning: the simultaneous decision of the court in the Dodge case required the Ford Motor Company to pay out $19 million in back dividends, although over half of this amount went to Henry Ford himself, and River Rouge was nearing completion. The burden was too great even for Ford, and, much as Henry Ford detested banks and the money market, the company had to borrow $75 million. Since Ford profits for 1919 were on the order of $70 million, the loan appeared unlikely to pose problems.

The year 1920, however, was a different story. Ford sales and earnings plummeted along with those of the rest of the automobile industry, and as the date for repayment of the loan approached (April 1921), the financial world eagerly anticipated a Ford Motor Company forced to go public and sell stock. However, that event would only take place a generation later, and for very different reasons. In early 1921, Henry Ford cut prices, canceled the company's orders for material, used up his existing inventory, and shipped the finished cars to his dealers unordered, with the usual sight drafts requiring immediate cash payment. The dealers could either accept or lose their franchises, and the reputation of Tin Lizzie still made a Ford dealership something to be prized. Some of the dealers were bankrupted, but most complied, and the resulting cash flow plus the economies from the curtailment of production kept the company safe.

Ford's maneuver had worked, and the Ford Motor Company retained its apparently unassailable leadership. It would have taken a bold and perceptive observer to suggest in 1921 that the Ford position was not as strong as it appeared to be. To millions of people Henry Ford had become a figure of legend, carrying an aura of infallibility. He was seriously considered as a candidate for president of the United States. True, his record in activities other than the manufacture of motor vehicles was somewhat less than impressive, but people at large in the United States and elsewhere saw him only as the genius behind the Model T and mass production. Yet the signs of future trouble were discernible. The Ford Motor Company was controlled by an autocrat who acted on impulse rather than on any rationally conceived program. The departure of able executives from an apparently prospering organization was a clear signal that all was not well. The loss of Couzens has been noted. In the 1919–21 period C. H. Wills and John R. Lee left and, most damaging of all to the Ford Motor Company, William S. Knudsen—all because of friction within the Ford organization. Wills and Lee formed their own company and built the Wills Sainte Claire, which they proudly and accurately advertised as being ten years ahead of its time. It was, but an automobile ten years ahead of its time is no more saleable than one ten years behind its time, and the Wills Sainte Claire was a financial failure. Knudsen was taken into General Motors by Alfred P. Sloan and put in charge of Chevrolet, which had not lived up to its early promise. What he achieved will be told in the next chapter.

As was suggested earlier, while Henry Ford and the Ford Motor Company made vital contributions to the American and world automotive industries, organization was not one of them.

CHAPTER SIX

The Coming of Mass Consumption

The ten years that followed World War I were a landmark period in the history of the American automobile industry. They saw General Motors wrest leadership from Ford and Chrysler emerge as the third member of a dominant "Big Three." The career of the Model T came to an end, and the used car market became a significant element in automobile sales. The growing role of motor vehicle transportation was recognized in the Federal Highway Act of 1921, which made the first effective provision for a national highway system. It created the routes designated as U.S. and contributed half the cost of their construction, the other half coming from the states. The states discovered what at the time seemed a painless way to finance road construction and improvement: taxes on gasoline, initially one or two cents a gallon. The more traffic, the more revenue; it was a financial servomechanism.

Above all, in the decade of the 1920s the automobile became an article of mass consumption and use. This phenomenon had several causes. After the 1920–21 depression the economy boomed until 1929, so that disposable income increased, and much of it went to foster America's blossoming love affair with the motor vehicle. Output increased, to reach a peak of over five million in 1929, and vigorous competition for the mass market kept car prices in that category low. In the middle of the decade a new Model T coupe could be bought for $290. Marketing techniques were introduced to make it easier to buy cars on credit, as well as to encourage existing owners to "trade upward." In addition, petroleum was plentiful and cheap, so that the cost of operating a car was low. As a result, by 1929 there was one motor vehicle for every six people in the United States. The only other country to share this extent of motor vehicle ownership and usage was Canada, where the larger American producers had all established branch plants. Ford had gone farther afield. It had begun assembly in Britain as early as 1911 and was the country's largest producer by 1914, but British automobile usage was far below the North American level.

War and Aftermath, 1917–22

World War I had little effect on the American automobile industry. Nonmilitary production continued unchecked until the middle of 1918, when shortages of steel and other materials led the War Industries Board to order passenger car output cut by 50 percent. The war ended before this order had any serious impact. The industry did make a substantial contribution to the war effort, although nothing comparable to the scale it attained in World War II. Understandably the most immediate service it performed was the building of vehicles for military use. The White Motor Company alone made 18,000 trucks for the United States and Allied forces and found this branch of the business so much to its liking that it gave up passenger car manufacture altogether. Motor vehicle companies also made aircraft engines in quantity, something that in those days their engine plants were equipped to do. Indeed, the Liberty motor was specifically designed so that it could be readily produced by the automotive industry. Expectations that automobile assembly plants could be readily converted to airframes failed to materialize; in both world wars it was discovered that aircraft are best put together in buildings designed for the purpose.

The end of the war brought a brief period of rapid expansion, interrupted by the slump of 1920–21. Interestingly, this postwar expansion brought very few new firms into the industry, and none of them succeeded. Three have been mentioned—Lincoln, Rickenbacker, and Wills Sainte-Claire; Lincoln remained in existence only as part of the Ford Motor Company. One other that achieved some reputation was Duesenberg, which produced a luxury sports car that remained in production through most of the 1920s.

Without exception these new entrants attempted to compete at the upper level of the motor vehicle market. It was not yet ten years since Henry Ford had introduced the moving assembly line but in that short time mass production and mass marketing had transformed the character of the industry. The time had definitely passed when motor vehicle assembly could be undertaken with a minimum of capital and equipment, trusting that cars could be built and sold before the suppliers' bills had to be paid. For a complete newcomer to enter the low-priced automobile market now required an investment in production and marketing facilities so great as to present a virtually prohibitive risk.

The industry had not yet hardened into the oligopolistic form that it would subsequently take. There were still more than 100 companies manufacturing motor vehicles in 1919, although many of them were in a precarious financial position and would disappear in the 1921 depression. The field was dominated by Ford, with half the total United States production. General Motors was second, with about a fifth of the market.

The experience of Ford, General Motors, Maxwell, and Willys during these immediate postwar years has been told. Behind them was a group of middle-sized producers—Dodge, Hudson, Nash, Packard, Studebaker—who maintained a reasonable stability during the postwar expansion and subsequent contraction. Hudson, ably managed by Roy D. Chapin and Roscoe B. Jackson, expanded its operations by introducing a lower-priced model, the Essex. It never sold at the price level of the Ford, but it found a market among the increasing number of Americans who were prepared to go to a somewhat higher price range in order to get an automobile with more amenities and style than the ungainly Tin Lizzie. Charles W. Nash for once lost his ordinary caution and tried to break into the luxury market with a car called the Lafayette. The venture failed but without doing the Nash Motor Company much harm. Dodge, Packard, and Studebaker maintained a steady growth and in common with Hudson and Nash were conspicuously unaffected by the 1921 panic.

What remained of the motor vehicle market was divided among a miscellany of producers. Some had historic names: Marmon, Pierce-Arrow, Locomobile, Reo, Kissel (built in Hartford, Wisconsin), Moon, Dort, Hupp, Cole (which was advertised as a fully assembled car, claiming that it thereby embodied all the special expertise of its parts manufacturers), Jordan (famous for its "somewhere west of Laramie" advertising), Peerless, Elcar, Velie, and Stutz, which made the most popular American sports car of that day, the "Stutz Bearcat." The rest of the industry was composed of unknowns who appeared briefly on the automotive scene and vanished, few of them remembered even by antique car enthusiasts. The 1920–21 depression devastated these minor firms.

The Emergence of the Big Three

When the panic of 1920–21 ended, the United States entered an economic boom period that lasted until the much greater market crash of 1929. Motor vehicle production and sales increased rapidly, from 1,116,119 in 1921 to 5,337,087 in 1929, a figure not surpassed for the next twenty years. However, the most significant feature of these years for the automobile industry was a major restructuring that resulted in a clear-cut oligopoly with three firms—General Motors, Ford, and Chrysler—dominating the industry, and a shrinking number of independents whose position became increasingly precarious.

The appearance of the Big Three represented an end of the Ford domination of the industry that had lasted since the introduction of Model T in 1908. It was quite unlikely that Ford could have retained its market position of over 50 percent indefinitely, but the decline was accelerated by Henry Ford's refusal to recognize that public taste had changed and that the Model T had had its day. People were becoming automobile owners in larger numbers, and in an economic boom they wanted more in their cars than Tin Lizzie had to offer. The customer who wanted somewhat more quality and style but was short of cash found it increasingly easy to buy on credit; perhaps more important, the market now offered a growing supply of used cars which offered the desired style and quality at no greater cost than the Model T. It should have been a warning sign for Ford that jokes about the Model T, formerly an invaluable advertising medium, now began to show a caustic quality: for example, "What does the Ford use for shock absorbers? The passengers." The company tried hard to keep the Model T in competition by adding such items as closed bodies, windshield wipers, electric starters, and other accessories—there was in fact a thriving business in accessories for the Model T—but in the automotive climate that had developed Tin Lizzie could never be made to look like anything but a poor relation in a hand-me-down outfit.

It would be misleading to suggest that Ford actually lost ground. Events would show that the Ford Motor Company had a devoted following, sublimely confident in Henry Ford's genius. Rather, what happened was that Ford was marking time while two powerful rivals were forging ahead. Under Sloan's managerial system General Motors cleared up its internal disorder and became a vigorous, efficient organization. It too had to face the problem of the used car. Sloan's solution was the annual model—a systematic change each year carefully calculated so that each new model would be recognizably different from its predecessors, but not so far different as to pose the threat that each year's model would be completely out of style a year later.

The policy of the annual model has been widely associated in the public mind with "planned obsolescence"—building a car so that it would last just for a limited length of time. The automobile industry's refusal to concede that it practices planned obsolescence is undoubtedly justified. Building a vehicle intentionally so that it will self-destruct in some calculated period of time (something like James Russell Lowell's "Wonderful One-Hoss Shay") should be distinguished from making one that is not meant to last indefinitely. Construction for permanence is necessarily very expensive; it is totally impractical if the manufacturer is seeking a moderate or low-priced market. The only American automobiles built to last indefinitely have been cars like Auburn, Packard, and Marmon, and they were unable to survive in the competitive conditions of the United States market. Cadillac and Lincoln can be put in this category also, but they have had the advantage of being parts of a much larger organization. Much of what has passed for planned obsolescence has been due to normal wear and tear, frequently aggravated by inadequate maintenance, and some of it should be attributed to careless workmanship and inadequate quality control, not to intent.

A step that hurt Ford badly was Sloan's appointment of William S. Knudsen, one of the great production men in the automobile industry, as head of the Chevrolet Division. Knudsen had left the Ford Motor Company in 1921 after a dispute over Henry Ford's methods of management and joined General Motors a year later. At that point Chevrolet was in trouble. The car had not lived up to its early promise; in fact serious consideration was being given to dropping it from the General Motors line. However, Sloan was reluctant to give it up and decided to give Knudsen a chance to see what he could do. Knudsen set out to make the Chevrolet fully competitive with the Model T—in his strong Danish accent he would exhort Chevrolet dealers, "I vant vun for vun"—that is, to match Ford. Under his driving leadership Chevrolet sales rose from about 300,000 in 1922 to over a million in 1927, putting it in first place on the American passenger car market. This feat clearly marked Knudsen as the man who would in due course succeed Sloan as president of General Motors.

The rise of Chevrolet at last convinced Henry Ford to recognize what his son and other Ford officials had been trying to tell him for some time. On 31 May 1927, the final Model T (number 15,007,003) came off the River Rouge assembly line, and all Ford manufacturing operations were shut down for over a year while Ford himself and a few assistants worked on designing a successor. The power of the Ford cult was then dramatically demonstrated. Buyers by the thousand waited for Henry Ford to repeat his Model T triumph; many of them placed orders sight unseen with Ford dealers for whatever car would eventually emerge from the great man's deliberations. The dealers themselves struggled to stay alive by selling used cars and waited patiently for the new car to appear.

They must have felt rewarded when the Model A Ford was put on the market for the 1929 model year and the demand was so great that Ford again outsold Chevrolet—for one year. The Model A was a good but quite conventional automobile, and once its novelty had worn off Ford dropped back to second place. The introduction of the V-8 in 1932 gave Ford the lead for another year and there have been occasional repetitions since then, but Ford has never lastingly recovered the position it once held.

Until the end of the 1920s it was by no means certain that there would be just three major motor vehicle producers. When the boom period began, Durant Motors, Studebaker, Hudson-Essex, Maxwell, and Willys-Overland could all conceivably have been competitors of General Motors and Ford. Durant's operation was ambitious and highly publicized. In the low-priced range it offered a car called the Star that sold a total of a million and a half units and seemed for a few years to have established a place alongside Chevrolet and Ford. But Durant Motors was a speculative enterprise, inadequately financed, and neither sales promotion nor financial manipulation could substitute for skill and efficiency on the production line or in management. Durant Motors was in trouble at the peak of the boom, and the stock market collapse put it out of business. The company was finally liquidated in 1933 and Durant himself went into bankruptcy in 1936. He had ideas for other ventures—none automotive—but age and declining health forced him into inactivity. He died in 1947, the same year as Henry Ford.

John N. Willys rebuilt his empire after the 1921 receivership, with the Overland as his low-priced entry, two high-priced cars, Willys-Knight and Stearns-Knight, featuring the Knight sleeve-valve engine, and a sports-type automobile called the Whippet. This grouping had the same weakness as the previous Willys combination in that there was no organic relationship among the separate parts. Willys himself provided what unity there was. In addition, the Knight engine was an expensive mechanism, more difficult to maintain and repair than the poppet-valve engine, and improvement of the latter had eliminated the advantages that the Knight formerly possessed. The Overland was a popular car and in fact lasted beyond World War II, but the Willys organization itself went into receivership again in 1933 and never really recovered.

Studebaker was the third largest automobile manufacturer in the United States at the outset of the 1920s. It was well behind Ford and General Motors but had twice the output of its next nearest rivals. The company's prospects seemed excellent: it was a long established firm with a respected name and a good product. But managerial mistakes in the middle of the decade started the company on a decline that cost Studebaker its strong position in the industry. The first of these steps was an attempt to compete in the low-priced car market. That decision was understandable under the circumstances, when the mass market was booming and Ford and General Motors were demonstrating the potential of the economies of scale, but Studebaker's offering, the Erskine, named for the company's president, Albert R. Erskine, was a failure. Erskine then went in precisely the opposite direction and in 1928 bought control of the

Pierce-Arrow Motor Car Company, makers of a well-known but unprofitable luxury car, which had lost three quarters of a million dollars in the boom year of 1927.

Hudson was another good prospect, especially with the Essex doing reasonably well in the medium-price range. The company scored an impressive first in 1922 by offering an Essex with a closed body, something hitherto reserved for high-priced cars. This first Essex body was a boxlike wooden structure on a metal frame. It had to be done that way because expensive cabinet work was out of the question and stamping presses for all-metal bodies had not yet come into use; but it was an innovation with profound effects on motor vehicle use. Naturally it had to be emulated by all of Essex's competitors, and it made the automobile for the first time a truly all-weather vehicle for the majority of owners, with all the potentialities that such a vehicle offered. However, the Essex was not a competitor of Ford and Chevrolet, and the fundamentally conservative Hudson management had no ambitious plans for expansion.

That left the field to Walter Chrysler. He wanted his own company and his own car, and the Maxwell Motor Corporation gave him his opportunity. With continued support from the banking group that had financed the Maxwell reorganization, he put the Chrysler car on the market in late 1924. It was designed to sell in the $1,500 range but to offer the style and performance of more expensive automobiles. To achieve this objective Chrysler's engineers used the knowledge of high-compression engines that had been gained in developing aircraft engines in World War I. The car was an immediate success, so that Chrysler had a financial base for subsequent growth, and in 1927 the Chrysler Corporation was organized. It replaced the Maxwell Motor Corporation and the Maxwell line was terminated.

This was by no means enough for Walter Chrysler. He was well aware that for his company to have a really solid position in the industry, it must expand its product line and in particular compete in the mass market with Chevrolet and Ford. But the Chrysler Corporation by itself lacked the production and marketing capacity for this purpose. Chrysler's opportunity came when the Dodge Brothers Manufacturing Company was put on the market. Its founders, John and Horace Dodge, both died in the influenza epidemic of 1920, and their widows were not interested in running an automobile manufacturing company. They sold it in 1925 to the banking house of Dillon, Read, and Company, which did not want to make Dodge cars either but held the company for a prospective buyer. After what must have been interesting bargaining, in which the buyer knew that the seller wanted to sell and the seller knew that the buyer wanted to buy, the Chrysler Corporation bought Dodge for $170,000,000 in Chrysler stock.

This transaction gave Chrysler both the manufacturing and marketing capacity he needed—the Dodge purchase added a well organized group of several thousand dealers to the Chrysler organization. The Dodge line was of course continued, and in 1928 Chrysler was able to put a low-priced car, the Plymouth, on the market in competition with Chevrolet and Ford. The move was well timed, whether accidentally or intentionally, because the Plymouth made its appearance in the hiatus between the demise of the Model T and the arrival of the Model A and so got itself established while competition was limited.

The Mass Market

By the 1920s the American automobile industry had mastered the technique of producing motor vehicles in large quantity; it was now grappling with the equally complex problem of selling them. Only half the retail price of a car represents the cost of manufacturing it; the rest is the cost of marketing and distributing it to the customer, and the industry was discovering at this time that economies of scale offered advantages in marketing as well as in production—another factor that worked in favor of the bigger companies. The industry was also realizing that the ability to manufacture in quantity was creating a selling problem for new cars by making available an accumulating number of serviceable used cars.

The system of selling motor vehicles through dealers holding exclusive franchises was well established by this time. The dealer was restricted by his franchise to selling a specified make or makes of new cars, always from the manufacturer granting the franchise; he had to accept quotas of vehicles fixed by the company and pay for them on delivery; and the franchise could be canceled at any time. He had some territorial rights but little effective protection against infringement. In short, the dealer was at the mercy of the manufacturer, but during the boom period new car sales were brisk and most automobile dealers were doing well enough so that the inequities of the system did not bother them. There was some grumbling among Ford dealers after 1924 because they were allowed a markup of 17½ percent on new cars while their General Motors rivals had just been raised from 17 to 24 percent so as to give them more scope for trading, but it was not until the depression started to bite in 1930 that Ford went up to 22 percent.

The importance of a strong dealer network was fully understood. It has already been mentioned that one of the attractions of Dodge for Chrysler was its dealer organization. Alfred P. Sloan spent much time as president of General Motors in visiting individual dealers, and in 1924 he established a General

Sales Committee whose functions included building the dealer organization and overseeing its operation. The Ford Motor Company received vital support from its dealers during the 1921 crisis and again in the interim between Model T and Model A. Policies for handling the used car problem varied widely. Ford insisted that its dealers make a profit on used cars. General Motors, on the other hand, felt that in some circumstances it might be good business for a dealer to take a loss on a used car, and so GM contented itself with establishing broad guidelines for its dealers to follow. The situation was complicated by the growth of a class of automobile dealers who did business in used cars only and over whom the manufacturers had no control.

When the depression came and both manufacturers and dealers were contending with lagging sales, the weaknesses in the system became more evident. The manufacturers put stronger pressure on their dealers and canceled franchises more freely and arbitrarily than in the past. Dealer protests led to the formation of the National Automobile Dealers Association, and the Federal Trade Commission investigated the motor vehicle industry, but there was no change in the basic situation. The automobile dealers lacked strong public support and they had very little consensus among themselves, except possibly on the cancellation issue, and even on that there was no accepted position on how to distinguish between arbitrary and justifiable revocation of a franchise.

The general prosperity of the 1920s in the United States provided a favorable atmosphere for the mass marketing of motor vehicles. Purchasing power in people's hands was amplified by generous use of installment buying. Thus the automobile industry had the stimulus of an expanding economy, but at the same time it was a significant contributor to the expansion. Apart from the direct stimulus afforded by the manufacture of steadily larger numbers of motor vehicles, the automobile industry became the country's principal consumer of steel, machine tools, and rubber, the last-named of course predominantly in the form of tires. Tire design was greatly improved. Cotton cord became the basic fabric, and during the 1920s the "balloon" tire, operating at 30 psi of air, replaced the tires that had used sixty pounds of pressure and thereby provided much smoother riding. The automobile industry's demand was responsible for the introduction of the continuous strip mill for rolling sheet steel and the continuous process method of making plate glass—the latter an innovation promoted directly by Henry Ford. About half the output of machine tools went to implement the production of motor vehicles, most of them custom-made to designs originating in the specialized needs of mass production.

The petroleum industry was transformed by the automobile in the twentieth century, from chiefly a producer of illuminants to predominantly a producer of gasoline, with both constant exploration to find new sources of supply and

continuous research for more efficient refining techniques. The earliest of
these steps was the Burton cracking process introduced by the Standard Oil
Company of Indiana in 1913. Named for William M. Burton, who directed
the research, the process used high temperatures and high pressures to double
the quantity of gasoline extracted from a given amount of crude oil, from 20
to 40 percent. This process was eventually replaced in the 1930s by catalytic
cracking. Meanwhile in 1922 Charles F. Kettering and Thomas H. Midgley
discovered that adding tetraethyl lead to gasoline virtually eliminated engine
knock. General Motors and the Standard Oil Company of New Jersey (now
Exxon) then combined to form the Ethyl Gasoline Corporation in 1924. General Motors subsequently decided that it should not be in the petroleum business and withdrew, but leaded gasoline continued to be the premium fuel for
motor vehicles until the antipollution agitation of the 1960s and 1970s led to
its gradual elimination. The octane scale for gasoline was worked out in 1926
by Graham Edgar of the Ethyl Gasoline Corporation.

The most obvious economic impact of the mass market for automobiles was
a massive program of road construction and improvement. This relationship
was very direct. As motor vehicle ownership and use became more general,
pressure for better roads became stronger, and as the mileage of improved
highway increased, automobile ownership became more attractive. This pressure, as has been pointed out, had actually begun in the latter part of the nineteenth century as an effort to do something about the generally appalling state
of American rural roads, and it was intensified by the popularity of bicycling
in the 1880s and 1890s. It produced some results, mainly in the Northeast, but
the development of a national network of good hard-surfaced highways had to
await the enactment of the Federal Highway Act of 1921. The road system
envisioned by this law was substantially complete, about a quarter of a million
miles, by 1935, and it was then already inadequate. The volume of motor
vehicle traffic kept increasing ahead of expectations, and these roads, much as
they contributed to facilitating travel, were still built to a concept of highways
going back to an earlier and simpler era. The idea of the superhighway specifically designed for fast-moving, self-propelled vehicles had come into existence by then from various sources, including such apparently unlikely personalities as T. Coleman du Pont in the United States and Hilaire Belloc in Great
Britain, and some urban parkways were designed accordingly, but for some
time the novelty and high cost deterred widespread adoption. Expenditures on
roads and streets in the 1920s from all sources—federal, state, and local—
averaged two billion dollars a year, a substantial contribution to the economic
boom of the period. In the next decade highway construction was used as a
means of combating unemployment.

The social impact of the automobile was just beginning to be felt. Cities were facing problems of traffic congestion, the toll of highway accidents was becoming a matter of increasing concern, and there was an awareness that social customs and living habits were undergoing change. However, none of this affected the industry in the sense that there was any pressure for restriction or restraint. There were not yet enough motor vehicles in use to create a problem of air pollution; in fact, the problem was not known to exist. The automobile was seen by most people as offering freedom from dependence on public transportation systems that were generally looked on as unsatisfactory.

Thus during the decade of the 1920s the American automobile industry operated under highly favorable conditions, not for all the individual firms but for the industry as a whole. The motor vehicle was welcomed in American life, along with the industry that produced it. The automobile was an asset to the American economy. Henry Ford was a folk hero, generally seen as a genius whose opinions on any subject deserved attention, although such political ambitions as he had disappeared early in the decade. Others like Durant, Willys, Chrysler, and Nash occupied somewhat lesser places in the same pantheon. Oddly enough, Sloan, who contributed more than anyone else to the growth of the automobile industry in that era, remained relatively obscure.

The national government's role in the automobile industry, apart from promoting highway improvement, consisted only of enacting protective tariffs, which were meaningless because automobile imports were negligible. State action, other than highway building, was limited to providing for registration of vehicles and licensing of drivers and establishing traffic regulations—at that time in some parts of the country decidedly on the exiguous side. There were some restrictions on truck weights and sizes, but essentially the industry was free to produce and sell whatever it chose.

Expansion Abroad

The expansive atmosphere of the 1920s stimulated interest in foreign markets among American motor vehicle producers. For most companies this was a matter of exporting vehicles made in the United States, and this business did in fact increase, reaching just over 11 percent of total United States production in 1929. The export market had drawbacks in that foreign countries imposed restrictions, notably those that were trying to foster their own automotive industries, and even in those days the standard American passenger automobile was too big to be generally acceptable elsewhere. Canada remained a special case. All the major American firms had Canadian subsidiaries and the Canadian market was dominated by American-type cars built in Canada.

The obvious way to get around restrictions on exports was to locate plants in countries that offered attractive market potential, although this was an option available only to the stronger companies. Ford, as stated, had pioneered successfully in Britain as early as 1911, and shortly afterward General Motors was making a British car on a Buick chassis under the name Bedford. During World War 1 Ford built a factory in Cork, Ireland, to make Fordson tractors, and after the war Ford expanded its European operations with assembly plants in Denmark, France, Germany, Italy, Spain, and Sweden. The company lost its first place in the British market during the 1920s but remained among the leaders. Ford of Britain had an exceptionally able manager in Percival L. D. Perry, later Lord Perry, who had the distinction of being the only individual of any prominence in the entire Ford organization to leave the company after a dispute with Henry Ford and later rejoin it.

The dispute occurred right after World War 1, when Perry insisted that American sales techniques would have to be modified for the British market and that the British company should design and build cars tailored to British needs and tastes, a position supported by Edsel Ford. However, Henry Ford was still committed to the Model T and convinced that Ford manufacturing and sales techniques would work anywhere. Perry resigned, but when Ford's British operations floundered, he was asked to return in 1928 as head of a new Ford Motor Company, Ltd., which took over all Ford interests in the United Kingdom and Ireland. The stock was sold publicly, something that would not happen to the Ford Motor Company in the United States for another quarter century. Construction was promptly started on a new plant at Dagenham, just outside London. Perry was also made general supervisor of all Ford's European activities, but the intense nationalism that came with the Great Depression prevented him from carrying out this function as had been hoped. In Germany Ford built a new factory in Cologne in 1930 but the effects of the depression and the rise of the Nazis limited its usefulness.

General Motors followed a different policy in Europe. Instead of establishing its own branch plants or subsidiaries, it chose to affiliate with the existing European industry. It bought Vauxhall in Britain in 1925 and Opel in Germany in 1929, both after the kind of intensive study that was characteristic of Sloan's methods. Opel was and has remained one of the leading German automobile manufacturers, while Vauxhall has had a somewhat lesser, albeit highly successful, role in the British motor industry. In addition Ford and General Motors established assembly plants in Japan in 1925 and 1927 respectively, and these between them accounted for the largest part of Japanese motor vehicle output during the 1920s. However, the Japanese market at that time was very limited, and government policy presently swung in the direction of actively encouraging the growth of an indigenous automobile industry.

The influence of the American automobile industry extended beyond exports to other countries and direct investment abroad. While it was true that American methods could not be transferred unaltered into differing social climates, the fact remained that the rest of the world, especially Europe, was profoundly impressed by the American achievement in mass production and paid it the high compliment of trying to imitate it. Germany in the 1920s had a cult of "fordismus," a term for the American mass production techniques and plant organization that seemed best exemplified by Henry Ford. The ability of American manufacturers to build motor vehicles in quantity and at low cost attracted attention and prospective imitators. The only one to make a start before the advent of World War I diverted European automotive production to military uses was William Morris, later Lord Nuffield. He was a bicycle mechanic in Oxford, England, who moved into motor vehicle repair and built up a group of service establishments under the name Morris Garages, from which a well-known sports car, the MG, later took its name.

In 1912 Morris decided to go into automobile manufacturing, with the hope of repeating in Britain what Henry Ford was doing in the United States. He went to Detroit to study Ford methods and found that he could buy components cheaper in the United States than he could at home. The war interrupted him but he returned to his concept afterward with a low-priced model called the Morris Cowley (the first Morris factory was in Cowley, adjoining Oxford). He found himself in close competition with Herbert (later Lord) Austin, whose Austin Seven was for some years the leading seller among low-priced British cars. The "Seven" referred to horsepower. Britain had imposed a tax on motor vehicles of ten horsepower or more, so that builders of automobiles intended for the popular-priced market had to keep their horsepower below the taxable minimum. The Morris Cowley thus was rated at 8 h.p. Since horse-power was calculated for tax purposes on a formula based on the diameter of the bore times the number of cylinders, British designers favored engines with narrow-bore and long-stroke cylinders, and as few cylinders as possible—both the Austin Seven and the Morris Cowley had two-cylinder engines. By contrast, American and most other automobile manufacturers preferred wide-bore, short-stroke engines, which gave more power.

These British efforts were matched in France by Louis Renault, who had been building motor vehicles since 1898, and Andre Citroën, who aspired to be the Henry Ford of France. After a spectacular rise, Citroën suffered a financial collapse, but his company survived and continued to be one of France's major motor vehicle producers. None of these efforts really achieved their hopes at that time. They did increase automotive production, but they did not reach the kind of mass market that Henry Ford did. Whether such a market existed or might have been created in either Britain or France at that time is a matter of dispute among historians. Britain became the world's second largest manufacturer of motor vehicles during the 1920s, but it was not until the early 1930s that Austin, Morris, or a third competitor, Hillman, attained sufficient volume of production to justify the installation of full-fledged moving assembly lines.

CHAPTER SEVEN
Depression and the New Deal

The collapse of the United States stock market at the end of 1929 signaled the arrival of the worst economic depression in the history of the modern world. The causes of this event are far too complicated to be discussed in any detail here; they are still a subject of controversy among economists and historians, with no sign of final agreement. They certainly include the aftereffects of World War I and its peace settlement, constraints on international trade by the multiplying of tariffs and other restrictions, prolonged agricultural depression in the 1920s, and injudicious expansion of credit during the boom period—credit to foreign governments, to business organizations, and to individual consumers alike.

The effect on the United States was devastating. At the depression's low point in 1932 there were between 13 and 15 million unemployed in a total population of about 130 million (there were no exact figures on unemployment), at least as many more people were working on short time, and wages had dropped steeply. Agricultural distress had reached proportions that provoked near civil insurrection in some areas. Bank failures were numerous, and early in 1933 a banking crisis reached such severity that all the banks in the country had to be temporarily closed until remedial measures could be taken.

This bank closing was the first official action of the newly elected president, Franklin D. Roosevelt. It was followed by the other sweeping measures that constituted the New Deal, which drastically altered the conditions under which industry operated in its relationships with both government and labor.

Adjustment to Depression

The economic crisis inevitably brought major changes to the American automobile industry, as it did to so much else throughout the world. Sales of new

73

cars shriveled, from the almost 5 ½ million of 1929 to a low of under 1 ½
million in 1932. There was a slow recovery after that, but it took until 1948 to
reach the five million mark again. The industry approached this figure in 1940
and 1941, but the outbreak of war interrupted passenger car manufacture. Motor vehicle use was not affected in the same way. Even at the bottom of the
depression in 1932, total motor vehicle registrations were only about 5 percent
lower than they had been in 1929. The same phenomenon appeared in later
downswings of the economy. Americans did not give up their cars when hard
times came; they simply deferred the purchase of new ones.

The shock of the depression accentuated the already existing trend to oligopoly. By 1929 the number of motor vehicle producers in the United States had
shrunk to forty-four, down from over a hundred ten years before. After the
stock market collapse the weaker competitors disappeared rapidly, and in the
process a number of well-known names vanished from the American automotive scene, among them Locomobile, Moon, Peerless, Franklin, and Jordan,
to cite a few. The Peerless factory in Cleveland became a brewery, completing
a rather remarkable progression from washing machines to bicycles to automobiles to beer. The luxury cars were the principal victims of the economic
collapse.

Two of the survivors, Studebaker and Willys, were badly hurt. Studebaker
was plunged into a spectacular bankruptcy by errors of judgment on the part
of its president, Albert R. Erskine. He appears to have aspired to raise Studebaker to the same class as General Motors, Ford, and Chrysler, a reasonable
enough hope during the boom period, but nothing went right for him. His
Erskine car was a failure and his purchase of Pierce-Arrow saddled Studebaker
with an unprofitable burden just as the depression arrived. Then Erskine made
his most disastrous blunder. He calculated that the depression would be brief,
and in the face of continuing economic decline continued to act on the assumption that the upswing was about to arrive, even to the extent of paying Studebaker dividends from capital in order to keep up the appearance of prosperity.
In 1931 Studebaker again tried to enter the low-priced market with a car named
the Rockne, after the famous football coach of Notre Dame University (the
Studebaker Corporation was based in South Bend, Indiana), but not even a
glamorous name could sell cars in 1931. A year later the company's condition
was desperate. Erskine tried to save it by buying control of the White Motor
Company, which had a reserve of working capital that might be used to tide
Studebaker over its crisis, but this effort was blocked by court action on the
part of minority White stockholders. Studebaker was forced into receivership
and Erskine committed suicide. The company was reorganized under the leadership of Harold S. Vance and Paul G. Hoffman, the latter to achieve distinc-

tion later as administrator of the Marshall Plan. They did well enough so that the Studebaker name remained in the automotive world for another thirty years, but it was never again the power that it had once been.

The fundamental problem with Willys-Overland was that the company had not recovered its financial health after its collaspe in 1921. John N. Willys retired from active management to become ambassador to Poland in the Hoover administration, but he had to give up that post in 1932 to attempt to rescue his company. He was unable to avert receivership and Willys-Overland was reorganized with its capitalization trimmed from $87 million to $15 million. Willys himself died in 1935. Just before the outbreak of World War II the company found a special place in the automotive market with the Willys Jeep, which would make itself universally popular during the war. The name came from the fact that the Army termed it a General Purpose Vehicle, abbreviated to GP, and thence easily converted to Jeep.

Hudson was also threatened with receivership, but it was saved by herculean efforts on the part of Roy D. Chapin, who had served briefly as secretary of commerce under President Hoover. This effort almost certainly contributed to undermining Chapin's health. He died of pneumonia early in 1936, at the age of fifty-six. Nash met the depression through diversification. It merged with Kelvinator, a manufacturer of electric refrigerators and other household appliances, as the Nash-Kelvinator Corporation in 1936.

The companies that survived had to compete among themselves for shares of a sharply reduced market. Some of the competitive technique took the form of innovative styling—for example, the unsuccessful "Dynaflow" of Chrysler's DeSoto models of this period and similar body styles claiming to reduce air resistance—but the most striking changes came in engineering. More power was added as the lower-priced cars climbed from four to six-cylinder engines and then to the V-8 pioneered by Ford in 1932. The V-8 engine as a mass production item was made possible by improvements in foundry methods that made it possible to cast the entire engine block and crank case as a unit. The same methods could also be used to cast crankshafts.

The Ford V-8 of 1932 developed 65 h.p. as compared with the 20 h.p. of the Model T. It gave Ford the lead over Chevrolet, but once again only temporarily, and it had consequences that can be considered regrettable. The competitive horsepower race of the 1930s laid the groundwork for the absurdities of the 1950s.

There were more useful technical innovations. Studebaker introduced freewheeling in 1930, a device whereby the transmission went into neutral when the throttle was released. It had a brief popularity, but it created the hazard that the car lost the braking power of the engine. Overdrive, a Chrysler innovation in 1934, was a better method of economizing on fuel and enjoyed longer lasting popularity. Automatic transmission was a more important step. It was first offered by Reo in 1934, but Reo gave up passenger car manufacture two years later to concentrate on commercial vehicles, so that General Motors became the effective pioneer of automatic transmission with the 1937 Buick and Oldsmobile lines.

Automatic transmission affords a good example of an interplay between technological and economic forces that is frequently overlooked. The basic principles were well known; the torque converter and hydraulic coupling were used experimentally in marine engines before World War I. But it took time to refine them to the stage where they could be used in the space limitations of a passenger automobile, and the technical development of the passenger automobile to the point it reached in the late 1930s was required for automatic transmission to be economically feasible. The Model T Ford had the epicyclic gearbox used in automatic transmission, but it would have been impractical and economically pointless to put an automatic transmission in a Model T. All the driver had to do to shift gears anyway was press or release the clutch pedal.

The larger companies had the best of the competition. At General Motors Kettering kept an active program of engineering research going, with Sloan's full support. "Boss Ket" was instrumental in getting General Motors into diesel engine development. At his instigation G.M. bought the Winton Engine Company and the Electro-Motive Company of Cleveland in 1930, both engaged in diesel development, and combined them as the Electro-Motive Division of General Motors. During the 1930s under Kettering's direction this organization improved the diesel, notably by using two rather than four cycles and devising a highly efficient fuel injector, so that by the end of the decade diesel power was beginning to replace steam on the nation's railroads and was becoming practical for highway vehicles.

Chrysler managed to emerge from the depression in good condition, although it had gone through periods when production was down to forty percent of capacity. Walter Chrysler took pride in the fact that his company had not cut its research budget even when things were at their worst, and this policy was reflected in Chrysler's leadership in innovations like overdrive. The 1930 Plymouth led the way in raising engine power for the low-priced cars, with a six-cylinder engine that was given three-point support on rubber mountings.

Ford did not do so well. True, the V-8 of 1932 was a technical and economic success, but then Chevrolet sales again forged ahead of Ford. The heart of the problem was that Henry Ford was an aging autocrat, increasingly a recluse under the influence of the notorious Harry Bennett, the head of the Ford Service Department. This department had nothing to do with taking care of motor vehicles. It was a totalitarian secret police; it may not have had life-and-death authority over Ford employees, but it had complete authority to discharge virtually anyone in the company. Bennett appears to have gained his influence in the first place by playing on Henry Ford's fears for the safety of his grandchildren after the brutal kidnapping and murder of Charles A. Lindbergh's baby son. When Henry Ford had a stroke in 1938, Bennett's ascendancy increased because he had access to Ford that no one else in the company enjoyed. He issued orders in Ford's name without anyone else, even Edsel, being in a position to know whether they actually came from Henry Ford or Harry Bennett. Under these circumstances effective management was impossible and the Ford Motor Company steadily lost ground. In fact, after 1933 it fell behind Chrysler in total sales. The introduction of the Mercury in 1938, intended to give Ford an offering in the medium-priced range, brought no appreciable improvement. Nevertheless, the Ford Motor Company retained a considerable latent strength, supported by persistent customer and dealer loyalty—the dealers remained loyal even though at the start of the depression the company had appointed hundreds of new Ford dealers in an effort to boost sales, without regard for the rights of existing dealers. Vigorous protests and a loss of dealers to Chevrolet and Plymouth forced Ford to give up this practice after two years.

By the end of the depression the "Big Three"—General Motors, Ford, Chrysler—were indisputably dominant in the American automobile industry. Together they controlled 85 to 90 percent of the market for new passenger cars, with General Motors alone having over 40 percent. Then came five intermediate-sized companies—Hudson, Nash, Packard, Studebaker, Willys-Overland—that shared most of the rest. One or two smaller companies completed the list of passenger car producers: Graham-Paige and Crosley (formed in 1939 to attempt to market a small car, foreshadowing the future but premature). Reo, as stated, turned to truck manufacture in 1936, and Marmon dropped passenger car manufacture at the same time to experiment with four-wheel-drive vehicles.

The market for commercial vehicles gave more scope for the smaller firms. The Big Three made trucks, as did other passenger car manufacturers, and they dominated the field in the production of the smaller types that could be turned out by assembly-line methods. However, big trucks and to some extent buses are products with individualized specifications and with limited production runs, so that the economies of scale are less important, sometimes nonexistent. The principal truck manufacturers were White, Mack, Autocar, and International Harvester, and there were several smaller firms. White was left in an uncertain financial state after its brief association with Studebaker, but it was rehabilitated by a new president Robert F. Black, who was brought in

(1935) from successfully rebuilding the insolvent Brockway Motor Truck Company after a career with Mack International. As Clevelanders later put it, "Black took White out of the red."

There were even additions to the number of commercial vehicle manufacturers, in sharp contrast to what was happening in the passenger car segment of the business. These included ACF-Brill, formed in the early 1920s when American Car and Foundry decided to supplement its declining railroad car business; Twin Coach, organized by the brothers Frank P. and William B. Fageol in Kent, Ohio, in 1923 to make the first modern motor buses, with the engines underneath; Divco, established in Detroit in 1932 and specializing in door-to-door delivery vehicles (taken over by the Fageols in 1938); and Flxible (so spelled to permit the name to be trademarked), initially a maker of motorcycle sidecars, but changed to small and medium sized buses in the mid-1920s. In addition, as already noted, Reo left the passenger car business in 1936 and successfully converted to truck manufacturing.

There was a major change in the 1930s that had nothing to do with the depression but was simply a result of the passage of time. The first generation of leaders in the American automobile industry was passing from the scene. Willys died in 1935 and Chapin a year later. Walter Chrysler retired from active management in 1935 and was succeeded by another self-taught engineer, K. T. Keller. Chrysler died in 1940. Alfred P. Sloan gave up the presidency of General Motors in 1937 and became chairman of the board. He was succeeded as president by William S. Knudsen, whose term of office was cut short when he was put in charge of military production in World War II. Charles W. Nash became board chairman of Nash in 1930 and later of Nash-Kelvinator. By the end of the decade Henry Ford was visibly failing, although he stubbornly clung to control of his company until 1943, by which time a sequence of strokes had left him incapacitated. William C. Durant was also in declining health, but he had ceased to be a factor in the industry.

These transfers of authority had been anticipated and planned for in most of the automobile companies so that they were smoothly carried through without any immediate effect on the companies affected. At Ford there was a power struggle, with Edsel Ford, still officially president of the company, and Sorensen aligned against Harry Bennett. It was obvious that the elder Ford would have to yield his power very soon and that the Ford Motor Company would join the rest of the industry in having a new generation of management.

This first generation of leaders in the motor vehicle industry had an impressive record of achievement. It remained to be seen if their successors would reach the same stature.

The New Deal and the Automobile Industry

The depression brought political as well as economic upheavals. It was directly responsible for the victory of Franklin D. Roosevelt in the presidential election of 1932, and the deepening crisis that followed between the election and the inauguration of the new president in the following March led to the adoption of the variety of measures known collectively as the New Deal. The program had three separate objectives, the "three R's: Relief, Recovery, and Reform," which occasionally conflicted with each other; but at the beginning the national mood was such that there was a general disposition to cooperate in any steps that offered a prospect of restoring the country's economic health.

The most important of the initial New Deal programs to affect the automobile industry was embodied in the National Industrial Recovery Act (NIRA) of 1933. This enormously complicated piece of legislation provided among other things for each business and industry to draw up a code of fair competition, an idea initially advocated by Herbert Hoover when he was secretary of commerce in the Harding and Coolidge administrations. These codes were to regulate competition and control prices—not, as is usual with governmentally imposed price controls, to keep prices from rising, but to keep them from getting any lower than they already were. Wages, hours of labor, and working conditions also came under the codes. Section 7(a) of the NIRA gave labor the right to organize and bargain collectively through agents of its own choosing. Pending drafting of the individual codes, the government had the power to impose a blanket code.

The whole program was put into operation through a National Recovery Administration (NRA) under the direction of General Hugh S. Johnson, whose nickname of "Old Ironpants" hardly suggested him as the ideal person to resolve critical problems of highly sensitive economic relationships. Things started off well enough, with enormous parades in support of the NRA (although the author can testify that the participants in the parade he marched in were simply advised that their presence was expected) and Blue Eagles, the insignia of the NRA, on display everywhere. The idea might have worked better if the codes had been limited to major industries, but the NRA attempted to impose codes on every form of business in the United States, no matter how small. The result was administrative chaos.

The code for the automobile industry was drawn up by a committee of the National Automobile Chamber of Commerce (later Automobile Manufacturers Association and then the Motor Vehicle Manufacturers Association), including a representative of the Ford Motor Company. The code included only the vehicle manufacturers and their subsidiaries; independent supplier firms and dealers had separate codes. This arrangement was probably the only way to handle the variety of industrial and business operations that went into the manufacturing and marketing of motor vehicles, but it unavoidably made for conflict among different code authorities.

Like the others, the automobile code regulated prices, wages, and hours and conditions of labor, and it was accepted by most of the industry without great enthusiasm. Price competition in the automobile industry was already limited, wages and working conditions generally compared well with other industries, and there was well-founded apprehension about the implications of section 7(a) of NIRA. Moreover, as everyone who knew him had anticipated, Henry Ford flatly refused to sign the code, so that the Ford Motor Company was not subject to the constraints that his competitors had accepted.

The company could have been prosecuted for noncompliance, but it was not. The government backed away for two reasons. First, Henry Ford himself made the point that Ford wage rates and hours of labor both bettered the requirements of the automobile industry code, so that all the company could have been charged with was failure to put a signature on a piece of paper. Second, the Ford mystique remained strong, and nonconformity was what the public expected of Henry Ford. Taking him into court on a technicality would not have been a popular step, and Franklin D. Roosevelt was always acutely sensitive to the potential political effect of his actions.

An alternative sanction provided in the law was to exclude Ford from government purchases of motor vehicles, but attempts to take this course ran into the marketing structure of the automobile industry. The Ford Motor Company did not sell vehicles to the government or the public. Ford dealers did that, but Ford dealers were independent businessmen who had all complied with the automobile dealers' code, so that there was no legal way to bar them from bidding on government contracts, or to refuse to buy from them if they were the low bidders. There is nothing to show that the Ford Motor Company suffered from its noncompliance with its industry code. It had other troubles; so did the NRA. In 1935 the United States Supreme Court in the so-called "sick chicken" case (*Schechter Poultry Corp.* vs. *U.S.*) put an end to a program already in collapse by ruling unanimously that the entire NIRA was unconstitutional.

The Rise of the UAW

Until the coming of the New Deal the motor vehicle industry was rigorously open shop. The I.W.W. was active just before World War I; the Ford Sociological Department was created in part to forestall threats from this source. The

American Federation of Labor made a few feeble attempts to organize the industry, but in the prosperous 1920s the labor movement was on the decline and the AFL lost membership and had no impact whatever on the automobile industry. The depression made labor much more favorable to unionization, but there was little progress until the New Deal brought in an administration committed to support collective bargaining, a position incorporated in section 7(a) of the NIRA.

Considerable industrial conflict resulted. Organized labor was naturally eager to take advantage of the opportunity offered by a friendly national administration and began to move into the nonunion industries, and industry equally naturally resisted. Collective bargaining had to be accepted in principle, but what constituted "agents of its own choosing"? Did the phrase mean that all workers in a given concern were obligated to accept the bargaining agent chosen by the majority, or were dissident groups entitled to have their own separate agents? Were company unions acceptable as bargaining agents? There were ample grounds for dispute on this issue alone, and it did not help that four different federal agencies had jurisdiction in such disputes, along with a fifth especially for the automobile industry.

There was friction within organized labor as well, basically a conflict between the craft unionism that dominated the AFL (organizing workers by crafts: for example, plumbers, electricians, etc.) and the concept of industrial unionism (having all workers in the same industry belong to the same union). The latter was clearly more suitable for assembly-line workers, who were neither skilled craftsmen nor in the mass of the unskilled that the AFL at that time preferred to ignore.

When the leaders of the existing industrial unions became impatient early in the New Deal with the organizing efforts of the AFL, they formed the Committee for Industrial Organization, which later left the Federation and became the Council of Industrial Organizations (CIO). In 1936 the AFL, after several futile attempts to get a foothold in the automobile industry, granted a charter to the International Union, United Automobile Workers of America (later United Automobile, Aerospace and Agricultural Implement Workers), or UAW, which went with the CIO when the separation occurred. The new organization was aggressively led by a former clergyman, Homer Martin, and the brothers Walter and Victor Reuther. They introduced the "sit-down" strike, borrowed from the French Popular Front of the period, in which the workers stopped work but remained in the plant. This technique caused some alarm and there were demands that the strikers be forcibly evicted, but Governor Frank Murphy of Michigan refused and concentrated his efforts on trying to find a peaceful settlement.

In the meantime the NIRA had ceased to exist, and section 7(a) with it. No effort was ever made to revive the code provisions, which had become increasingly unpopular and unworkable, but the guarantee of collective bargaining was revived and reinforced in the Wagner-Connery Act, or National Labor Relations Act of 1936, which was more specific than 7(a) had been and provided for more adequate enforcement. The constitutionality of the Wagner Act was sustained in 1937 (*U.S.* v. *Jones and Laughlin Steel Corporation*). Even before that happened, Alfred P. Sloan, with General Motors tied up by a massive strike and in the face of Roosevelt's overwhelming victory in the 1936 election, decided that industrial warfare was a profitless occupation for everyone. Consequently, in February 1937 General Motors accepted the UAW as the bargaining agent for its work force, which was a fitting piece of industrial statesmanship to conclude Sloan's term as president of General Motors. Chrysler, also strike-bound, did the same thing two months later, and the rest of the industry followed rapidly, except Ford.

The Ford position offered further evidence of the decay of a once-great figure. Henry Ford persisted in believing, or at least asserting, that his entire work force was "loyal" and had no interest in labor unions. He would not negotiate with any union, nor would he tolerate any union activity among Ford workers. To enforce this policy, early in 1937 he put Harry Bennett in full charge of all labor matters in the Ford Motor Company—a step that deserved Winston Churchill's remark about a British cabinet appointment of this same era: "There has been no worse appointment since Caligula made his horse a consul." Edsel Ford disapproved of his father's policy. He would have negotiated with the UAW, but as usual he was overruled, and on the labor issue Sorensen and Bennett were in rare agreement. The hard line undoubtedly appealed to Sorensen, but in any case he never ventured to dispute Henry Ford's decisions. Certainly he disliked Harry Bennett intensely, but then there were few people whom Charles E. Sorensen liked, and probably fewer still who liked him. In justice to Sorensen, he has to be given credit for being the individual most responsible for keeping the Ford Motor Company from going to pieces during these difficult years. He was genuinely devoted to the company and to the interests of the Ford family as he understood them. Unlike Bennett, he had no aspirations about becoming head of the company himself and on most issues he was in sympathy with Edsel Ford in his resistance to the autocratic and increasingly unrealistic policies of Henry.

Bennett's philosophy of dealing with labor unrest was soon demonstrated. On 25 May 1937, Walter Reuther and other UAW organizers were attacked and badly beaten by thugs from the Ford Service Department while they were distributing union literature on an overpass leading into the River Rouge plant. Trouble had been anticipated, so that reporters and cameramen were on hand,

and the "Battle of the Overpass" shocked the country. On a subsequent Ford Sunday Evening Hour, a radio program of classical music, a company spokesman, W. J. Cameron, asserted that the attacks had been spontaneous acts by "loyal Ford employees," a lame explanation unless it was customary for ordinary Ford employees to carry items like blackjacks and brass knuckles in the normal course of their duties. Cameron was the editor of Henry Ford's newspaper, the *Dearborn Independent,* during the 1920s when Ford made it the vehicle for an anti-Semitic campaign.

The violence continued. There were similar attacks on union organizers and sympathizers at Ford plants in other parts of the country, the worst being in Dallas and Kansas City. None of this was good for the reputation or business of the Ford Motor Company, but it took four years for a settlement to be reached, largely because the UAW became involved in an internal power struggle. The upshot of this was that Homer Martin, whose administrative abilities did not match his militancy or his eloquence, was ousted and Walter Reuther became head of the union. In one important respect this delay was advantageous to the union, because during this time its complaints against Ford for violation of the Wagner Act were sustained by the National Labor Relations Board and the courts. Also, by 1941 the shadow of war was hanging over the country, and the Ford Motor Company was losing defense contracts because of its intransigence. In addition to the Wagner Act, there was now the Fair Labor Standards Act of 1938 as well, which denied government business to companies that failed to meet its specifications.

The showdown came in April 1941 when dismissal of a number of Ford employees for union activity touched off a company-wide strike. Henry Ford appealed to the government to protect the company from violence, but there was very little violence, and this appeal was merely a symptom of how far he had become dissociated from political realities. This time, for once, Edsel had his way. Negotiations were opened with the UAW, the strike was called off, and an election under the auspices of the National Labor Relations Board gave a convincingly overwhelming majority to the UAW. The elder Ford remained disgruntled. He spoke of terminating all his company's activities and letting the government take it over, but he was talking nonsense and his wife was able to tell him so.

Thus, after five years of bitter and frequently violent conflict, the United Automobile Workers became the sole collective bargaining agent for the entire American automobile industry. The management of the industry was certainly not happy about this outcome; it was accepted at best with gloomy resignation. Yet the results were generally satisfactory. Under Reuther the UAW became a well-run, responsible organization that drove hard bargains but then kept its agreements meticulously. Wildcat strikes are almost unknown in the American automobile industry. By comparison, in the British motor industry union contracts mean little and most strikes are called by shop stewards on the spur of the moment and often for trivial causes that would be settled as a matter of routine by normal grievance procedures in American plants, like the occasion when Ford's British Dagenham plant was struck because the tea served during breaks was not hot enough. The UAW wants to get all it can for its members, but it has also been aware that the self-interest of those members calls for keeping the American automobile industry as healthy as possible.

Diversification Efforts

One effect of the depression and the New Deal on the automobile industry that has been overlooked was their discouragement of some attempts at diversification. An exception has to be made of Nash's merger with Kelvinator in 1936, which was depression-stimulated, and possibly of the move of General Motors into diesel development, but the diesel is after all an internal combustion engine, and so this was not complete diversification. Otherwise the tendency was for the motor vehicle companies to withdraw from other fields. Ford, the only automobile company to have any success with tractors, stopped manufacture of the Fordson in the United States in 1928, before there was any sign of depression, although it continued to produce Fordsons in Britain and for some years Ireland, first at Cork and then at Dagenham.

The most ambitious ventures into other areas by motor vehicle companies were in aviation. Henry Ford was the pioneer here also. In 1924 he bought the Stout Metal Airplane Company, founded a year earlier by a colorful engineer-journalist named William B. Stout to make airplanes with the aluminum alloy duralumin. There was much excitement over the prospect that Ford was going to do for aviation what he had done for highway travel. He did not go that far, but the Ford trimotor, termed the "Tin Goose," was the first successful American all-metal transport plane and it became well known on the country's still embryonic airways. Ford and Stout quarreled in 1930 (this was now a recurrent theme in Ford history) and Stout left the company. Two years later the enterprise was losing money and Ford simply abandoned it. With Boeing's 247 and Douglas's DC-1 and 2 about to arrive on the aeronautical scene, this act born of impatience emerged as good judgment, even if coincidental.

General Motors went more deeply into aviation. The Kelly Air Mail Act of 1925, providing subsidies for commercial aviation, along with steady improvement in aircraft design and construction, and the overall economic euphoria of the period led to the organization in the late 1920s of a number of ambitious combinations of aircraft manufacturing and air transport companies. The most important were United Aircraft and Transport, North American Aviation, and the Aviation Corporation. Of these, United was created by William E. Boeing and did not involve the automobile industry.

General Motors entered aviation independently of these combines by buying stock interests in 1929 in the Bendix Aviation Corporation and the Fokker Aircraft Corporation and acquiring outright the Allison Engine Company, manufacturer of aircraft engines. Then through a complex series of corporate reorganizations, the Fokker and Bendix holdings were exchanged for North American Aviation Stock. The depression hit these combinations hard, but United, North American, and AVCO would probably have stayed in operation if it had not been for an alleged scandal over the award of air-mail contracts that surfaced early in the New Deal (no scandal was ever actually proved—nothing but arbitrariness on the part of President Hoover's postmaster-general). President Roosevelt canceled all air-mail contracts in an equally arbitrary action and tried an unhappy experiment of having the Army Air Corps carry the mail.

The investigation that followed produced a new Air Mail Act in 1934 that broke up the combinations by requiring manufacturing and transport activities in aviation to be separated. In the reorganization that this act required North American Aviation became an airframe manufacturer and Bendix became independent again, but still with General Motors holding a substantial minority stock interest in both. This situation lasted until 1948, when General Motors sold its North American holdings. With Allison and Bendix manufacturing aircraft engines and parts, the General Motors management concluded that for it to remain a major participant in an airframe company put it in the position of competing with its own customers.

AVCO became involved with the career of Errett Lobban Cord, who for a time seemed to be creating a promising automotive empire. A salesman and racing car driver, Cord in 1924 gained control of the Auburn Automobile Company of Auburn, Indiana, maker of a high-priced car that had a respectable run in the American automobile industry (1903–36). Two years later he took charge of the Duesenberg Motor Company of Indianapolis, which had been in receivership, and announced that it would build the world's highest-priced passenger car. Cord's salesmanship made these companies profitable during the boom period, and he began to expand into aviation. He also put the Cord car on the market in 1929, a beautifully designed vehicle with the then unique feature of front-wheel drive. Cord chose to concentrate on luxury cars. Unfortunately 1929 was the wrong year to offer another high-priced model, and the Cord car remained on the market only briefly.

All these enterprises were consolidated as the Cord Corporation in 1929. Two years later the Cord Corporation became affiliated with AVCO in circumstances that put Cord in control of AVCO. Then came the New Deal and the Air Mail Act of 1934. The AVCO combination was broken up, and Cord was left with his original corporation. By this time expensive automobiles were no longer selling—even Packard had to offer a lower-priced model in the 1930s—and when Cord found himself in a dispute with the new Securities and Exchange Commission he simply abandoned the automotive industry altogether. Auburn and Duesenberg ceased production, and E. L. Cord eventually went into uranium mining in Nevada.

CHAPTER EIGHT
The Automobile Industry at War

The record of the American motor vehicle industry in World War II requires a separate chapter not just because of the immense volume of output that it achieved but because it was, up to that time certainly, a unique phenomenon in the history of warfare. The automobile industry was not alone in making a prodigious effort in the United States, and its counterparts in other belligerent countries were similarly heavily involved in military production, but the American industry outstripped all others in the total volume of production and the diversity of its output.

It should have been the leader; the American automobile industry was the greatest concentration of industrial capacity anywhere in the world, and to some extent its wartime performances had been anticipated. While war was still a threat rather than a reality, it was taken for granted—too easily taken for granted by government, the military, industry, and the public alike—that if the need arose the tremendous resources of the motor vehicle industry could immediately be converted to make weapons of war. In particular there was the same easy assumption as in World War I that motor vehicle factories were readily convertible to the manufacture of airplanes, this although both aircraft and aircraft engines were far bigger and more complicated in 1940 than they had been in 1917. When the time came, conversion was neither immediate nor easy, but it was done, and the results far exceeded the expectations.

Preparatory Steps

Until the outbreak of war in Europe in 1939 and for some time thereafter very little was done toward industrial mobilization. The mood of the country in the mid-1930s was markedly isolationist, as evinced by the neutrality acts of the

87

period. When hostilities began American public opinion was definitely anti-Nazi and anti-Fascist, but isolationism remained strong and those who favored aid to the British and French adopted the slogan, "All aid short of war." In this climate any steps resembling military preparation were suspect, and there was little pressure on the automotive or any other industry to get ready for conversion to military production. The aircraft industry was an exception, but it was increasing its military output largely under the stimulus of British and French orders.

The German blitzkrieg in the spring of 1940 came as a massive shock. France fell in a matter of weeks, it appeared that Britain was in grave danger of defeat, and the United States was suddenly faced with the prospect of facing an aggressive Germany on one side, in complete control of Western Europe, and an aggressive Japan on the other, threatening to dominate East Asia. Two steps became urgent: one, to keep British resistance alive; and two, to build up America's defenses. The majority of the American people felt this way, but there remained a substantial and vociferous minority who believed that the United States should withdraw behind its defenses and ignore the rest of the world.

To meet this situation President Roosevelt announced a dramatic expansion of armament production, featured by a goal of 50,000 airplanes a year. It took two years to reach this figure, and it was meaningless anyway because it took no account of the kind of airplanes to be built, but it provided a target and a challenge. To help organize this effort Roosevelt in May 1940 created a National Defense Advisory Council (NDAC) with William S. Knudsen as chairman, picked because he was regarded as the ablest production man in the automotive industry and that industry's resources were critical to the program.

The NDAC had no authority, so that the best Knudsen could do was appeal to the automobile companies to suspend major model changes for 1941 so as to release machine tool capacity for military production. In October 1940 he further asked them to undertake the task of turning out half a billion dollars worth of urgently needed airplane parts and subassemblies, items that few automobile men had ever seen, let alone manufactured. The response to this appeal was to form an Automotive Committee for Air Defense in order to coordinate the industry's efforts in this direction. At about this same time Walter Reuther proposed an ingenious plan whereby idle automotive capacity was to be converted to aircraft production under the joint supervision of the government, the industry, and the UAW. Knudsen thought the scheme was impractical, and his knowledge of production gave weight to this opinion. At any rate after much publicity the Reuther Plan simply disappeared.

At the beginning of 1941 Roosevelt attempted to meet the need for more efficient organization of military production by forming the Office of Production Management (OPM), with Sidney Hillman, president of the Amalgamated Clothing Workers, as director and Knudsen as associate director. It was a poor administrative arrangement that worked only because Hillman and Knudsen exerted themselves to make it work. The OPM, like the NDAC, still had to work by persuasion, but industry generally cooperated. The automobile industry was asked to cut its 1941 production by 20 percent to conserve steel, and compliance appears to have been satisfactory, although there was criticism from the more enthusiastic proponents of rearmament that too much attention was still being given to civilian production and not enough to the critical international situation. The atmosphere of those days is not easily reconstructed. American opinion was markedly anti-Axis, but it was by no means clear how far that opinion was prepared to go toward active intervention in the war. Indeed, within the industry itself, Henry Ford repeated his isolationist-pacifist stand of World War I. He flatly refused to accept a contract to build Rolls-Royce Merlin aircraft engines for the Royal Air Force, in spite of the urging of the government and the protests of Edsel and Sorensen. This particular difficulty was resolved by having the Ford Motor Company agree to build Pratt and Whitney engines while Packard made the Merlins, but it illustrates the dilemma that industrial management faced. Memories of the congressional investigations of the 1930s were still very recent, and industrial leaders had no desire to be labeled "merchants of death" or "warmongers." They were more than willing to serve their country's needs, but until the Japanese attack on Pearl Harbor their country was confused about just what its needs were.

With the attack on Pearl Harbor, full industrial mobilization could be undertaken. The OPM was reorganized with a single head (Donald M. Nelson) and power to enforce its decisions. Knudsen was appointed a lieutenant general and given a roving commission to expedite production for the War Department as special advisor to Undersecretary of War Robert P. Patterson. He was the only civilian ever appointed directly to that rank, and in 1942 not many military men had ever been appointed to it either.

The personnel problems that had to be solved in this conversion process were enormous. It was necessary not only to replace the many thousands of men who went from the factories into the military services but also to find new employees for the expanded production programs and for the new plants that the motor vehicle companies were asked to operate. When the process began, estimates were that twice as many people would be needed as the industry had ever employed before. This problem was shared by all industry and the solutions followed much the same course. The most obvious resource was to recruit women, and this was done extensively. "Rosie the Riveter" had her innumerable counterparts on every assembly line. The unemployment that had been reduced but not eradicated in the late 1930s filled some of the gaps, and others who would not ordinarily have been part of the labor force—retirees, students working part time, people whose peacetime jobs disappeared—were drawn into the war effort. There was even a major demographic change in American society as large numbers of blacks moved from the South to seek the alluring opportunities and presumably better environment offered in the industrial centers of the North and West.

There was also expanded resort to subcontracting, which had the additional merit of bringing into the war effort many small firms that would otherwise have had to stay in what was left of the civilian market or go out of business altogether. Of subcontracting Donald M. Nelson, head of the War Production Board, observed that Detroit knew much more about it than Washington.

The recruitment of workers from these new sources involved delicate relationships between the automobile industry, the UAW, and the government. All three were equally committed to doing everything possible to bolster the nation's defenses and, after Pearl Harbor, to win the war, but the union naturally wanted to safeguard its position and the rights of its members in the face of this influx of new employees. Few of them had any union affiliation or any marked feeling about union membership, and most of them saw their wartime employment as temporary. Government policy sought to promote defense production and maintain the New Deal's commitment to collective bargaining. These complexities had to be worked out, but once the nation was at war those who were involved wanted to see them solved, and it was done well enough so that labor disputes caused no obstruction of the war effort in any segment of the automobile industry.

The drain on manpower affected management as well as labor. The major problem here for the motor vehicle companies was to spread their managerial talent over their expanded operations under conditions where procurement of additional executive strength was well-nigh impossible. The Ford Motor Company put Charles E. Sorensen in charge of its new aircraft assembly plant at Willow Run and then found itself in a major crisis when Edsel Ford died in 1943. By then his father was both physically and mentally incapable of running the company and it was necessary to get the Navy to release Edsel's oldest son, Henry Ford II, so that he could take charge. The further development of the Ford story is told in chapter 9.

There were losses to government and military service as well. Conspicuously, General Motors had to replace its president when William S. Knudsen resigned to become chairman of the National Defense Advisory Council. His successor was an engineer, Charles E. Wilson. A tendency to unguarded loquacity later made Wilson a controversial secretary of defense in the Eisenhower administration, but he was one of the great presidents of General Motors. At the end of 1943 he was able to report that every defense contract given to General Motors was in production, on schedule, and yielding more output than the government had considered possible. The strain proved too much for Wilson's health. He had to take a three months' leave, and he suffered from circulatory troubles and migraine headaches for the rest of his life.

Mobilization and Production

With the country at war, the course for the automobile industry was finally clear. There could be no further question of dividing effort between military and civilian production. Immediately after Pearl Harbor the manufacture of passenger automobiles was suspended for the duration. Their use, other than for wartime needs, was restricted anyway. The rapid Japanese overrunning of Southeast Asia and Indonesia cut off supplies of natural rubber and necessitated strict rationing, and the destruction of tankers by German submarines, due to failure to provide for convoys along the Atlantic seaboard and to shut off lights along the east coast of Florida, required rationing of gasoline.

By the end of December the industry, working through the Automobile Manufacturers Association, had formed the Automotive Council for War Production for the purpose of assisting to organize the resources of all the automotive firms—vehicle manufacturers and parts and component manufacturers alike—for maximum efficiency and volume of production. The president of the Council was Alvan Macauley, president of the Packard Motor Car Company and in 1941 the senior in length of service among automobile company presidents. The managing director was an AMA official named George Romney, just at the beginning of a great automotive career. The Council had twelve divisions, whose titles neatly illustrate the scope and diversity of the automobile industry's participation in the war effort: (1) Machine and Tool Equipment Service; (2) Tooling Information Service; (3) Contract Service; (4) Aircraft Engines; (5) Airframes; (6) Ammunition Components; (7) Artillery; (8) Small Arms; (9) Marine Equipment; (10) Military Vehicles; (11) Propellers; (12) Tanks and Tank Parts.

Turning out military vehicles was a minor problem for the industry that had introduced mass production for the making of motor vehicles. Over 2.5 million trucks and 660,000 jeeps (the latter mainly by Willys-Overland and Ford) headed the list in this category. Most of the military trucks were given four-wheel drive. The automobile industry was also the principal builder of tanks. Chrysler was the first company selected for this purpose. Others were drawn in rapidly, but Chrysler remained the leading American producer of tanks and continued to hold that position after the war. Besides tanks, trucks, and jeeps, the industry's output ranged from quarter-ton reconnaissance cars to forty-ton tank transporters, along with items like mobile kitchens, machine shops, and hospital units.

Engines naturally were also a major item. In addition to engines for vehicles, the automobile industry made over 450,000 aircraft engines and almost 170,000 marine engines, including the major proportion of the diesels used by the Navy. The rest of the list is long and variegated. A summation appears in table 8–1. Another way of describing what was done is that General Motors delivered approximately $12 billion worth of military material during the war years, and two thirds of this total consisted of items the company had never made before.

Aircraft Production

Participation in aircraft manufacturing proved to be the most troublesome part of the automobile industry's participation in the war effort. There were two basic difficulties. First, the aircraft companies had misgivings about automobile firms entering their highly competitive industry and possibly remaining in it after the war. Extensive new plant construction was going to be needed to reach the levels of production that the government wanted, and these facilities might well give new competitors a foothold. This problem actually never became serious. When Knudsen first invoked the help of the automobile industry he took pains to assure the aircraft companies that this assistance would be strictly in the form of subcontracting, and this assurance was adhered to. Indeed, the program from the beginning planned that the new wartime aircraft assembly plants would be operated by airframe manufacturers, with about 75 percent of the parts and subassemblies to be fabricated by automotive firms. This policy was followed except for the operation of Willow Run by the Ford Motor Company and the manufacture of a number of fighter planes by General Motors, both described later in the chapter. This contribution of subassemblies and parts made the role of the motor vehicle industry in aircraft production substantially greater than it appeared to be; without it the goals set for the aircraft program could not possibly have been attained.

As things turned out, when the war ended there was a tremendous pent-up demand for cars and thus very little temptation for any automobile company to divert its efforts from the booming market for its own products and enter the

Table 8–1

Military Production by U.S. Automotive Industry in World War II

Items	Value*	Percent of Total
Aircraft, aircraft subassemblies, and parts	$11,216,487	38.7
Military vehicles and parts	8,612,173	29.7
Tanks and parts	3,808,626	13.1
Marine equipment	1,944,533	6.7
Guns, artillery, and parts	1,587,736	5.5
Ammunition and components	909,335	3.1
All other war products	907,495	3.1
Total	**$28,986,385**	

*In thousands of dollars
Source: Freedom's Arsenal: The Story of the Automotive Council for War
    Production (Detroit: Automobile Manufacturers Association, 1950, p.
    193).

visibly shrinking market for airplanes. The war-built aircraft plants were financed by the government and operated under lease. Only one (Willow Run)
became part of the automobile industry afterward, and it was never used for
aircraft manufacturing after World War II ended.

The other and more serious difficulty was that the two industries had almost
completely divergent attitudes about production. The automobile men thought
primarily in terms of quantity and were justifiably proud of their achievements
in mass production. Their training was to get a design worked out and then
make large numbers of the same model, with as much use as possible of sin-
gle-purpose tools. They were quite sure, at times even cocky about it, that they
could transform what they saw as the antiquated methods of the aeronautical
industry. This attitude showed in extreme form in Henry Ford's announcement
in May 1940 that his company could readily convert to the manufacture of a
thousand airplanes of standard design a day, provided he had the advice of men
like Charles A. Lindbergh and Eddie Rickenbacker and complete freedom
from "meddling" by government agencies. Walter Reuther estimated that his
plan could produce 500 fighter planes a day, and Knudsen, somewhat more
realistically, spoke in these same early stages of General Motors turning out a
thousand planes a month.

On the other hand, until the spring of 1940 no American aircraft manufacturer had ever received any single order for more than two hundred airplanes. Production as they saw it was a matter of high precision, of very fine tolerances, and, especially with military aircraft, of constant modifications in design. This was particularly so in war, when a constant stream of information was pouring back from the combat areas regarding changes and improvements that needed to be made. The aviation people doubted that any automobile company could work to their standards. But fortunately the participants on both sides were patriotic individuals who were fully aware that the most important consideration was to win the war; and most were open-minded enough to be willing to learn from each other.

The building of aircraft engines was one of the earliest tasks undertaken by the motor vehicle industry. It appears to have offered no special difficulties, even though the engines were different products from what the autombile companies were accustomed to manufacture. The automotive industry had nothing to do with jet engines, which were a recent invention and still very much in the developmental stage, but the radial piston engines used by World War II airplanes were still far more elaborate and complex mechanisms than even the 12- or 16-cylinder motors that went into the luxury cars of the 1930s. New plants had to be built for this purpose; the existing automobile engine facilities were not only unsuitable but were already working to capacity on engines for military vehicles.

Automotive companies turned out twelve different types of aircraft engines, including the biggest radial piston engines ever built, the 2,800 h.p. Pratt and Whitney Wasp and the Wright Cyclone. The Allison Division of General Motors was the principal producer of liquid-cooled engines for the Army Air Force, and Packard made Rolls-Royce Merlins. In the process the automotive people were able to introduce production techniques that speeded production and cut costs, such as devising jigs for the automatic grinding in groups of engine parts that had previously been ground separately by hand.

Complete airplanes were another story. The automobile industry did very well in fabricating aircraft parts and components, but in the main the final assembly proved to be best done by the companies that were accustomed to doing it and in plants designed for the purpose. Altogether some 300,000 airplanes were built in the United States between 1940 and 1945, and automobile companies contributed 20,000 of these, exclusive of helicopters and gliders. The Eastern Aircraft Division of General Motors made 13,500 and the Ford plant at Willow Run, in Ypsilanti, Michigan, almost seven thousand. The General Motors operation was a combination of five plants in New Jersey,

New York, and Maryland, which were converted to make fighter planes under licence from the Grumman Aircraft Corporation.

Since Willow Run was constructed to build B–24 Liberators, Ford was the leading automobile firm in airframe weight produced, but nevertheless the Willow Run operation has to be classed as a failure. Construction of the factory was begun in 1941 on a site apparently chosen at the insistence of Henry Ford himself, but Ypsilanti had no local supply of labor. The work force had to be recruited in already labor-scarce Detroit. In fact, Michigan's Industrial Expressway was started at this time specifically to provide fast transportation between Detroit and Willow Run, and in the end the plant never reached the employment level it was supposed to. In addition, when Reuben Fleet, the founder and head of Consolidated Aircraft, the designer of the B–24, visited Willow Run to inspect the factory, he was startled to find an enormous L-shaped structure, so that the assembly line had to make a right-angled turn. The Ford officials explained that to have continued in a straight line would have taken the building into the next county, with consequent complications for the Ford Motor Company in legal and tax matters.

Charles E. Sorensen was put in charge of Willow Run, which was logical from the Ford point of view, since he was the Ford Motor Company's top production man. Sorensen found ways to improve assembly technique. At Consolidated the B–24 fuselage was assembled and then the wiring and piping was brought through the door to be installed, a technique described by Sorensen as being like a bird building its nest while sitting in it. At Willow Run the fuselage was assembled in two longitudinal halves and the wiring and piping installed. Then the two sections were put together.

On the other hand "Cast-iron Charlie" was hardly the best possible person to deal with a difficult labor situation or with people from the government and another company, who were under no compulsion to take orders or abuse from him. He was further handicapped because while Willow Run was trying to get into operation, Harry Bennett was working to keep the UAW out, so that labor relations were poor from the beginning. Then in 1943 Edsel Ford's sudden death threw the Ford Motor Company into confusion.

By that time Willow Run was being referred to sardonically as "Will It Run," and there was serious consideration of having the government step in and take over. The final decision was to give the new administration at Ford a chance, and in 1944 the operation finally swung into something resembling the expectations that had been held out for it, although it never produced at its planned capacity and it reached its maximum output at the time the Liberator was being superseded by bigger and better airplanes. The situation demanded a scapegoat, and "Cast-iron Charlie" was it. In 1944, after forty years of service in the Ford Motor Company, he went the way of so many Ford executives. After the war he became president of Willys-Overland but served only briefly before the company was taken over by Kaiser-Frazer.

Reconversion

The Automotive Council for War Production performed a notable service in getting its industry organized for military production; it also performed an equally notable but less well publicized service in coordinating preparations for the return of the industry to its normal peacetime pursuits. It had been a complex process, technically, financially, and otherwise, to switch the assembly lines from motor vehicle chassis and bodies to gun-mountings, airplane wings, and so on; it was just as complex to switch them back again.

The process started in the latter part of 1944, when the success of the Normandy invasion justified hopes that the end of the war was in sight. Both government and industry were anxious to have as smooth a transition as possible from war to peace and above all to avoid repeating the mistakes of World War I, when no preparations for the ending of hostilities had been made and war contracts were abruptly canceled without regard to the consequences. Legislation to facilitate reconversion was passed in 1944 and in October of that year an Office of War Mobilization and Reconversion was established. On its side the Automotive Council for War Production set up a Contract Termination Committee for the purpose of assisting its members through the legal, financial, and other complexities of reconversion. This was the Council's last important activity. It was dissolved on 11 October 1945.

In 1944 also the output of nonmilitary trucks was raised to 18,000, as compared with 3,000 for all of 1943, but this was not really a step toward peacetime production. It was done because the trucks were required for urgently needed transportation purposes at home, and production was cut back again when the hopes for an end to the European war in 1944 proved to have been oversanguine. However, in the following spring the surrender of Germany reduced the demand for military production and made an early peace a real prospect. In May 1945, shortly after the German surrender, the War Production Board authorized the manufacture of 100,000 passenger automobiles during the remainder of the year. Only 70,000 were actually made, but this was still in sharp contrast to the 139 of 1943 and 610 of 1944.

Then came the atomic bombs and the surrender of Japan. The American public promptly littered the streets with torn-up gasoline coupons and looked forward eagerly to replacing the cars that had been limping along for four years on retreaded tires and frequently with rebuilt engines. That took time. It was 1949 before the automobile industry returned to its full peacetime capacity. Shortages of materials persisted, so that priorities remained in force through 1946 and price controls for a year after that. The outbreak of war in Korea brought back controls and shortages, but the scale and duration of the conflict were well below the level of World War II. There was a lessening of motor vehicle production, but the overall impact on the automobile industry was slight. No one paid attention to the fact that a fair amount of the requirements for trucks in Korea was filled by two Japanese companies that were just resuming production after the devastation of World War II: Nissan (Datsun) and Toyota. The war in Vietnam brought no interruption of civilian motor vehicle production; the administrations responsible for waging it decided (in retrospect it would appear unwisely) to conduct the war without restricting the civilian economy in any way.

CHAPTER NINE
The Triumph of Bigness

The fifteen years after World War II saw motor vehicle production in the United States rise to new heights while at the same time the number of producers continued to shrink. The independent firms that survived the depression and the war tried to remain competitive by combination, but only one of these combinations survived. In addition, several attempts at new entry were made immediately after the war, but only one, Kaiser-Frazer, was still in business by 1950, and it left the field in 1955. By 1960 there were only four manufacturers of passenger automobiles in the United States: the Big Three and American Motors, which was formed by merging Hudson and Nash.

During this same period American passenger automobiles grew rapidly in size and horsepower. The emphasis in selling was on style, on selling the car as a "status symbol," with the result that styling became extremely elaborate, with lavish use of chrome and exaggerated tail fins. The latter were justified on the ground that they were needed to house the lights required at the rear of the vehicle—tail, directional, and backup—and that they gave the car aerodynamic qualities. Both claims can be dismissed as unfounded.

Ownership and use of automobiles was further encouraged by federal and state governments through extensive road-building programs that now emphasized the controlled-access, dual-roadway type of express highway variously termed "freeway," "expressway," or "thruway." ("Freeway" is the term officially used by the Federal Highway Administration for any highway that has complete control of access, separate roadways, and no crossings at grade. It has nothing to do with whether tolls are charged or not.) Some mileage of this kind was built in the 1930s, but most of it came after World War II. First, a number of states constructed toll roads, predominantly in the Northeast and eventually reaching about 3,600 miles. At the same time California provided for a freeway system financed by gasoline taxes. Then in 1956 Congress passed the Interstate Highway Act, which established a Highway Trust Fund from gasoline and other highway user taxes, to be used for the construction of a nationwide network of express highways that would eventually reach fifty thousand miles. Construction of toll roads lapsed soon after the Interstate system was begun.

Postwar Readjustment

When the war ended, the market for motor vehicles was decidedly a seller's market. After four years in which very few passenger automobiles had been built and people had high wartime earnings with limited opportunities for spending them, the demand for cars was insatiable—preferably new cars, but anything with wheels and a motor would sell. It took three years for supply to begin to catch up with demand. The whole national economy was going through the same readjustment from war to peace, and the process was constantly being interrupted by shortages of materials and labor disputes, so that restoring normal production was anything but easy.

In the automobile industry this situation at first favored the independents, whose share of the market reached a peak of 18.4 percent in 1948 and remained at about 15 percent until the end of the Korean War, a share they maintained by virtue of the fact that production quotas during the Korean conflict were based on market shares since 1945. Ford, as will be seen, was undergoing a major and critical reorganization, while General Motors was badly handicapped by strikes. However, the principal reason for this temporary rise in the independents' market share was one that backfired on them later. In order to take advantage of the immediate postwar demand, they paid premium prices for materials and accepted high-cost labor contracts, and their competitiveness suffered accordingly when normal conditions returned.

The conditions of the 1945–50 period also attracted newcomers to automobile manufacturing. The market was there for anyone who could produce, and low-cost plant facilities were available in the war-built factories that the government was now trying to dispose of. Several such projects were announced when the war ended, but practically all were stillborn. Of those that appeared on the market, one had actually started before the war. This was Crosley Motors, Inc., launched in 1939 by Powell Crosley, a manufacturer of radios, to build a small four-passenger car with a four-cylinder engine, something that had been virtually extinct in the American industry for ten years. The war came before the company could get into production, so that the Crosley's effective appearance on the market was postwar.

Crosley was ahead of his time. A car with an 80-inch wheelbase, which made it smaller than the Volkswagen, was probably too small for the kind of driving that most Americans did, and the American public was not as yet ready to buy small cars in quantity. The Crosley reached a peak of just over 25,000 sales in 1948 and then steadily declined. The company was sold in 1952 to the General Tire and Rubber Company and automobile manufacture was discontinued. The plant was converted to make military material for the Korean War.

Two of the new aspirants died in infancy. The Playboy Motor Corporation planned to produce a sports car and did make a few in 1947–48, but it could not raise capital. A proposed $20 million stock issue was whittled down to $3.5 million and even that found few takers. Another two million was raised by selling franchises, but this was well short of what was needed and Playboy faded from the automotive scene. A more ambitious effort, the Tucker Torpedo, designed as a rear-engined sports car, lasted just about the same length of time. The promoter, Preston Tucker, leased a war-built plant in Chicago where Dodge had built aircraft engines, for a rental that started at $500,000 a year for the first two years and was to rise to $2.4 million, with an option to buy for $30 million. The original cost of the factory had been $76 million. Tucker raised $7 million from the sale of franchises and $15 million from the sale of stock, most of which had to be sold directly to the public at a dollar a share because brokerage and investment houses, distrusting Tucker's flamboyant methods, refused to handle it. Entry into the automobile industry could not be achieved for $22 million. The most reliable estimates for what would have been required to make a start in the 1950s run from a quarter of a billion to over a billion dollars, exclusive of the dealer organization, and the lower figure was regarded as very risky. At any rate the Torpedo never went into effective production, so that it was left for Volkswagen to introduce the rear-engine car to the United States market a few years later.

Only one of these attempts at entry lasted any length of time, and it appeared for a while to have some prospect of succeeding. This was the Kaiser-Frazer Corporation, founded in 1945, just before the end of the war, by Henry J. Kaiser and Joseph W. Frazer, chairman of the board of the Graham-Paige Motor Car Company. Kaiser was a businessman who had established a reputation in construction during the New Deal and became a national figure during the war by building ships on a mass production basis, achieved through extensive use of prefabrication. He built the first steel plant west of the Rocky Mountains, in Fontana, California, when the government decided that steel for the war effort should be made on the Pacific coast. The announcement that "Henry J." proposed to manufacture automobiles therefore stimulated considerable interest.

The new company bought Graham-Paige, but this was a small firm with limited production capacity. For its main plant Kaiser-Frazer leased, of all places, Willow Run. The rental started at $500,000 for the first year and rose to $1,250,000 in the third, after which the company bought the property for $15 million—the original construction cost had been on the order of $100 million. The company floated stock issues in 1945 and 1946 for $54 million, and borrowed $44 million from the Reconstruction Finance Corporation in 1949, along with bank loans for about another $30 million.

This seemed to be a promising start and in its first two years of production (1947 and 1948) Kaiser-Frazer led the independents with a 5 percent share of the market, but then difficulties began to accumulate. There was insufficient capital. Kaiser later said that the company's initial stock offerings should have been at least three times as large as they were and could have been successfully floated while public interest was still strong. Then, like other independents, Kaiser-Frazer paid premium prices for materials to get into production, and there are indications that its assembly operations were inefficient. Financial stringency compelled the company to give up ideas for innovative designs and make quite conventional automobiles.

In time these troubles might have been surmounted, but Kaiser-Frazer found the marketing problem insoluble—and this is the major problem for anyone trying to enter the motor vehicle industry. The American purchaser normally trades in one car when he or she buys another and expects to trade in that one in due course, which is the fundamental reason why each year's model must be just enough different from its predecessor to be distinguishable but not so much as to impair trade-in value. Consequently there is a reluctance to become committed to cars that might become "orphans," and this is beyond question the most severe handicap any newcomer in the industry must face. Kaiser-Frazer recruited about five thousand dealers to begin with, when Henry Kaiser was regarded as a prospective new Henry Ford, but then the numbers began to shrink. In 1953 Kaiser-Frazer became the Kaiser Motor Corporation and took over Willys-Overland in the first of the mergers by which the independent manufacturers tried to survive in the motor vehicle industry. Four years later the company became Kaiser Industries and withdrew from all motor vehicle manufacturing except jeeps. Willow Run, which had begun with Ford, was bought by General Motors and used for making transmissions. The jeep business was sold to American Motors in 1970, so that technically the Kaiser entry into the automobile industry can be claimed to have lasted twenty-five years.

The Rebirth of Ford

While the independents were striving for their place in the postwar automobile market and the would-be new entrants were making their unsuccessful bid for a foothold, the Ford Motor Company was undergoing a massive transformation. Reference was made earlier to Edsel Ford's death in 1943 at the age of forty-nine, a premature death caused by a combination of "stomach cancer, undulant fever, and a broken heart" (Nevins and Hill, *Ford: Decline and Rebirth, 1932–1962,* 247–48). The cancer came from stomach ulcers brought on by frustration and harassment at the hands of his father and Bennett, the broken heart from the same source, and the undulant fever from drinking unpasteurized milk from his father's farm. After his son's death Henry Ford resumed the presidency of the company, but he was then eighty and had been incapacitated by strokes. Since the Ford Motor Company was vital to war production, there was talk of the government taking it over and operating it. Instead, Edsel's oldest son, Henry Ford II, was released from service in the Navy to take charge of the company. Harry Bennett seems to have believed seriously that he would take control, but he made the fatal error of ignoring the women in the Ford family. Clara Ford, Henry's wife, resented his influence over her husband and was determined that her grandson would not be denied his heritage. Edsel's wife held Bennett responsible for her husband's early death and was equally determined that her son should be head of the company. The family stock, which was all the voting stock in the Ford Motor Company, was consequently voted unanimously to make Henry Ford II executive vice president early in 1944, and a year later he became president. Harry Bennett's connection with the company was severed shortly afterward.

The reference to voting stock deserves further mention. In 1936 Henry and Edsel Ford became aware that increased estate taxes meant that in the event of their deaths their heirs would have to sell control of the company to pay the taxes. They therefore divided Ford stock into two classes, of which 5 percent was voting and the rest nonvoting, established the Ford Foundation for philanthropic purposes, and bequeathed their nonvoting stock to it. Consequently, after the deaths of both Edsel and his father, the latter in 1947, the Ford Foundation became the owner of 95 percent of the stock of the Ford Motor Company.

The Foundation in time became wealthy, but before that could occur the Ford Motor Company had to be completely reorganized. When Henry Ford II took over, the company's affairs were perilously close to chaos. The accounting system was elementary; no one really knew the financial position, except that it was poor. The best available estimate put losses at about $10 million a

Courtesy of the Henry Ford Museum, The Edison Institute

Edsel Ford
(1893–1943)

Courtesy of the Henry Ford Museum, The Edison Institute

Henry Ford II
(b. 1917)

month. Management was in the hands of executives whose responsibilities were vaguely defined and who were bitter antagonists, and labor relations, in spite of the 1941 settlement with the UAW, could best be described as unsatisfactory.

The new president, a young man not quite thirty, knew something of the condition of his company and suspected more, but he was still shocked by what he found. He realized that he had to have help and had also decided that the rehabilitation of the Ford Motor Company required that it should be given a General Motors type of organization. The logical source of assistance was therefore General Motors. The man he wanted, and persuaded to join Ford as executive vice-president, was Ernest R. Breech, at that time president of Bendix Aviation. Breech had previously been president of North American Aviation and before that had been with General Motors in various capacities. Breech became executive vice-president of the Ford Motor Company in 1946; he later became chairman of the board and retained that post until he resigned in 1960. He and Henry Ford II together gave the company a thoroughgoing reconstruction along the lines of General Motors, including efficient financial controls and a more enlightened labor policy. In a remarkably short time they succeeded not only in restoring Ford to profitability, but also in recovering the company's position as second among American automobile producers.

They were materially assisted in this effort by a group of eight former Air Force officers who joined the company after the war and became known collectively as the "Whiz Kids." They had worked on managerial and financial controls for the Air Force and had decided to stay together after the war. They selected Ford because it obviously could use their services and because they felt that in a giant organization like General Motors they might well be lost. The group broke up after a few years with Ford, but it contributed substantially to the rehabilitation of the company and two of its number, Robert S. McNamara and Arjay Miller, in time became presidents of the Ford Motor Company. McNamara left in 1961 to become secretary of defense for John F. Kennedy and later for Lyndon Johnson.

The Completion of Oligopoly

When an armistice ended the fighting in Korea in 1953, the American automobile industry was free to expand for the first time in almost twenty-five years, unburdened by depression, price controls, shortages of materials, and other limitations. The gloomy forecasts of massive unemployment during the postwar readjustment had failed to materialize—their worst manifestation was to induce Congress to pass the Full Employment Act of 1946, which finally

emerged as a statement of policy that committed the government to nothing—
and by 1953 the economy was flourishing. The readjustment period saw numerous labor disputes, triggered largely by the fact that prices remained high
and labor wanted wages raised accordingly to compensate for the loss of the
overtime pay of the war years.

In the automobile industry this labor unrest particularly affected the Big
Three and was a retarding factor in their return to full-scale production. One
reason, as we have seen, was the independents' readiness to make concessions
in order to take advantage of the booming postwar market. More important,
the UAW developed a policy of focusing on a single company when contract
negotiations came due, with the idea of using that settlement as leverage for
the rest of the industry, and it made sense to take one of the Big Three for this
purpose. There were some painful strikes, but by the early 1950s several critical issues had been resolved. First there was a settlement (1948) tying wage
increases to the Department of Labor's cost of living index, along with an
"improvement factor," allowing for increased productivity resulting from
technical advances. Then came an agreement, initially with Ford in 1949,
guaranteeing a minimum retirement income for employees with thirty years
service. Finally in 1955 provision was made, again initially with Ford, for the
automobile companies to supplement government unemployment benefits
when workers were laid off, up to a stipulated proportion of the worker's normal earnings.

The effect was that by the mid-1950s the motor vehicle manufacturers were
in a period of relative labor peace. Some features of these settlements were not
necessarily to the long-range advantage of the automobile industry or the economy at large—conspicuously, tying wage increases automatically to the cost
of living index resulted in a continuous upward movement in wages, which in
turn pushed prices up and so stimulated an inflationary spiral. However, in the
1950s the outlook for motor vehicle manufacturing was bright and the conditions that created this situation worked overwhelmingly to the benefit of the
largest companies.

By 1953 they had set their houses in order and were ready for full-scale
peacetime production. Neither General Motors nor Chrysler had to face anything like the upheaval that Ford had gone through. General Motors had lost
Knudsen, who died in 1948, overstrained by his efforts for his adopted country. The new president was Charles Erwin Wilson, called "Engine Charlie" to
distinguish him from Charles Edward Wilson, "Electric Charlie," who was
president of General Electric. Paradoxically, "Engine Charlie" had been educated as an electrical engineer, while "Electric Charlie" was a financial man

with no engineering training whatever. Highly articulate, Wilson had a propensity for letting his tongue run away with him. He attracted worldwide attention by a much-misquoted remark made during hearings on his nomination as President Eisenhower's secretary of defense: "I have always believed that what's good for the country is good for General Motors, and vice versa." Actually Wilson was a capable industrial statesman, responsible, for example, for the "improvement factor" in the 1948 agreement with the UAW.

Chrysler's major change was that Lester Lum Colbert replaced K. T. Keller as president in 1950—a lawyer for an engineer. But Chrysler dropped back to third place among motor vehicle manufacturers, mainly because of bad judgment in the design of its models, based on the assumption that practicality would rule consumer motivations in the 1950s.

By 1953 the pattern for the rest of the decade had been established. The Big Three held about 90 percent of the United States market for passenger automobiles, with General Motors taking half or more of the total, Ford about a fourth, and Chrysler ranging around 12 to 15 percent. These proportions fluctuated, but never by much. What was left, usually less than 10 percent, went to the independents and a slight but growing trickle of imports from Europe. The domination of General Motors was reflected in the pricing policies of the industry: the other passenger car manufacturers simply followed the lead of General Motors. This control was limited. General Motors could not set prices so low as to put its competitors out of business, as it undoubtedly could have done, nor could it appear to be establishing prices by agreement. Either course would have incurred the disapproval of the Federal Trade Commission and the Anti-Trust Division of the Department of Justice.

As the dominant producer in the motor vehicle industry, with at least half the total output, General Motors has had to be acutely sensitive to the antitrust laws. This fact was vividly demonstrated in 1957 by a decision of the United States Supreme Court requiring Du Pont to divest itself of the 23 percent stock interest in General Motors that it had had since 1921, on the ground that this holding might give Du Pont an unfair advantage in the sale of automotive paints and lacquers. There was no evidence that Du Pont had ever had such preferential treatment, but the court ruled that under the Clayton Act of 1914 a stock interest that might restrict competition was illegal whether such restriction existed or not. This decision created an acute financial problem. Dumping almost a quarter of the shares of General Motors on the market would have had an upsetting effect, to say the least, and the capital gains taxes would have been close to confiscatory. Eventually legislation had to be enacted to make special provision for the disposal of the Du Pont holdings.

Ford had a happier financial problem to deal with. The successful reform of the Ford Motor Company after 1946 proved a bonanza for the Ford Foundation, which after the death of Henry Ford in 1947 became the owner of 95 percent of the company's stock. The Ford Foundation became by far the wealthiest of the great American philanthropic foundations. By 1955 the foundation's directors decided that its holdings should be diversified; it was not desirable to have all its assets in the stock of a single corporation no matter how well it might be doing. So in that year Ford Motor Company stock—class B, nonvoting—was offered to the public for the first time, and immediately snapped up.

This year, 1955, was a banner year for the American automobile industry and typified the atmosphere of the period. Total motor vehicle sales were over nine million, of which almost eight million were passenger cars. This total was a good two-thirds of the entire world output of motor vehicles for that year. Competition from imports was still minor, and government regulation on the subjects of safety, emission control, and fuel economy was ten years and more in the future. It was a near-ideal situation for the Big Three. An approximate breakdown of market shares for 1955 shows General Motors with 50 percent, Ford with 27, Chrysler with 17, and American Motors and Studebaker-Packard and all imports with 2 per cent each.

The independents were taking the only course open to them, which was to try to survive by merging. If bigness was the route to success in the motor vehicle industry, then that was the direction for them to take, or at least to try to take. Kaiser-Frazer, as noted, absorbed Willys-Overland in 1953, but this expedient failed. A year later Hudson and Nash combined as the American Motors Corporation and Studebaker and Packard as the Studebaker-Packard Corporation. With the latter, as with the Kaiser-Willys combination, two weak companies could not add up to one strong one. The Packard name was dropped in 1958 and in 1964 Studebaker motor vehicle manufacturing was moved to Hamilton, Ontario, where it lasted only two years longer.

American Motors had better fortune, or rather better management. The president of the new corporation was George Romney, the man who had been the efficient executive director of the Automotive Committee for War Production. Automotive operations were concentrated in the Nash plant at Kenosha, Wisconsin, and the Hudson name was abandoned. Romney realized that it was futile for his company to try to compete with the Big Three; its future depended on finding a niche in the market for passenger automobiles that they had not preempted. That, as he saw it, was in making and selling small cars, something for which a market scarcely existed in 1954. His efforts in this direction will be described in chapter 10. They were neither as profitable nor as lasting as Romney may have hoped, but they kept American Motors alive as one of the four remaining passenger car manufacturers in the United States.

The trend to concentration emerged among the manufacturers of commercial vehicles, with the White Motor Company in the role of General Motors—but on a radically smaller scale. White took over the Autocar Company of Ardmore, Pennsylvania (1953), one of the oldest of American motor vehicle manufacturers (1898) and a manufacturer of heavy duty trucks exclusively since 1908. White added Reo in 1957 and Diamond T in 1958, leaving International Harvester, Mack (taken over by Signal Company, a conglomerate, in 1967), and Flxible as the only other important separate producers of commercial vehicles. Flxible became part of the Grumman Corporation in 1978. White thus became the biggest firm in the field of strictly commercial vehicles, but it still was much smaller than General Motors, Ford, Chrysler, and American Motors, and it had to compete with their truck divisions.

On the other hand, the trend to oligopoly in the assembly and sale of motor vehicles did not conspicuously affect the supplier firms who made parts and components. There was some increase in integration, as could have been expected, but no one in the business of making automobiles came anywhere near Henry Ford's ideal of total vertical integration, nor did they particularly want to. General Motors was about 50 to 55 percent integrated, with the others in descending proportions according to size. There are advantages to having independent suppliers: they may offer special skills that would be difficult and expensive to duplicate; they offer a check on the efficiency of the firm's own operations; and the investment needed to make the part internally may be unjustifiably high. As the 1960s began, when passenger car manufacturers were being reduced to four, these four were supplied by more than three thousand independent concerns.

The Era of Large Cars

Big companies made big cars. There was no necessary relationship, but the conditions of the 1950s worked that way. It was a prosperous period, with the American economy expanding and both Europe and Japan making a remarkable recovery from the effects of World War II. There was money to spend and much of it throughout the world was being spent on motor vehicles. In the United States the private automobile had become far more than a means of transportation. It was a status symbol, the most universal demonstration of conspicuous consumption in American life. This aspect of automobile ownership had existed at least since the introduction of the annual model and the demise of the Model T in the 1920s, but it was magnified in the 1950s to the point where it superseded all other considerations in the design and marketing of passenger cars. Styling became the principal factor in design, with power coming next. It was all important that a car should *look* luxurious, and this requisite was interpreted as demanding ornateness in appearance and lavish use of chrome. It was almost as important that the car should have plenty of power, with quick pickup and rapid acceleration. These characteristics were justified on grounds of safety, in that the vehicle could respond promptly in an emergency that called for a quick burst of speed. The cars sold; style, size, and power were what the public wanted.

In 1957, when the era of the automotive dinosaurs was at its peak, the low priced cars ran to wheelbases of 118 inches and overall lengths of 208 inches, and at the top of the list the Cadillac had a wheelbase of 130 inches and an overall length of 225. Engine horsepower ranged from 190 for Chevrolets, Fords, and Plymouths to over 300 for Cadillacs and Lincolns and as high as 375 for Chryslers. (These were brake horsepower ratings achieved by engines in bench tests; they were not necessarily reproduced in the vehicle.) These horsepowers were attained by using the high compression ratios of 8:1 to 10:1. These were V-8 engines, but even the six cylinder engines used in some of the low priced cars were rated well over a hundred horsepower, and sixes were becoming increasingly rare.

The cars also added items like automatic transmission, power brakes, power steering, and air conditioning that were considered extras at first but by the late 1950s were becoming standard equipment. The first three certainly made it easier to handle the high-powered behemoths, but all of them increased fuel consumption. That, however, was a minor problem, with gasoline selling for about thirty cents a gallon and apparently in limitless supply. None of these devices represented any new technology; they simply had not been worth introducing until the time was reached when competition was based on style and luxury rather than price and the public was willing to accept high prices for its automobiles.

This state of affairs could not be expected to last indefinitely. As cars became larger and mechanically more complicated, repairs became more difficult and expensive, and when remarks started to circulate about how buying a new car meant building a new garage to accommodate it, this might have been seen as a sign that the limit of size had been reached. The failure of Ford's Edsel in 1958 was perhaps another portent, although allowance has to be made for the fact that 1958 was a recession year. The Edsel was intended to come between the Lincoln and the Mercury, competing with Buick and Oldsmobile. Market research at the time it was projected—1954 and 1955—appeared to show that there was a place for a Ford product in this class, and none for a

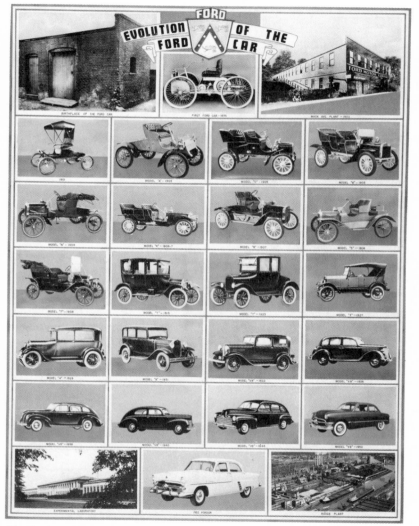

The Evolution of the Ford Car, 1896–1952.
Courtesy of the Henry Ford Museum, The Edison Institute

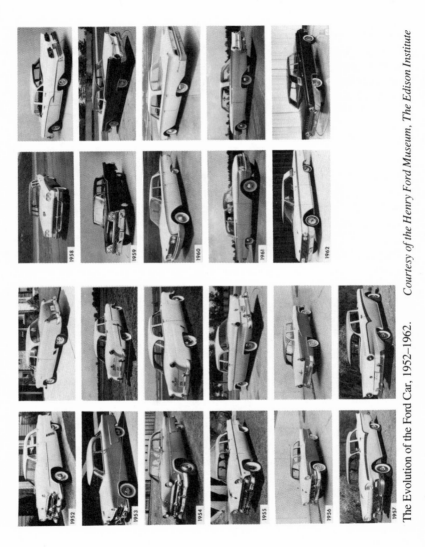

The Evolution of the Ford Car, 1952–1962.   Courtesy of the Henry Ford Museum, The Edison Institute

small, low-priced model. But the record sales of 1955 temporarily glutted the market for new automobiles, and the subsequent decline in production contributed to the recession that ensued. Consequently, the Edsel arrived on the market at the worst possible time.

A more telling portent was the increasing sales of small foreign cars and of American Motors' offer of the Rambler. They still occupied a very minor segment of the market, but they were making gains. The Big Three were watching this development but were not alarmed by it. They were complacently confident that if the small cars became a threat, they could meet it by making their own. What actually happened is the subject of chapter 10.

Diversification

The generally prosperous atmosphere of the 1950s and 1960s encouraged some motor vehicle companies to expand their operations into other fields. General Motors moved cautiously, since it always had to weigh any contemplated expansion against the possibilities of antitrust action. It was already making aircraft engines and diesel locomotives, and it chose to remain in the automotive field. GM's one major acquisition in the 1950s was the Euclid Road Machinery Company, builder of off-highway dump trucks and other earth moving equipment, and it sold that to the White Motor Company in 1968. Chrysler continued to be the country's principal manufacturer of tanks until 1982, when it sold its tank division to General Dynamics, but did not diversify otherwise. Chrysler was having trouble enough holding its position in the motor vehicle market and had no incentive to push into other areas. The Plymouth was frequently outsold not just by Chevrolet and Ford but by the medium-priced lines like Buick and Pontiac, and Chrysler's own medium-priced model, the DeSoto, had to be dropped in 1960.

The Ford Motor Company characteristically followed a different course. First, it returned to tractor manufacturing. This had began in 1939 with a "handshake agreement" between the elder Ford and an inventor and salesman from Northern Ireland named Harry Ferguson (actually Henry George Ferguson, but he never called himself anything but Harry). Ferguson was an enthusiast who shared with Henry Ford the dream of flooding the world with tractors that could be used on small farms, and he had designed both a tractor and a linkage system that would enable a variety of implements to be pulled by and operated from the tractor. The agreement between Ford and Ferguson was purely verbal, and when it became an issue later only Ferguson was alive to testify to its provisions. Basically Ford was to manufacture the tractor and Ferguson was to sell it through a company called Harry Ferguson, Inc.

This venture lost money consistently for the Ford Motor Company, and in 1946 Henry Ford II and Breech, after trying vainly to reach a more definite arrangement with Ferguson, who was a difficult person to get along with, terminated the agreement with him and made plans for manufacturing an exclusively Ford tractor. To sell the Ford product a distributing company, Dearborn Motors, Inc., was formed. This organization served a second purpose, which was to give Breech and other Ford executives at least some of the opportunity for stock ownership and options that executives in large American corporations customarily have. It would be nine years before anyone other than the Ford family or the Ford Foundation could own shares in the Ford Motor Company, but stock in Dearborn Motors could be made available to Ford executives. When Ford stock was finally put on the market in 1955, Dearborn Motors was dissolved. This new line of Ford tractors was built for some years in the Highland Park factory where the moving assembly line became a complete system of production.

Meanwhile Harry Ferguson turned to making his own tractors and did fairly well at it. But he was not the type to take his dismissal quietly, and in 1948 he sued the Ford Motor Company for $251 million, of which $246 million was claimed as treble damages under the Sherman Antitrust Act for alleged conspiracy to put Harry Ferguson, Inc., out of business. The rest was for alleged infringement of Ferguson's patents in Ford tractors. Four years later this suit was settled by a consent decree that awarded Ferguson $9.25 million. Ferguson then merged his company with the Canadian farm implement firm of Massey-Harris, the new combination becoming Massey-Ferguson although Ferguson himself remained in it for only a year.

Ford also became involved in antitrust action when it bought part of the properties of the Electric Autolite Company in 1961. This concern made automotive electric equipment, and in this case Ford was required to dispose of its Autolite holdings in 1973. In the same year as the Autolite purchase Ford expanded into electronics through acquisition of the Philco Corporation, a well-known manufacturer of radios and televisions. This transaction presented no legal difficulties. Earlier, in 1956, Ford had entered missile and space technology by establishing an Aeronutronics Division, which was merged with Philco in 1964 as the Philco Division of the Ford Motor Company.

The other automotive firm to expand into other areas on a substantial scale was White. Its truck acquisitions have been noted. During the 1960s White became a major manufacturer of farm equipment by the acquisition of the Oliver Corporation (1960), Cletrac (1961), maker of crawler tractors, and Motec Industries (1963). These were consolidated as the White Farm Equipment Company. Then in 1968, as previously mentioned, White bought the Euclid Road Machinery Company from General Motors.

This transaction was symptomatic of a reverse trend that appeared in the late 1960s, with some companies deciding to spin off their nonautomotive operations. American Motors left the refrigerator and household appliance business in this same year (1968) by selling its Kelvinator Division to White Consolidated Industries. GM had sold its holdings in the Ethyl Corporation some years earlier (1962), and we have seen how it withdrew from the airframe business shortly after World War II. The Ford Motor Company joined this movement by selling the home entertainment section of its Philco Division to Sylvania Electric, then an affiliate of General Telephone and Electronics, in 1974.

Diversification has not been a really important part of the American automobile industry. Most of the motor vehicle companies have ventured into other fields at one time or another, but seldom on any large scale or with satisfactory results. Ford's persistent involvement with tractors may be regarded as an exception, and this interest was an enthusiasm of the senior Henry Ford that became a company tradition. Tractors and farm machinery can in any case be considered as automotive equipment, as can diesel locomotives, but among the automobile companies only Ford has had any real success with the former and only General Motors has attempted to build the latter. A withdrawal from nonautomotive operations became very noticeable in the 1970s.

Consequently these moves toward diversification in the automobile industry attracted little attention from either the public or the government. The antitrust action against Ford for its Autolite purchase was exceptional and obscure. On the other hand, the obvious concentration within the industry became a matter of concern by the beginning of the 1960s. The arrival of oligopoly was associated with the visible absence of effective price competition. There was a connection, of course, but it was not generally appreciated that the system of administered prices practiced by the automobile industry served to keep competition alive rather than suppress it. If there had been unrestricted price competition Chrysler and American Motors would have been out of business and Ford's position would have been threatened. General Motors was the obvious target for critics of the industry's structure, and from at least the latter part of the 1950s there was agitation to break up General Motors. Nothing came of it, mainly because no one could quite calculate how to separate the component parts of a very well coordinated organization without severe financial disruption and loss of efficiency in production, and as time passed it became increasingly evident that competition for American motor vehicle manufactures did exist, in the form of a rising tide of imports from Europe and Japan.

CHAPTER TEN
The Rise of the Small Car

The American predilection for large automobiles was not a phenomenon pe-culiar to the 1950s. American cars had generally been bigger than others since early in the century, for several reasons: cheaper fuel, the absence of the taxes that discriminated against high-powered cars in other countries, and the fact that automobiles in the United States were likely to be used more intensively and driven for greater distances (but not at higher speeds) than elsewhere in the world, except for Canada. The manufacturers encouraged this preference, because as the size of a car increases, its price rises more steeply than the cost of manufacturing it, and big cars thus yield more profit per unit than small cars. Furthermore, attempts at marketing cars of substandard size in the United States had a poor record.

In the 1950s the emphasis on size and power was carried unreasonably far. The public could not be expected to disregard the rising costs of buying and operating an automobile indefinitely, so that some reaction was inevitable. At the end of the 1950s small cars, domestic and foreign, had gained a firm foot-hold in the American market and were gradually expanding it, but it still took twenty years and major changes in the United States and world economic sit-uation before American motorists definitely turned away, or were pushed away, from their preference for the bigger vehicles.

Interest in the sales possibility of a passenger automobile smaller than the six-passenger sedans that were the standard offering of Chevrolet, Ford, and Plymouth existed well before the oversized vehicles of the 1950s were being produced. As far back as 1930 an attempt was made to introduce an American version of the British Austin Bantam two-seater, but the "Baby Austin" was mainly a curiosity. Then in 1939 Powell Crosley began his experiment with a four-passenger vehicle, which was just appearing when World War II intervened. The subsequent history of the Crosley has already been told.

At the end of the war there was uncertainty about precisely what the public was going to want when it resumed buying automobiles, so that both General Motors and Ford prepared designs for small cars. These were shelved when it developed that they would offer no real saving in price and that Americans were continuing to show their usual willingness to buy the larger vehicles. The General Motors design became the Australian Holden, so that the effort was not altogether wasted. By 1948 the Big Three had lost interest in the small car field, but the independents continued to eye it as a possible place for themselves in the motor vehicle market. All of them brought out small cars in the early 1950s—Hudson's Jet, Kaiser's Henry J., Nash's Rambler, and Willys's Aero. The results were discouraging. The independents found what Ford and General Motors had calculated in their planning, that the price differential between their offerings and the standard-sized models was not great enough to attract customers. The standard-sized vehicle could offer more in style and comfort, and the price of gasoline was low enough so that the smaller vehicle had no real advantage in economy of operation. The makers of these small cars may have been overcautious in their pricing policies—none of the smaller companies felt secure enough to cut its prices substantially and hope to attract volume sales thereby.

The Aero and the Henry J. were short-lived, and the Jet, like the Hudson itself, disappeared in the American Motors merger. The Rambler lost money at first, but it remained in production because of George Romney's conviction that the compact car—the term was just beginning to be used—was the route to salvation for American Motors. He was right. Rambler sales rose encouragingly to 80,000 in 1955, about 1 percent of the total domestic passenger car sales, a creditable showing at the point when the tail-finned behemoths were at their peak of popularity. It was still losing money at that level, but with the ensuing recession and the partial turning away from high-priced cars, Rambler sales shot up to 186,000 in 1958 and American Motors was operating in the black. Studebaker-Packard followed the American Motors example with two compacts, the Scotsman (1957) and the more successful Lark (1958), which gave it a brief period of profitability before it left the automotive scene. By 1960 the Big Three had their own compacts on the market and competitive conditions became difficult for the independents, although American Motors managed to stay alive. Romney left the automobile industry for a political career in 1961, and with his departure some of the drive at American Motors was lost.

The Arrival of the Imports

The decision by the Big Three to enter the compact field after a decade of reluctance was due only in part to the rising sales of the Rambler and the Lark. A more important factor was the pressure they were feeling from the increasing popularity of foreign cars in the United States. This was a novel phenomenon. At the beginning of the automotive era some Americans bought Daimlers and Panhards in preference to the clumsy horseless carriages that their own manufacturers were turning out, and wealthy Americans continued to buy Rolls-Royces as the supreme status symbol of motordom. But by 1910 foreign cars were a rarity on American roads, and American motor vehicles were becoming an important export item.

After World War II the nations of Western Europe were desperately in need of dollar credits, and one obvious way of earning them was to export motor vehicles to the United States, where buyers were clamoring for cars of any kind and production remained short of demand for several years. It was an alluring prospect, but a difficult one to realize. European automobile manufacturers had far greater problems than the Americans in returning to peacetime production. Plants had been bombed, machinery was worn out, the political situation was frequently uncertain, and invading the market of the giant American motor vehicle producers was a risky enterprise.

Consequently, while some British and French makes began to appear on the American market in the late 1940s, their numbers were slight, even though the Ford Motor Company tried to promote sales of its British models in order to help the acute British dollar shortage. As the 1950s began and Europe was returning to normal production, import car sales in the United States were less than one half of one percent of the total. Two categories of foreign passenger cars gained a special place in the United States market, a position which did not appreciably fluctuate and was not really competitive with domestic production: the luxury makes like Rolls-Royce and Mercedes, and the sports cars such as Jaguar, Porsche, Ferrari, MG, and Austin-Healey. The problem that developed was with the family-type small cars.

The major part of this problem at first was an odd-looking German product named the Volkswagen, with an air-cooled, four-cylinder engine in the rear and a body shape that gave it the nickname "Bug" or "Beetle." Since the Volkswagen was the first foreign car to become part of the United States automobile industry, its origins can appropriately be included here. It began as a dream of Adolf Hitler, to provide Germany with a "People's Car" (which is what "Volkswagen" means) that would play the role of the Model T in the

United States. The vehicle itself was designed by Ferdinand Porsche and the project was financed by the German government. World War II intervened before this dream could be realized, and the new factory in Wolfsburg was devoted to the production of military vehicles comparable to the American jeep.

When the war ended the Volkswagen operation was considered for its value to the allies as reparations, but no American or British automobile company was willing to take it over. With the plant in ruins and a prewar design to work with, they considered it an unpromising prospect. So Volkswagen had to start over again on its own, under the joint ownership of the German federal government and the länder of Lower Saxony. Subsequently, when the enterprise had succeeded beyond expectations, half the stock was sold to private investors. Dr. Heinz Nordhoff was put in charge of the company. He had been managing director of Opel but was discharged by the occupation authorities after the war on the ground that he had collaborated with the Nazis. Apparently it was felt that he would be harmless in devastated Wolfsburg. Beginning production on a small scale, with some of the work carried on in tents, he exhorted his work force to make their contribution to the economic rehabilitation of their country, and gradually the ungainly Beetle became a familiar sight on roads in Germany and elsewhere. Like the Model T Ford before it, the VW did not have a new model each year. Every Volkswagen looked like every other, year in and year out, its marketing strategy differing from that of the Model T in just one feature: a Volkswagen could be bought in a number of colors other than black.

Penetration of the United States market started very slowly, until Nordhoff and his associates took a hard look at the problem and realized that if a foreign automobile, other than a specialized type like a sports car, was to compete effectively in the American market, its seller must be able to answer satisfactorily the question, "What if it breaks down in Dubuque?" Volkswagen thereupon put time and effort, well beyond any other foreign car manufacturer at that point, into building a sales and service network capable of guaranteeing that a purchaser of a VW could be sure of prompt and efficient service anywhere in the United States. That, plus economy of purchase and operation, and the unexpected phenomenon of antisnobbism, wherein its ostentatious lack of style made it a special kind of status symbol, put the Volkswagen at the top among import cars in the United States.

The results became apparent as early as 1955, when Volkswagen accounted for almost half of all sales of import cars in the United States. The totals were still small—28,000 VW's in a year when over eight million motor vehicles were sold altogether—but this was just a beginning. United States automobile imports mounted rapidly, to 600,000, or 10 percent of the motor vehicle market, in 1959, and while the Volkswagen lead declined, it remained comfortably in first place among the imports and its American sales reached 160,000 in 1960. Furthermore, three of the first five import makes in 1955 were sports cars (Metropolitan, a two-seater made for American Motors by the British Motor Corporation, Jaguar, and MG). VW was in first place and the British Hillman was fifth. By 1958 the sports cars had fallen behind and the top five imports in order were VW, Renault, British Ford, Fiat, and Hillman.

The appearance of the American compacts at this point slowed imports for a year or two, after which they picked up again and continued to grow steadily, still with Volkswagen in the lead. The VW predominance continued through the 1960s, reaching a peak of 62 percent of all import car sales in 1968 and total sales of almost 570,000 vehicles in 1970. At that point, for reasons to be explained later, the company's fortunes suffered a decline.

The Response of the American Industry

There has been a widespread belief that the United States automobile industry, especially the Big Three, was either oblivious to the growth of the market for small cars or deliberately ignored it and attempted through high-pressure sales techniques to continue to foist big cars on a buying public that did not want them; neither assumption is valid. We know that General Motors and Ford looked carefully into compact cars at the end of World War II and decided they could not be priced competitively with their standard low-priced models, and the attempts of the independents to market compacts in the early 1950s confirmed this judgment for that time. Nor was there a noticeable public clamor for small cars. As late as 1955, when Rambler and Volkswagen were beginning to attract attention, compact sales of domestic and foreign makes together came to just about 2 percent of the total passenger automobile market.

In those conditions it was good business sense for the Big Three to stay with their standard models. They had no incentive to promote small cars, and it would not have been to their advantage to do so, because the higher profit margins were with the larger cars. There was little concern then about fuel economy on the part of either the government or the public, so that there was no compulsion to limit vehicle sizes and weights on that account. It was certainly not necessary to force big cars on the buying public, nor would it have been possible; the failure of the Edsel offered proof enough of that. The small car market, such as it was, could be left to American Motors and the imports until such time as it became a more serious threat.

The American companies therefore had valid reasons for acting as they did, but in retrospect it is clear that they overestimated the strength of their position. They dominated the automotive world. They were all, including American Motors, far larger than any foreign motor vehicle manufacturer at that time, and they had become somewhat complacent about the superiority of their managerial and technical skills. They were confident that if it became necessary for them to make small cars, they would have no trouble in "sweeping the imports into the sea." Criticism of the size and cost of American automobiles of the period was brushed aside with reiterated statements that, "When you downsize a car, you take out quality faster than you take out cost," or, "A good used car is the answer to the American public's need for cheap transportation." Both remarks are attributed to General Motors; whoever dreamed up the second one was either being humorous or had never owned a used car. The first statement indicates a flaw in the approach of the American automobile companies to the small car problem that would persist for twenty years. They saw compacts primarily as cut-down versions of standard models, thus as inferior copies of the large cars their makers really preferred to sell; the manufacturers had strong reasons for wanting purchasers to be convinced that bigger was better. On the other hand, their European and later their Japanese competitors designed their vehicles from the start to be small-sized, with the appropriate dimensions and performance characteristics.

When the economy softened in the late 1950s, Rambler sales surged upward and imports not only reached the supposedly unacceptable 5 percent of the market but went up to 10 percent in 1959. The Big Three responded at first by offering their own foreign-made models. Ford intensified its efforts to sell its British-built cars and in 1958 introduced the German Taunus, which never sold well in the United States. General Motors imported Opels from Germany, sold through Buick dealers, and Vauxhalls from Great Britain, sold through Pontiac dealers. Chrysler entered the competition by selling the French Simca (made by the Societé Industrielle de Mecanique et Carroserie Automobile) and bought the company in 1958, thereby beginning a process of overseas expansion that in the end overstrained Chrysler's resources. American Motors was already in this race with its British built Metropolitan; Studebaker tried to stay competitive by becoming the distributor for the German Mercedes-Benz, which was a high-priced automobile and not a compact, and the DKW-Auto Union, a low-priced German car.

This policy was not enough. As small car sales continued to climb, the Big Three concluded that their only course was to enter the compact field themselves. They all had designs in preparation, so that the Chevrolet Corvair, the Ford Falcon, and the Plymouth Valiant were all put on the market in 1959.

They were very successful, probably more because of their novelty than because of any pronounced change in buyer tastes, and they were the precursors of a bewildering variety of compacts, near compacts, subcompacts, and intermediates. Yet they were only temporarily effective in reducing the volume of imports. That was partly because the economy recovered and the whole motor vehicle market expanded, to the point where the nine-million-unit record of 1955 was surpassed by an eleven-million year in 1965. A more direct factor in the competition between domestic and foreign cars was that American purchasers wanted the same amenities in their compacts—automatic transmissions, air conditioners, etc.—as they had become accustomed to in their larger automobiles, and the easiest way to meet this demand was to make the American compacts just a little bigger. But that in turn again left a gap at the lower end of the passenger car scale that the imports could fill with minimal competition from domestic sources. Import passenger car sales declined in 1960 and 1961 but they started a steady climb that carried them from their former high of 10 percent of the market to 15 percent as the 1970s began.

The impact of import cars may have been reduced in the eyes of the United States producers by the fact that between 50 and 60 percent of the small foreign automobiles were bought during the 1950s and early 1960s as second cars for families who already owned a large American car, so that to the automobile industry's market research agencies the number of "buying units" in the market was not greatly affected. Data compiled at this time also showed, however, that half the purchasers gave economy of operation as their chief reason for buying, as against only a fifth who cited low initial cost. This was an item whose significance seems to have escaped the notice of the American manufacturers.

The worst sufferers from the domestic compacts were in fact their own companies' "captive" imports. Evidently when it came to a choice between pushing one's own small cars or those of a foreign subsidiary, the home-grown product had first claim. British Ford, Opel, and Simca dropped out of the top ten import leaders, although they returned in the latter part of the 1960s. The Metropolitan ceased production in 1962, and Ford's Taunus left the American scene. Vauxhall was only a minor participant. Sales figures also indicate that for Ford and Chrysler the success of their compacts was at the expense of their standard models (see table 10–1).

The Newcomers

The ability of the foreign automobile producers to expand their share of the United States market in the face of competition from the much larger Ameri-

Table 10–1

Sales Comparison, Selected U.S. Standard and Compact Cars, 1959–63

YEAR	1959	1960	1961	1962	1963
GENERAL MOTORS					
*Chevrolet	1,349,552	1,614,342	1,201,914	1,495,476	1,625,931
**Chevelle	—	—	—	—	113,774
***Chevy II	—	—	86,310	369,246	312,097
***Corvair	79,441	259,276	316,600	296,687	251,513
*Pontiac	388,856	418,154	244,391	401,674	481,652
**Tempest	—	32,052	115,945	145,676	143,616
FORD					
*Ford	1,352,112	917,087	710,392	722,642	911,496
**Fairlane	—	—	60,392	386,192	318,018
***Falcon	100,757	507,199	486,079	381,558	341,871
*Mercury	156,765	161,787	109,775	109,347	118,815
**Comet	—	198,031	185,844	144,886	150,694

YEAR	1959	1960	1961	1962	1963
CHRYSLER					
*Plymouth	393,213	252,453	188,170	177,651	274,735
***Valiant	19,991	231,516	122,275	153,428	221,677
Dodge	192,798	362,808	166,158	216,518	246,425
**Lancer	—	48,858	54,621	35,546	—
***Dart	—	—	—	—	174,876 (1)
AMERICAN MOTORS					
***Rambler/American	378,064	485,745	134,369	117,003	129,665
***Classic	—	—	214,084	297,885	321,916
STUDEBAKER	153,823	105,902	78,664	86,974	67,918

*Regular **Intermediate ***Compact
(1) Negligible sales other than compacts.

Source: Automobile Facts and Figures, 1964.

can manufacturers can be attributed in part to the fact that small cars were still a minor interest of the American firms, but much more to significant changes in the import car situation that intensified competition in the small car field. The Volkswagen leadership carried on through the 1960s, but under increasing pressure. European rivals Renault and Fiat (Fabbrica Italiana Automobili Torino, founded 1899) were pushing vigorously for greater American sales, and a new arrival, the Swedish Volvo, quickly gained a respectable place in the American market. The British companies, British Motor Corporation and Leyland Motors, lagged behind, or at any rate failed to advance. They were handicapped by the chronically unstable labor conditions in the British motor industry, where constant unexpected and unauthorized strikes made orderly production difficult, and still more, where United States sales were concerned, by the fact that the British automobile firms never succeeded in establishing the kind of nationwide service and repair system that VW had found so important. Sports cars were a different matter; BMC sold 90 percent of its output of sports cars in North America, but although it was a prestigious market, it was not a high-volume one.

Far more important in its effect on the import car market was the appearance of Japanese automobiles, an event that passed virtually unnoticed at first. Few people were aware of the fact, or paid much attention if they did know about it, that the two largest Japanese motor vehicle manufacturers, Toyota and Nissan (Datsun), began to sell cars and trucks in the United States in 1957 and 1958 respectively. They were the biggest automobile companies in Japan, but they were small by either American or European standards; Japanese production of four-wheeled motor vehicles reached 100,000 for the first time in 1956, including passenger automobiles, trucks, and buses. The vehicles themselves were well built and sturdy, but under-powered for American driving conditions and ungainly in comparison with the elaborate styling of most American and European automobiles. For some time, indeed, Japanese cars were jokingly alleged to be made out of discarded beer cans.

But the Japanese meant business. Neither Toyota nor Nissan entered the United States market lightly. Both studied the situation carefully before they committed themselves, including examination of the Volkswagen experience in detail. They also had available to them the expertise of those unique institutions, the Japanese trading corporations like Marubeni and Mitsubishi. Getting established in the United States was still a long process; in fact, Toyota was virtually out of the passenger car market for a year or two in the early 1960s while it redesigned its models to meet American tastes and standards. The pickup trucks that both companies sold were of great help in attracting American buyers to Japanese vehicles, because a good many American servicemen had become familiar with them in Japan and Korea and knew them to be durable and economical.

By the mid-1960s Toyota and Datsun sales were growing rapidly and in 1970 Toyota was second and Datsun third in sales of import cars in the United States, an advance that signaled a revolution in the automotive world. In 1968 Japan passed the German Federal Republic as the world's second largest producer of motor vehicles, a phenomenal feat for a country whose automobile industry had been almost negligible ten years before. Other Japanese cars besides Datsun and Toyota were appearing in strength on the American scene. Honda, initially a manufacturer of motorcycles, offered an automobile with a stratified-charge engine, designed for greater efficiency in combustion and the reduction of pollutant emissions, and the Mazda, made by Toyo Kogyo, used the German Wankel rotary piston engine. Both makes sold well, although their engines never came up to the claims that had been made for them. Subaru, made by Fuji Heavy Industries, was a later arrival. In addition, there were three "captive imports" from Japan that sold well; the Dodge Colt, built by Mitsubishi, the Ford Courier pickup, made by Toyo Kogyo; and the General Motors Luv, also a pickup, from Isuzu, in which General Motors had a 35 percent interest.

In 1970 sales of foreign cars reached 15 percent of all sales of passenger automobiles in the United States. The percentage was somewhat lower (about 13.5) if all motor vehicles, including trucks and buses, were counted, but the passenger car figures mattered most. The response of the American automobile manufacturers, specifically the Big Three, to this renewed import surge was almost exactly what it had been ten years before, except that the alarm went off when the imports reached the 10 percent level rather than 5 percent. The American firms first tried to ignore the trend, then they pushed their own "captive" imports, and finally, in 1969 and 1970, all except Chrysler came out with a new line of "subcompacts." These were the Ford Maverick and American Motors Hornet (1969), and the Chevrolet Vega, Ford Pinto, and American Motors Gremlin (all 1970). Chrysler did not have a subcompact until 1972.

Here the analogy between the 1960 and 1970 situations ceases. The new subcompacts sold well, but they had no effect on the rising tide of imports. Motor vehicle sales continued to increase, and the small car segment of the market expanded steadily, so that there was business for both domestic and foreign makes. There was not as yet anything resembling a stampede to small cars. Table 10–2 presents the situation clearly and goes far to clarify the policies followed by the American automobile industry. Until the oil embargo of 1973–74, the United States market in passenger automobiles was divided ap-

Table 10–2

U.S. Automobile Market Shares by Size Class and Imports in Percent, 1970–80

Year	SMALL CARS		MID-SIZE CARS	FULL-SIZE CARS
	Import	Domestic		
1970	15.1	23.1	21.8	40.0
1971	15.3	23.6	19.9	41.2
1972	14.8	24.1	21.7	39.4
1973	15.4	27.2	22.5	34.9
1974	15.9	32.4	24.6	27.1
1975	18.2	35.3	23.5	23.0
1976	14.8	33.2	27.0	25.0
1977	18.4	28.8	27.7	25.1
1978	17.7	30.8	27.9	23.6
1979	21.9	34.8	23.3	20.0
1980*	26.9	38.0	19.8	15.3

*Through May

Source: Unpublished data from U. S. Department of Commerce, Bureau of Economic Analysis.

proximately 60 percent larger cars and 40 percent smaller. The domestic small cars outsold the foreign, and regular compacts outsold subcompacts.

The American manufacturers were therefore justified in believing that they were doing all that was needed to meet the demand for small cars, and they must have been sure they were doing the right thing when 1973 proved to be a record year, with factory sales of 9,676,000 passenger cars and 1,915,000 trucks and buses, for a grand total of 12,591,000 vehicles. This was a very satisfactory situation and overshadowed whatever threat the growth in imports may have posed. The foreign cars, after all, were selling mainly in the segment of the motor vehicle market that interested the American producers least. There was some grumbling about the growing influx of foreign-made automobiles, but nothing very serious, and neither management nor labor in the American automobile industry was prepared to advocate restrictive tariffs on imports. They had an interest in exporting their own products to other countries.

It was recognized that buyer preference was swinging toward smaller cars, but the swing was very gradual, certainly not enough to warrant a drastic shift in the product line of the automobile manufacturing companies. Such changes as were needed were expected to be made slowly. Few could have foreseen that events that were external to the industry and outside its control would in less than ten years bring about a massive transformation affecting motor vehicle production not only in the United States but throughout the entire world. In the meantime one fact was definitely established. Apprehension that the oligopolistic structure of the United States automobile industry might eliminate effective competition was now needless; the growth of the import car business was providing all the competition that anyone could want.

CHAPTER ELEVEN

The Government and the Automobile Industry

While the American motor vehicle industry was wrestling with the problem of what kind of passenger automobiles it should build and worrying about import competition, it was also being subjected to governmental controls on a much broader scale than it had ever before encountered. The principal issues dealt with were air pollution, traffic safety, and fuel economy, all of which became critical in the 1960s and 1970s. There were also some lesser matters that became subjects of governmental concern, and the body of legislation that resulted created a regulatory structure that had marked effects on the design of motor vehicles and the operations of the automobile industry as a whole.

Dealer Problems

The first of these issues to come up was the matter of relationships between the automobile manufacturers and their dealers. This was not, of course, a new problem. It had simply lain dormant during the war years and the period immediately afterward when there was a booming sellers' market. In the 1950s the National Automobile Dealers Association (NADA) was a stronger and more aggressive organization than it had been earlier, able to exert influence at both the state and national levels.

The dealer problem continued to revolve about the two questions of territorial rights and cancellation of franchises. This time the NADA was well organized and powerful enough to get some positive action. Only five states had had any sort of protective legislation before World War II (Wisconsin, Iowa, North Dakota, Florida, Mississippi). After the war this number increased to twenty, and seventeen others considered but did not enact such legislation.

These laws for the most part tried through licensing requirements to protect dealers against being required to take unordered cars and against arbitrary cancellation of their franchises. The word "tried" is used purposely; by and large implementation of this legislation appears to have been ineffective. There never was a satisfactory solution to the territorial problem, largely because the dealers themselves took customers as they found them, without worrying about whose territory they properly belonged in.

Dealer complaints increased as the postwar sellers' market disappeared and the producers were again competing vigorously for sales, so that the dealers came under stronger pressures. The problem attracted congressional attention in the early 1950s and was the subject of several committee investigations. The principal figures in these were Senators Estes Kefauver of Tennessee, A. S. "Mike" Monroney of Oklahoma, and Joseph J. O'Mahoney of Wyoming. Whether they were instigated by concern for the plight of the dealers, or by the opportunity to appear before the public as champions of the little man against General Motors, or by the hope of gaining political advantage for the election of 1956 is an unanswerable question. Certainly General Motors was the principal target of criticism, and the company's management did little to diminish this criticism when it acted as if congressional committees could be ignored at will.

The outcome was the "Dealers Day in Court" Act of 1956, passed after prolonged discussion which showed the dealers themselves to be divided on just how much legislative protection they ought to have. As enacted, the law prohibited actual coercion or intimidation of dealers by manufacturers but recognized that a manufacturer could properly employ "recommendation, endorsement, exposition, persuasion, urging, or argument" (15 U.S. Code, 1963, sec. 1222).

Like the state legislation, the Dealers Day in Court Act had only a limited effect on the issues it was supposed to resolve. Its existence undoubtedly inhibited some of the arbitrary practices that dealers had complained of, and it inspired some restructuring of dealer relations in the automobile industry in order to avert more stringent legislation in the future. During the hearings that preceded the passage of the law George Romney stated that the industry had abandoned the enlightened policies of Alfred P. Sloan. His fellow executives publicly disagreed, but they all proceeded to head off their various critics by providing for freer access for dealers to top management, less arbitrary power for manufacturers' field representatives, and closer cooperation with the NADA.

The difficulties remained what they had been since the problem first arose. The dealers were not a coherent, unified body. Those who were doing well preferred to maintain good relations with their manufacturers; others who might have been dissatisfied avoided making their complaints public rather than risk reprisals, because there were ways in which an "uncooperative" dealer could be penalized without infringing the law. He might, for instance, find that shipments of the best-selling models were not reaching him while others in his general area were well supplied.

More important, there was at least as much support for protecting the public from the automobile dealers as there was for protecting the dealers from their producers. This was particularly true in the selling of used cars, and most states came to require dealers to provide accurate information on the condition of the vehicle to prospective purchasers of used cars. It was usual also to prohibit tampering with a car's odometer. Senator Monroney was also concerned with this problem of protecting the consumer and sponsored the law, the Monroney Act, which requires all new motor vehicles offered for sale in the United States to have a sticker attached to them (the "Monroney Label") stating the suggested retail selling price, specifying the items that are standard equipment, and listing individually the options that the vehicle contains and their suggested prices. The retail prices have to be "suggested." For an automobile manufacturer to impose a retail price on its dealers would be restraint of trade. A dealership is legally an independent business; it must be free to negotiate with its customers on price, a process that usually occurs in bargaining over trade-in allowances.

Air Pollution

Pollution of the atmosphere over large cities is as old as the cities themselves. Whenever large numbers of people have congregated in limited areas, there has been some air pollution from cooking and heating fires and effluvia from human and animal wastes. Industrialization brought a more intensive outpouring of smoke, conspicuously coal smoke, and new pollutants in industrial wastes pouring from factory chimneys. The term "smog" initially had nothing to do with motor vehicle exhaust emissions; it was coined to describe the combination of coal smoke and fog that periodically blanketed nineteenth-century London. In short, air pollution existed long before the advent of the automobile and would have continued to exist even if the automobile had never been invented. The responsibility of the gasoline-powered motor vehicle for polluting the atmosphere should certainly not be minimized, but it should not be exaggerated either.

Automobile exhaust emissions were first recognized as a source of air pollution about 1950, when the yellowish-brown haze that is now called smog began to appear in the Los Angeles basin. Until then, however it may have appeared to motorists in rush hour traffic, there had been no concentration of motor vehicles consistently intense enough to produce perceptible effects on the atmosphere. Los Angeles had special conditions: a high concentration of motor vehicles, ample sunlight to create the chemical reactions needed to convert exhaust and industrial emissions into smog, frequent temperature inversions to keep the emissions from rising into the upper atmosphere, a semicircle of high mountains, and prevailing winds off the ocean with insufficient velocity to blow the smog over the mountains.

The relationship of motor vehicle exhaust emissions to this photochemical smog was established in the early 1950s by Dr. A. J. Haagen-Smit of the California Institute of Technology, when he identified the principal components of this atmospheric aberration as unconsumed hydrocarbons, carbon monoxide, and nitrous oxides. He estimated that about 70 percent of the Los Angeles smog was produced by automble exhausts. There was considerable discussion about the appropriate action to be taken, and finally in 1960 California required that motor vehicles sold in the state have devices that would keep pollutant emissions within prescribed limits. The automobile companies disliked this requirement, because it meant that they would have to install special equipment on cars destined for California, and the California market was too big to be ignored.

The overall response of the motor vehicle industry regrettably followed a pattern that applied to every major public issue affecting the industry during approximately the twenty years from 1955 to 1975. First, industry spokesmen denied that the problem existed; they then conceded that it did exist but asserted that it had no solution; finally, they conceded that it could be solved but that the solutions would be very expensive, difficult to apply, and would require a long time to develop. In this third position the industry was usually right, more so than its critics were willing to admit, but in the meantime steps 1 and 2 had created a public image of an industry that was unwilling to accept any social responsibility and was not open to fresh ideas. This image was not fully accurate, but the fact remains that in facing the social effects of their operations the American automobile manufacturers were poorly served by their policy planners and their public relations staffs.

In the 1960s air pollution rapidly became a national issue. After preliminary legislation in 1963, Congress passed the Motor Vehicle Air Pollution Control Act in 1965, instructing the secretary of health, education and welfare to establish emissions standards for new motor vehicles on the basis of technological and economic feasibility. The first federal standards were based on those of California, limiting emissions to 275 parts per million (ppm) of hydrocarbons

(HC) and 1.5 of carbon monoxide (CO), to become effective with the 1968 model year. By the Air Quality Act of 1967 the federal government assumed sole responsibility for establishing clean air standards, although California was allowed to have somewhat more stringent emission controls than were required nationally.

Shortly after the passage of the 1967 law emission levels were set at 2.2 grams per million (gpm) for hydrocarbons and 23 gpm for carbon monoxide. The change from ppm to gpm illustrates one of the complications of legislating on imperfectly understood technical problems. The makers of small cars, including the imports, protested that measuring emissions in ppm discriminated unfairly against them. Installing emission controls was more difficult for them because they had less space to work with, so that a car with a four-cylinder engine might be emitting more ppm of pollutant than the vehicle with the V-8 engine in the adjoining lane, although the smaller engine was producing less total pollutant.

There were other examples of the same problem. Because hydrocarbons and carbon monoxides were the earliest components of photochemical smog to be positively identified, the first emission control regulations emphasized reducing hydrocarbons and carbon monoxide and tended to disregard oxides of nitrogen (NOx). The most direct method of reducing HC and CO emissions was to use higher engine temperatures and the manufacturers took that route. Then it developed that hotter engines produced more NOx and that it was in fact a very important element of smog.

Above all, there has never been an accurate, agreed-on criterion of what should constitute clean air. Attempting to achieve 100 percent purity would be prohibitively expensive as well as unrealistic; completely pure air does not occur in nature. But no one knows at what level of air quality the optimum balance is struck between costs and benefits. The automobile industry had legitimate grounds for protesting against the burden of regulations that kept imposing more stringent standards without any indication of what the ultimate goal might be. When the consequences of the oil crisis of 1979 plunged the American automobile industry into a prolonged slump, it was found that the public interest could accept some relaxation of schedules for reaching prescribed emission levels.

In addition, the United States motor vehicle manufacturers were not permitted to cooperate in the development of emission control techniques. They were advised that any such collaboration would be considered to be in violation of the antitrust laws. The argument offered by the government agencies involved, including the Department of Justice, was that requiring each company to develop its own system would keep prices competitive. By contrast, Japanese motor vehicle manufacturers were encouraged to pool their resources and did, with a considerable saving in research and development cost to each individual company. The Japanese method also guaranteed that every Japanese car would be equipped with the best emission control system the country's automobile industry could produce.

The phase of the Clean Air Program that involved the automobile industry can be adjudged a partial success. Pollutant emissions from individual motor vehicles have been appreciably reduced, but some of the gains have been off-set by the fact that the number of cars on the road has been increasing along with the population.

Available information indicates that atmospheric pollution in the United States has been checked, possibly even somewhat reduced by the steps that have been taken to control automotive and industrial exhausts, but an exact assessment of what has been accomplished is difficult to make because there has been no definite statement of the goals.

Highway Safety

At just about the same time as Congress took action on the issue of air pollu-tion, it also began to legislate on the subject of highway safety. The incentive in this case was less obvious. Admittedly it was distressing that some fifty thousand people were killed on American roads every year, with much larger numbers injured and a horrendous toll in property damage, yet an analysis of accident statistics (see table 11–1) plainly shows that in the 1960s the accident rate had been steadily declining for thirty years and that American highways were considerably safer than others. The aggregate numbers of accidents, fa-talities, and injuries grew because the number of vehicles in use was steadily increasing, but the ratio of fatalities to vehicle miles traveled, for example, was a third lower in the 1960s than it had been in the 1930s. Comparisons with traffic conditions elsewhere are complicated by differences in methods of com-piling the data; however, in 1961 the ratio of highway fatalities to registered motor vehicles in six countries with substantial traffic was: Italy, 1:375; West Germany, 1:430; Japan, 1:526; France, 1:934; Great Britain, 1:1,410; United States, 1:2,000. These particular figures drew from an authoritative British source the comment: "This is slender evidence on which to generalize, but the ratio for the United States suggests that, in some way, matters are better con-trived than in Europe" (*Traffic in Towns* [London: HMSO, Ministry of Trans-port, 1963], p. 19).

Nevertheless the accident toll was a matter of concern. The aggregate num-bers of highway casualties appeared unacceptable. Public feeling was stirred up when an antibusiness lawyer named Ralph Nader published a book in 1965 claiming that unsafe vehicle design was a major contributor to highway accidents and picked out the General Motors Corvair as a particular culprit. The federal government had already undertaken to promote automotive safety by having the General Services Administration impose safety requirements for vehicles purchased by the government. These included padded instrument panel, recessed instrument panel, impact absorbing steering wheel, four-way flasher, dual braking system, and specifications for tires.

The National Traffic and Motor Vehicle Safety Act and the Highway Safety Act followed in 1966, the first designed to require the incorporation of safety features in all motor vehicles and the second to develop comprehensive programs of traffic safety. Both were administered by the National Highway Traffic Safety Administration (NHTSA) of the Department of Transportation, which began by adapting the GSA requirements and then issued further regulations covering the installation of seat belts, the design of door knobs and latches, and numerous other matters relating to safety.

The automobile industry reacted to safety agitation with the same three-stage response as it had used with the air pollution question, this time with rather more justification. The requirements of the NHTSA unavoidably added to the cost of building cars, and the industry had grounds for arguing that some were excessive. Certainly when the NHTSA ruled that cars must be designed so that they would not start unless the seatbelts were fastened, there was so much public protest that the offending regulation had to be withdrawn. Unfortunately the principal member of the automobile industry displayed an astonishing ineptitude on the safety issue. The Corvair could have been defended; the charges against it were hardly irrefutable. Instead, General Motors chose to hire an investigator to look into Nader's private life, and the job was done so clumsily that the company was sued and compelled to make a substantial out-of-court settlement. In addition, the president of the company, testifying before a United States Senate committee studying the highway safety problem, confessed ignorance of how much General Motors spent on safety each year and indeed gave the impression that he had no idea why he had been called to Washington in the first place. None of this helped the automobile industry's credibility when it tried to present its case on safety matters.

As with air pollution, the safety regulations did have a beneficial effect. The ratio of highway fatalities to vehicle miles traveled has continued to decline, but allowance has to be made for factors other than the equipment mandated for the vehicles. The effect of the establishment of a national highway speed limit of 55 mph as a result of the Arab oil embargo in 1973 shows plainly on the table, and some allowance has to be made for the expansion of the Inter-

Table 11–1

Traffic Fatality Rates

Year	Total Deaths	Death Rates Per 10,000 Motor Vehicles	Per 100,000,000 Vehicle Miles	Per 100,000 Population
1980	53,300	3.23	3.53	23.5
1979	52,800	3.30	3.45	24.0
1978	52,411	3.41	3.39	24.0
1977	49,510	3.33	3.35	22.9
1976	47,038	3.28	3.34	21.9
1975	45,853	3.33	3.45	21.5
1974	46,402	3.44	3.59	21.8
1973	55,511	4.28	4.24	26.5
1972	56,278	4.60	4.43	27.0
1971	54,381	4.68	4.57	26.4
1970	54,633	4.92	4.88	26.8
1969	55,791	5.19	5.21	27.7
1968	54,862	5.32	5.40	27.5
1967	52,924	5.35	5.50	26.8
1966	53,041	5.53	5.70	27.1
1965	49,163	5.36	5.54	25.4
1964	47,700	5.46	5.63	25.0
1963	43,564	5.22	5.41	23.1
1962	40,804	5.12	5.32	22.0
1961	38,091	4.98	5.16	20.8
1960	38,137	5.12	5.31	21.2
1959	37,910	5.26	5.41	21.5
1958	36,981	5.37	5.56	21.3
1957	38,702	5.73	5.98	22.7
1956	39,628	6.07	6.28	23.7
1955	38,426	6.12	6.34	23.4
1954	35,586	6.07	6.33	22.1
1953	37,955	6.74	6.97	24.0
1952	37,794	7.10	7.36	24.3
1951	36,966	7.13	7.53	24.1
1950	34,763	7.07	7.59	23.0

Table 11–1

Traffic Fatality Rates (continued)

Year	Total Deaths	Death Rates Per 10,000 Motor Vehicles	Per 100,000,000 Vehicle Miles	Per 100,000 Population
1949	31,701	7.09	7.47	21.3
1948	32,259	7.85	8.11	22.1
1947	32,697	8.64	8.82	22.8
1946	33,411	9.72	9.80	23.9
1945	28,076	9.05	11.22	21.2
1944	24,282	7.97	11.42	18.3
1943	23,823	7.71	11.44	17.8
1938–42 ave.	33,549	10.41	11.49	25.4
1933–37 ave.	36,313	13.50	15.55	28.6
1928–32 ave.	31,050	12.10	15.60	25.3
1923–27 ave.	21,800	11.10	18.20	18.8
1918–22 ave.	12,700	13.90	NA	11.9
1913–17 ave.	6,800	23.80	NA	6.8

Source: Motor Vehicle Facts and Figures, 1981, p. 50.

state Highway and other freeway and expressway systems, since freeways are about six times as safe to drive on as ordinary roads. And as with air pollution, the question of how far to go with safety equipment has remained unanswered. Mandating the installation of seat belts was simple, but getting people to use them was not, and the proposed solution of requiring either air bags or seat belts that fasten automatically has been bogged down in controversy.

Energy Conservation

During the 1960s the United States reached a historic turning point, of which most of its people were totally unaware. A nation that formerly produced a surplus of oil became an importer, and in the middle 1960s imports for the first time exceeded domestic production. The cause was straightforward enough:

gradual depletion of domestic sources combined with greatly increased consumption. The number of motor vehicles rose continuously, and ever since the 1920s there had been a steady conversion from coal to oil in industry, rail and water transportation, and space heating. Warnings from oil companies that this new situation could mean higher prices and might call for some rethinking of American policy in the Middle East, where most of the imported petroleum came from, went unheeded.

Then in October 1973 the Yom Kippur War broke out and the Arab members of the Organization of Petroleum Exporting Countries (OPEC) imposed an embargo on exports of oil to countries deemed to be sympathetic to Israel, a list that included the United States and Canada, all of Western Europe, and Japan. The embargo lasted until the spring of 1974. While it was in effect there were long lines of cars waiting at gasoline stations, limits on purchases, panic buying that made the situation worse, and much ill feeling. Many Americans refused to believe that there was any shortage of oil. They were convinced that the whole thing was a conspiracy on the part of the oil companies to raise prices and accepted fantastic stories of loaded tankers waiting offshore for prices to go up (an inordinately expensive method of storing oil) and supplies of gasoline concealed in the tanks of abandoned service stations.

The government responded to the crisis by imposing a 55 mile an hour national speed limit and authorizing the Department of Energy to allocate oil supplies and control prices. It was also found possible to overcome environmentalist objections to the construction of the pipeline across Alaska that would transport oil from the recently discovered North Slope field, so that the project was eventually completed at a cost ten times what it would have been if the pipeline had been built when it was first proposed.

To the automobile industry the oil embargo came as an unexpected and very rough jolt. The embargo had little effect on the United States in 1973 because oil already in transit continued to arrive, and in fact 1973 was another banner year for the industry. Passenger car sales were almost 11.5 million, the highest figure ever reached, and this did not include another 1.75 million import cars. The next two years were a different story. Buyers turned away from the larger cars, not merely because of the immediate impact of the embargo but because when shipments of petroleum resumed, the OPEC countries proceeded to raise the price of crude oil sharply, so that the price of gasoline at the pump went up three- and four-fold. (Some allowance has to be made for inflation in these increases.) Many potential purchasers obviously held off until the situation became clearer and they could determine better what they should buy.

These conditions should have been made to order for the imports, but they were not, for the simple reason that foreign automobile manufacturers were also adversely affected by the oil crisis. Steel production was limited by lack of fuel, and shipping space was curtailed by shortages of bunker oil. The result was that aggregate import car sales in the United States declined in 1974 and 1975, although their share of the market increased slightly as domestic cars lost ground more rapidly than the imports.

By late 1975 concern about a recurrence of the oil shortage had subsided; there was even a complacent attitude that the crisis had passed and would not return, and a continuing widespread belief that the crisis had been artificially contrived anyway. Motor vehicle sales turned upward again, this time featured by a surge in the market for trucks and buses that helped set a new record in 1978—close to thirteen million units, of which over 3.7 million were commercial vehicles. Passenger cars did not quite reach the 1973 total, but there was a revival of consumer interest in the larger models.

Nevertheless there was no real reversion to pre-embargo conditions. For one thing, the price of oil for all purposes had increased sharply, which meant that not only was the out of pocket cost of operating a car higher, but so was the cost of producing it. The rise was less in the United States than elsewhere because oil prices were controlled by law. In fact, between price controls and the sharp inflation of the late 1970s, in constant dollars the price of gasoline in 1979 was not appreciably greater than it had been at the time of the oil embargo, but since people do not do their day-to-day business in terms of constant dollars, the public perception was that prices had gone up.

The oil price controls were a product of the Energy Policy and Conservation Act of 1975, which formalized the emergency controls imposed at the time of the embargo. The act also continued the elaborate system of allocations and entitlements established during the embargo, a system that further confused an already confused situation and had the net effect of subsidizing oil imports. It is open to question whether controlling prices was the wisest policy that could have been adopted. It was politically popular of course, but if the United States was to become independent of foreign oil, it would have to increase domestic production, and this meant using secondary and tertiary recovery methods in existing fields and finding new supplies by drilling in such places as the Continental Shelf, the Overthrust Belt of the Rocky Mountains, or the Arctic Ocean—all extremely difficult and expensive to reach. It was easy to penalize the oil companies, although they had nothing to do with the shortage and had tried vainly to warn that it was coming, but penalizing them did nothing to provide more energy and in fact militated against it.

For the automobile industry the most important feature of the Energy Act was its provisions for achieving fuel economy in motor vehicles. Under this law all new automobiles in the United States were to reach a fuel consumption of not less than 27.5 miles per gallon in 1985, the goal to be attained in stages. Enforcement was in the hands of the Environmental Protection Agency, which was logical because the EPA was already the controlling agency for pollutant emissions, and it was highly significant of the new era that had come to the automotive world that EPA mileage ratings became an indispensable factor in automobile advertising. The EPA was thus placed in the anomalous but not especially exceptional position for a government agency of having to enforce two conflicting sets of laws. One required greater fuel economy in motor vehicles; the other required the same vehicles to be equipped with emission controls that increased fuel consumption. The fuel economy standards did not have to apply to each individual vehicle but were calculated on the basis of Company Average Fuel Economy, or CAFE.

These provisions of the Energy Act imposed on the automobile industry an extensive task of redesigning. The cars of the future were going to have to have more efficient engines, to be built of lighter materials where possible, and to be smaller, since reduction of weight was the most direct method of improving fuel economy. Until 1979 this law was the principal influence in moving the American automobile industry toward reducing the size of its products, because there was little public pressure in that direction. The warning of the embargo had faded from people's consciousness, and after 1975 there was even a decline in the share of the market held by compact cars. The beneficiaries were the medium-sized automobiles, not the very big ones. As late as 1979 80 percent of all American-made passenger automobiles had V-8 engines.

The manufacturers therefore had every reason to expect a period of gradual changeover. Then came the revolution in Iran in the spring of 1979 and with it a striking demonstration of how delicately balanced the supply of oil really was. A reduction of just 5 percent in crude oil imports precipitated another crisis, although this one was localized. On the East and West coasts the lines at the gasoline stations formed again and some emergency measures had to be taken, but the middle of the country was not as seriously affected.

By far the most important consequence of this crisis was that in a matter of a few weeks the American public's preference in passenger automobiles changed radically and apparently permanently. Large cars became unsalable, and there was a stampede toward compacts, which the domestic manufacturers could not satisfy because they had not anticipated any such drastic changes in demand. The effects will be discussed later in connection with other changes that were occurring in the motor vehicle industry.

For the government this crisis brought deeper involvement in the affairs of the automobile industry. For the Chrysler Corporation, which had been losing ground for several years—the result of a sequence of managerial misjudgments—the collapse of the market for standard American automobiles in 1979 was a near-final blow. In 1980 the corporation presented the federal government with a choice—either Chrysler went bankrupt and out of business, or it got a federal loan guarantee of $1.5 billion. Faced with a similar situation a few years before, the British government had taken over the British Leyland Motor Corporation (now BL), but no one in the United States advocated that option. There was a substantial body of opinion that was willing to let Chrysler go rather than set a precedent for having the government bail out mismanaged enterprises. It was suggested that other companies, including the foreign producers, could take over Chrysler's operations. In the end the loan guarantee was granted, almost too late to be useful, on terms that put Chrysler's finances under close governmental supervision until the loan should be fully repaid.

On a broader scale, the domestic industry simply could not meet the demand for small cars because it was not prepared for this sudden change in consumer preference. Buyers turned in large numbers to the imports, which by this time were predominantly Japanese. While sales of American-made passenger automobiles shrank, imports rose to 27 percent of the passenger car market; 99 percent of imported trucks were Japanese. With automobile plants shutting down and unemployment rising to alarming levels in the motor vehicle industry and its ancillary supplier firms, pressure mounted to impose restrictions on automobile imports, especially Japanese, or else to require the larger Japanese companies to establish assembly plants in the United States.

In 1980 the Ford Motor Company and the United Automobile Workers petitioned the International Trade Commission for protection from motor vehicle imports from Japan and elsewhere, but the Commission rejected the plea on the ground that imports were not the principal cause of the automobile industry's troubles. Since annual sales of imported automobiles rose by half a million between 1978 and 1980 while sales of domestic cars declined by two and a half million, the ITC was on firm statistical ground. The losses to the United States producers were in the area of large cars, where the imports offered little competition. American-built compacts consistently outsold small foreign cars by three to two and continued to do so in 1979 and 1980.

The ITC ruling did not by any means close the issue. There was agitation in Congress to take some action, but it turned out that both congressional and public opinion was divided. A substantial segment felt that the plight of the American automobile manufacturers was of their own making, and that the UAW had contributed to it by constant demands for higher wages and other benefits. This group argued that to cut off imports and thereby compel purchasers to turn to the larger American automobiles would simply increase the consumption of energy and needlessly raise costs to consumers.

Neither the Carter nor the Reagan administration particularly desired to become involved with restraints on motor vehicle imports. Any such action was certain to disturb relations between the United States and Japan, which both administrations wanted to keep as harmonious as possible. Fortunately, early in 1981 the Japanese government, in the interest of maintaining good relations, moved on its own to limit exports of automobiles to the United States. Announcement of plans for building Honda cars at the company's motorcycle plant in Marysville, Ohio, and for the construction of a Nissan (Datsun) truck factory in Smyrna, Tennessee, helped to relieve the tension as well. The likelihood of Congressional action faded, but it could hardly be said that the issue was completely dead. For one thing, the Japanese policy depended on voluntary cooperation by the Japanese motor vehicle industry, and it was not certain that this would be forthcoming for any extended period.

CHAPTER TWELVE
The Industry in Turmoil

The gasoline crisis of the spring of 1979 appears to have marked a watershed in the history of the American automobile industry. The long period when the United States had held undisputed first place in the automotive world came to an abrupt end. Even the giants like General Motors and Ford found themselves in a grim competitive struggle and faced with the necessity for making drastic and expensive changes in their operations. There were many facile explanations for this dramatic upheaval: short-sightedness on the part of management, particularly in the matter of switching to smaller automobiles; excessive demands for wages and fringe benefits by the UAW; poor workmanship in American cars; price controls that kept the price of gasoline artificially low; failure to keep pace with technical developments abroad. There were others, but these were the explanations most frequently offered.

Like most facile explanations, these all had some basis in fact but were oversimplifications. The management of the American automobile companies was in general reluctant to turn to smaller cars because there was more profit in the larger ones, and there is evidence that the long years of unchallenged domination of the United States market for motor vehicles, the biggest in the world, had induced a certain complacency and lack of interest in innovation. This complacency was vividly displayed in the industry's attitude toward foreign cars. It was casually taken for granted that as soon as the big American companies got around to taking small cars seriously, they would "drive the imports into the sea." They tried, several times, and it never worked, but the belief remained an accepted article of faith, weakened a little by the middle 1970s; then the imports were to be "driven back to the shores"—no longer into the sea.

In labor relations, during an inflationary era when price increases were commonplace, it was a little too easy to make concessions to the UAW rather than face a prolonged strike while competitors were still in business. The extra cost would be added to the price of the vehicles with little customer protest, and the competitors were certain to be presented with very similar terms in the immediate future.

The quality of American cars as compared with foreign is more difficult to determine. Spokesmen for the industry of course insist that American cars are at least as good as any others, and they can produce some impressive supporting evidence. Volkswagen, which manufactures in both the United States and Germany, asserts that there is no significant difference in workmanship between the two countries. On the other hand, probably a majority of Americans believe that "planned obsolescence" has been an integral feature of the design of American automobiles since the concept of the annual model first appeared, and there have been allegations that in some assembly plants minor deficiencies were allowed to pass rather than allow production schedules to be jeopardized—the deficiencies could be corrected by the dealer. What hurt the industry when the crisis began in 1979 was that a great many prospective buyers *believed* that American cars were inferior and acted accordingly.

The effect of gasoline prices on the purchase and use of automobiles is still more difficult to evaluate. Two facts can be accepted as certain: first, that the retail price of gasoline multiplied three or four times between 1973 and 1980; second, given the accelerating inflation that occurred after 1976, the price of gasoline in constant dollars actually did not rise significantly, and this circumstance has been advanced as a reason why Americans turned back to large cars once the panic of the Arab oil embargo had subsided. Perhaps it was. The market swung somewhat away from compacts between 1975 and 1979, but as table 10–2 shows, the beneficiaries were the medium-sized automobiles, not the really big gas guzzlers. To the motorist driving into a service station "constant dollar" is an academic abstraction; what matters is the actual dollars that have to be paid out to fill the tank, and as far as the public in general was concerned, the price of gasoline was sharply higher than it had been.

To what extent the cost of fuel affected buying choices is uncertain. The demand for gasoline in the United States appears to be basically price-inelastic. Until 1982 there was little change in the average number of miles traveled per vehicle each year. Figures for later years are not available, but the decline in overall gasoline consumption that has occurred is attributable to increases in fuel efficiency rather than to any decrease in the use of motor vehicles. To the extent that gasoline has been a factor in consumer choices, the sharp turn to smaller automobiles that began in 1979 was motivated more by concern over the availability of gasoline than by its price. In periods of shortage it was a considerable convenience to have a car that would go a long way on a tank of gasoline, reducing the amount of time spent waiting in line at service stations.

Developing Problems

The critical conditions that ushered in the 1980s for the United States motor vehicle industry had been building up for some time. They were not an overnight consequence of the oil shortage of 1979; that simply precipitated a crisis that was going to come anyway, although meeting it would have been easier if it had continued to develop at a slower pace. Nor was it simply a question of large versus small cars. Some of the problems would have existed even if that particular issue had not arisen. In fact, some would have developed quite independently of the inroads of the import cars in the United States markets.

One fundamental problem was that the impetus of concentration carried on. From the resumption of civilian production of passenger automobiles in 1945 until the oil crisis of 1979, sales of motor vehicles in the United States moved steadily upward, exclusive of sales of imported cars. There were fluctuations, of course, in periods of economic decline, but the slumps were invariably of short duration and when they ended, motor vehicle output tended to be higher than before, as could have been expected in a period of rising population and general prosperity.

The trouble was that the benefits of the growth were unevenly divided. General Motors was the principal beneficiary, with its market share frequently going up to 60 percent. Ford held its position at about 25 percent, with its Ford line usually close behind Chevrolet among the popular-priced cars. Both companies made mistakes, but both could afford them. The failure of the Edsel was a disappointment, but it did only minor damage to the Ford Motor Company, and General Motors could survive the bad reputation that the Corvair acquired. It might have been considered an ominous sign that in the 1960s Ford began to shed executives in a manner reminiscent of the days of Henry Ford, Sr., but the company seemed to be coming to no harm.

The situation was different for Chrysler and American Motors. The latter had a surge of success with the Rambler in the late 1950s, but then the Big Three moved into the compact car market and American Motors had to contend with competition from bigger rivals. It was helped by the acquisition of Kaiser's Jeep Division in 1970, a step that gave American Motors a product with a market of its own that was not threatened by Big Three competition. Roy D. Chapin, Jr., chairman of the board of American Motors from 1967 to 1978 and son of the founder of the Hudson Motor Car Company, followed a policy of eliminating the unprofitable lines and concentrating on jeeps and compacts. This policy kept American Motors alive, but the company was always in a precarious situation.

Chrysler, the smallest of the Big Three, was in a stronger position than American Motors, but the company entered the 1970s with a spotty record. As was mentioned earlier, in the 1950s the Plymouth had several poor years because of unappealing designs and the once-popular DeSoto completely lost favor and went out of production. Chrysler entered the compact car market at the same time as Ford and General Motors, and its Valiant was well received, but definitely at the expense of Plymouth sales. The same thing happened with the Ford and the Falcon, but the Ford Motor Company's considerably larger sales volume made the change easier to absorb. At the end of the 1960s Chrysler was slow to produce subcompacts and thus lost ground in the growing small car market.

The Fluctuating 1970s

The decade began in depression, with a sharp drop in motor vehicle output in 1970, followed by a rapid recovery over the next three years, to the record passenger car production of 1973. The American subcompacts were coming on to the market, adding to an already bewildering variety of models for consumers to choose among. Buyers were presented with such names as Mustang, Fury, Monaco, Concord, Sportsman, Cougar, Lynx, Malibu, Firebird, Riviera, Le Mans, Eldorado, in a profusion that made it almost impossible to know who the producer was and whether the vehicle was luxury, standard, intermediate, compact, or subcompact. Indeed, it appeared that the competition of the 1950s in tail fins and chrome had been replaced by competition in elaborate nomenclature, obviously selected to suggest speed, power, and luxury.

The rise of sales to a new high was undoubtedly very satisfying to the American motor vehicle manufacturers, but there were problems in the situation as well. Import cars now held 15 percent of the passenger car market, and there was no indication that this share would decline, even with the domestic subcompacts doing well. There was a decisive change among the foreign cars too, in that Volkswagen had lost its predominance and the leading sellers were now Japanese.

The import threat in a number of commodities, not just motor vehicles, was one of the key factors in the economic program adopted by the Nixon administration in mid-1971 in an attempt to combat the current recession conditions and also control the inflation that has plagued every American administration since the 1960s. The salient features of this program as they affected the automotive industry were: (1) suspension of dollar convertibility, which was a *de facto* devaluation of the dollar, subsequently confirmed by legislation in May 1972; (2) a surcharge of 10 percent on imports; and (3) wage and price controls.

The Nixon program had little effect on the United States automobile industry, whose production was markedly on the upswing well before the new policies were adopted. The share of the market held by foreign cars declined slightly in 1972, but the total number of import cars sold increased. The import surcharge was terminated late in 1972, and the price and wage controls followed soon afterward. The devaluation of the dollar had the greatest impact. It threw the world's currency exchanges into confusion, only partially remedied when the other major industrial nations agreed to let their currencies float within specified limits. The result was that foreign cars lost much of the price advantage they had had in the American market. The Japanese motor vehicle industry suffered least from that situation, because its rapidly growing domestic market enabled it to keep production costs down and remain competitive in the United States, although Japanese sales organizations in the United States had to make continual price adjustments through 1972 and 1973.

The American automobile companies, in the meantime, were enjoying a rapidly rising market, to a high point of 12.6 million vehicles in 1973. Then, in October of that year, came the outbreak of the Yom Kippur War and the Arab oil embargo. The three-year boom in automobile sales abruptly ended, for domestic and foreign cars alike. The demand for American cars plummeted as buyers turned away from "gas guzzlers." Import sales reversed their performance of 1972; in 1974 their share of the market rose, but the total number of vehicles sold was substantially less than it had been in 1973, for the reasons explained in the previous chapter.

In the second half of the 1970s the American automobile industry had entered a new era, although as is customary with new eras in history, the signs of its arrival were blurred and uncertain. It is only in retrospect that the coming of a new era can be clearly discerned. The industry was being urged to shift to smaller cars by a clamorous section of public opinion and by those who feared further embargoes, and it was being pushed in the same direction by the requirements for fuel economy imposed by the EPA under the Energy Conservation Act. On the other hand, as the memory of the embargo faded, American consumers showed a continuing preference for automobiles with power and speed—something with an eight-cylinder engine—and more interior accommodation than a compact had to offer. This was still the most profitable segment of the market, and the automobile manufacturers had the natural propensity of any privately owned business not only for pursuing the most profitable course but for offering its customers what they appeared to want. Consequently, while there was some progress toward reducing the size and weight of American automobiles, it was certainly slower than it would have been if buyers had given a more definite signal that they wanted the industry to move in that direction. Whether there was a lack of foresight in management is a matter of opinion. Large organizations like the American motor vehicle companies are likely to be slow to change, and there was an understandable reluctance to give up the most profitable part of their operations in the absence of any visible and compelling reason for doing so. The gift of prophecy is very rare.

The structure of the industry was undergoing changes also. General Motors and Ford remained comfortably in first and second place and were able to ride out the crisis of the oil embargo without undue difficulty. The smaller passenger car manufacturers were in a less happy position. Chrysler was having increasing trouble holding its share of the domestic market even though it added to the Chrysler line compact cars made in Japan by Mitsubishi, and its European ventures became so burdensome that in 1978 Chrysler sold both its British operations and the French Simca company to Peugeot, which had previously taken over Citroën. This transaction made Peugeot the largest single passenger car manufacturer in Europe; the British Chrysler lines and the Simca production were continued for a time under the name Talbot.

American Motors remained in the grim struggle for survival that has marked most of its existence. Even in the prosperous years from 1975 to 1978 its sales steadily declined, and in 1977 it sought outside support by entering into an agreement with Renault to market the French company's Le Car through American Motors dealers and eventually to manufacture the vehicle in Kenosha, Wisconsin. This agreement provided for financial support from Renault and led to Renault's acquisition of a substantial interest in American Motors. These relationships offered some evidence of the probable future course of the automotive industry: namely, that it would develop in time from a collection of national industries into a group of supranational organizations.

The import car business in the United States underwent a far more drastic restructuring during the 1970s than the domestic automobile industry. At the beginning of the decade both Toyota and Nissan (Datsun) moved ahead of Volkswagen, and by the mid-1970s Japanese automobiles accounted for well over half of the sales of foreign passenger cars in the United States. Japanese pickup trucks had 99 percent of the market for imported light trucks. This Japanese achievement was assisted by the fact that the mid-1970s were a period of weakness on the part of the principal European competitors.

Table 12–1

Domestic and Import Passenger Car and Truck Retail Sales by Types, 1978–82

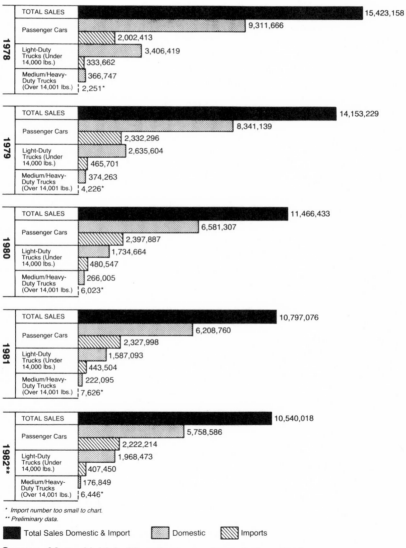

1978

TOTAL SALES	15,423,158
Passenger Cars	9,311,666
	2,002,413
Light-Duty Trucks (Under 14,000 lbs.)	3,406,419
	333,662
Medium/Heavy-Duty Trucks (Over 14,001 lbs.)	366,747
	2,251*

1979

TOTAL SALES	14,153,229
Passenger Cars	8,341,139
	2,332,296
Light-Duty Trucks (Under 14,000 lbs.)	2,635,604
	465,701
Medium/Heavy-Duty Trucks (Over 14,001 lbs.)	374,263
	4,226*

1980

TOTAL SALES	11,466,433
Passenger Cars	6,581,307
	2,397,887
Light-Duty Trucks (Under 14,000 lbs.)	1,734,664
	480,547
Medium/Heavy-Duty Trucks (Over 14,001 lbs.)	266,005
	6,023*

1981

TOTAL SALES	10,797,076
Passenger Cars	6,208,760
	2,327,998
Light-Duty Trucks (Under 14,000 lbs.)	1,587,093
	443,504
Medium/Heavy-Duty Trucks (Over 14,001 lbs.)	222,095
	7,626*

1982**

TOTAL SALES	10,540,018
Passenger Cars	5,758,586
	2,222,214
Light-Duty Trucks (Under 14,000 lbs.)	1,968,473
	407,450
Medium/Heavy-Duty Trucks (Over 14,001 lbs.)	176,849
	6,446*

* Import number too small to chart.
** Preliminary data.

■ Total Sales Domestic & Import ▨ Domestic ▧ Imports

Source: Motor Vehicle Manufacturers Association, 1983.

The European motor vehicle manufacturers suffered from the devaluation of the dollar more than did the Japanese, since the latter had a rapidly growing domestic market to support them. In addition, Fiat and British Leyland were at this time handicapped by severe labor problems and strikes. Fiat recovered and returned vigorously to the American market by the end of the decade. BL, however, had managerial and financial difficulties to cope with as well as the chronic propensity of British trade union members to walk off the job (or be called off by their shop stewards) as the first step in any industrial dispute, no matter how trivial. The company had to be taken over by the British government to prevent the economic calamity that would have resulted if BL had gone out of business.

Volkswagen also encountered problems. It was hurt by the devaluation, since the deutschmark remained stable and may even have been overvalued. In addition, the company had managerial and labor problems, and it repeated Henry Ford's mistake with the Model T by keeping the Beetle in production too long. In the United States other companies, notably the Japanese, were offering automobiles that were competitive in price, at least as good in technical quality, and more attractive in style. Volkswagen met its problems head-on. New management was brought in, organizational changes were made, and the product line was brought up to date. Most important in its effect on the motor vehicle industry in the United States, Volkswagen decided to deal with the currency handicap by manufacturing in the United States and in 1978 opened an assembly plant in New Stanton, Pennsylvania, buying a former Chrysler facility for this purpose.

There was much more than luck behind the Japanese ascendancy in the import car market. The first Japanese automobiles to be offered to American buyers lacked the power and styling that most American buyers preferred. In less than twenty years this attitude was turned completely around, to the point where Japanese cars were widely considered to be better built and more reliable than their American competitors. The question, "What if it breaks down in Dubuque?" was no longer asked, because networks of dealerships and parts depots made prompt service available anywhere in the country. Japanese firms were innovative, as Volkswagen had been when it introduced the rear-engined car. Honda introduced the stratified-charge engine and Toyo Kogyo (Mazda) the German Wankel rotary-piston engine. In 1980 Nissan brought out its NAPS-Z (Nissan Anti-Pollution System) engine, a computer-designed mechanism with a hemispherical combustion chamber, which gave more efficient combustion without increasing emissions of nitrous oxides.

Nothing comparable appeared in American automobiles. Front-wheel drive and disc brakes appeared first on European cars. The Volkswagen popularized the rear-engine design, although this had its drawbacks and was not generally adopted. American trucks and buses adopted diesel power extensively after World War II, but European firms made more use of diesel engines for passenger cars. As long as gasoline was plentiful and cheap, the diesel had no great advantage in the lighter vehicles. Chrysler experimented with gas turbine engines in the 1960s and had some success, but technical problems made it evident that the gas turbine was not yet ready for large-scale use in an automobile power plant. In addition, the larger Japanese companies, specifically Nissan and Toyota, were well ahead of American production techniques in using robots on their assembly lines. The foreign car share of the passenger automobile market in the United States rose to a high of 18.5 percent in 1977, and then fell to 17.8 in 1978. Domestic compacts still outsold the imports, so that although the American producers disliked the constant increase in foreign car sales, they did not see them as a major threat. Their own passenger car sales were growing steadily, and their truck sales were setting new records. The overall picture is shown in table 12–1.

Crisis

There can be very few incidents in the history of business comparable to the reversal of fortune that struck the American automobile industry in the spring of 1979. For the first quarter of the year the market continued strong, even running slightly ahead of the comparable period in 1978, and sales of standard-sized passenger cars were holding up satisfactorily (see table 12–2). In fact the Ford Motor Company was having difficulty keeping up with the demand for V-8 engines, and General Motors was considering the conversion of one of its compact car plants to larger models.

Then came the revolution in Iran with the consequences previously referred to—long lines at service stations, frantic efforts by national, state, and local authorities to curb panic buying and allocate supplies equitably, even the same stories about how the whole thing was a conspiracy on the part of the oil companies to force prices up. Interestingly, the countries of Western Europe were exposed to the same shrinkage of their oil supplies, but none of them imposed price controls or allocations, and they had no waiting lines or panic buying. In the United States the crisis was less severe than during the Arab oil embargo. The shortages were local rather than nationwide, the most severe occurring on the Atlantic and Pacific seaboards, and in a few weeks conditions were reasonably well back to normal, as far as gasoline supplies were concerned.

Not so in the automobile industry. There the minor petroleum crisis of 1979 did what the major crisis of 1974 had failed to do—completely changed Amer-

Table 12-2

U.S. Passenger Car Retail Sales Reported by U.S. Manufacturers, Excluding Imports (By Months, 1971–82)

Month	1971	1972	1973	1974	1975	1976
January	586,162	609,732	736,021	551,384	462,999	588,262
February	636,587	698,241	774,702	567,795	535,808	651,114
March	755,906	771,894	963,671	653,717	523,620	815,915
April	736,654	774,133	862,642	702,829	517,879	788,352
May	747,677	887,737	971,889	766,943	603,012	793,555
June	797,744	876,539	908,948	697,630	618,968	829,498
July	668,176	769,119	808,395	691,220	636,902	737,119
August	565,835	656,000	685,872	667,681	534,490	615,959
September	755,639	740,659	753,985	591,222	590,634	644,800
October	934,131	932,182	857,506	628,124	773,942	730,679
November	847,955	891,283	778,016	505,932	655,293	721,230
December	648,943	719,257	574,143	429,506	599,469	694,771
Year Total	**8,681,409**	**9,326,776**	**9,675,790**	**7,453,983**	**7,053,016**	**8,611,254**

Month	1977	1978	1979	1980	1981	1982
January	601,767	545,291	645,025	588,001	469,993	368,189
February	666,434	628,436	676,092	591,502	543,839	457,219
March	895,779	883,327	864,604	670,390	719,246	575,974
April	822,242	863,289	764,041	540,984	533,777	498,915
May	833,701	963,338	797,463	498,744	524,298	584,461
June	919,486	950,154	701,306	511,072	517,918	451,863
July	731,422	762,074	688,772	542,397	497,445	430,035
August	726,875	753,034	705,486	486,755	602,172	409,411
September	656,979	662,529	600,897	486,064	518,854	488,454
October	870,348	884,389	729,683	664,237	491,554	487,871
November	737,758	769,992	606,535	529,558	432,084	558,146
December	646,231	645,813	561,235	471,603	357,580	448,048
Year Total	**9,109,022**	**9,311,666**	**8,341,139**	**6,581,307**	**6,208,760**	**5,758,586**

Source: Motor Vehicle Manufacturers Association, 1983.

ican buyer preferences in motor vehicles. In just about a month the market for large cars almost vanished; customers were looking for vehicles with good fuel economy, and these the American motor vehicle manufacturers were unable to provide in anything approaching sufficient quantity. The myth has now become firmly established that the American producers were caught in a bad situation because they had totally ignored the growth of the market for small cars. It is a myth, one of those that gets accepted as fact.

The American automobile companies were well aware that the demand for smaller automobiles was growing, but it had been growing slowly, and until the gasoline crisis of 1979 there was no reason to expect that the pace would change in the foreseeable future. Managerial judgment in the automobile industry may have preferred this view of the automotive future because it was reluctant to give up the more profitable larger cars as long as there was an obvious willingness to buy them.

Yet the automobile companies were in fact working on new and improved compacts. Chrysler's Omni and Horizon, front-wheel drive vehicles, were already in production, the General Motors X-cars, also front-wheel drive, were on the way, and Ford had a similar vehicle in preparation. Front-wheel drive was becoming popular for small cars, because it allowed more interior space in the vehicle. Thus there was planning for the future, but no one had expected the future to arrive overnight. Chrysler had decided to use Volkswagen engines in its Horizons and Omnis and ordered 300,000. When the crisis came, many more of these vehicles could have been sold, but VW's engine capacity was fully absorbed in meeting the demand for its own cars and no more engines were available for Chrysler. The new General Motors and Ford compacts would not come into production until 1980 and 1981.

The consequences appear vividly in the tables in this chapter. Sales of American-built automobiles went into a prolonged decline. Factories were closed down and workers were laid off in large numbers—some 300,000 before the end of 1979. The slump continued through 1980 and 1981 and into 1982 because the whole national economy went into a recession to which the ailing condition of the automobile industry largely contributed. Plant closures and mounting unemployment spread to supplier firms and supporting industries, and as economic conditions deteriorated, purchases of new cars suffered still more, which in turn depressed the economy further. When the new Big Three compacts made their appearance, sales fell below expectations because of the recession.

The Big Three were therefore in the awkward position of having to face massive capital outlays to change over to making smaller cars and to introduce the up-to-date production techniques the Japanese were using, and to do it with reduced earnings because the vehicles they were currently turning out were not selling. American Motors was adversely affected also and would almost certainly have gone under except for its new relationship with Renault. To complicate matters, much of the automotive production plant in the United States was aging, the most conspicuous example being Dodge Main in Hamtramck, Michigan, which was built in 1917 and remained in operation until 1980. It is a significant feature of the development of the industry that new facilities have in general been constructed elsewhere than in the Detroit area. In the 1970s Chevrolet production was transferred to a modern plant in Lordstown, Ohio, and other General Motors production has been located in Oklahoma City. Lower land values, tax advantages, and availability of labor have been the principal motives.

All the Big Three firms were hurt. The strongest, General Motors, lost money in 1981 for the first time in sixty years. The Ford Motor Company was sustained for a time by profits from its foreign operations, but these shrank also as the recession spread to other parts of the world, and at the end of 1981 Ford passed a dividend for the first time since the company went public in 1955. Chrysler was hardest hit of all, not surprisingly in view of the fact that Chrysler was the weakest of the Big Three and had been floundering for some years.

The biggest loss of business was in sales of passenger automobiles, but truck sales suffered also, and the White Motor Company, the largest independent manufacturer of commercial vehicles, withdrew from the field. It filed for bankruptcy in 1980 and sold its truck operation to Sweden's Volvo in 1981. As with Chrysler, White's plight was not exclusively a consequence of the 1979–80 crisis. The company's business in commercial vehicles had been losing ground for some time; the sudden slump in the motor vehicle market simply brought matters to a head. White's principal competitor, Mack, remained in the truck field with support from Renault, which bought 46 percent of Mack's stock in 1979.

Protectionism and Response

The conditions that brought disaster to the domestic motor vehicle manufacturers were, for a time at any rate, a boon for the foreign producers, especially the Japanese, because they had the small, economical cars that people now wanted. Sales of foreign-made passenger automobiles in the United States rose appreciably in 1979 and again in 1980, when they took 27 percent of the passenger car market, and four fifths of these imports were Japanese. In fact, total Japanese motor vehicle production in 1980 put Japan in first place among the world's motor vehicle manufacturers. Under the circumstances it was inevitable that a demand should arise for protection of the home industry, even though the American automobile industry had a long-standing commitment to free trade. The United Automobile Workers and others began by insisting that the principal Japanese producers (notably Toyota and Nissan) should be required either to have a specified percentage of American-made components in their vehicles or still better, to follow the Volkswagen example and open assembly plants in the United States.

The Japanese companies disliked the assembly plant idea because it would mean a heavy capital investment and the plants could not be in production before the new Big Three compacts arrived on the United States market. The Big Three might be struggling, but Japanese motor vehicle executives had a healthy respect for their inherent strength and ability to compete.

The appeal of the Ford Motor Company and the UAW to the International Trade Commission (ITC) has been described in chapter 11. In 1980 sales of foreign passenger cars in the United States were about 400,000 greater than they had been in 1978; in the same period sales of domestic passenger cars fell by 2,700,000. Obviously there was much more to the plight of the American automobile industry than increased sales of imported cars.

Some of the pressure on the Japanese manufacturers was relieved when both Honda and Nissan announced plans in 1980 to produce in the United States. Honda already had a motorcycle factory in Marysville, Ohio, and it proposed to add an automobile assembly plant on the same site. This decision was only partially a concession to American protectionist opinion. Honda needed to expand its capacity, and because of restrictions on land use it was unable to find a suitable site in Japan. The Nissan project, organized in 1980 as Nissan Motor Manufacturing, U.S.A., was a factory to build light trucks, located in Smyrna, Tennessee, and designed to produce 10,000 units a month beginning in 1983. In 1984 plans were announced to build passenger cars at Smyrna as well.

Another factor in this decision was a ruling by the United States Tariff Commission that a chassis with cab was to be classified as a complete vehicle. Previously it was classified under "Parts," and both Nissan and Toyota followed the practice of shipping cab and chassis and truck beds separately, and then assembling them after arrival in the United States. Under this system they paid a duty of 4 percent, but the new ruling subjected the cab and chassis to the 25 percent "Chicken War" Tariff. This name came from a dispute between the United States and the European Economic Community in 1962 over alleged discrimination against exports of American poultry to Germany. In reprisal the United States raised its tariff on imported light trucks. The intended target was Volkswagen, but in a few years VW trucks virtually disappeared from the American scene and the Japanese, who had had nothing to do with the original dispute, became the principal victims. The Tariff Commission's ruling doomed the Nissan and Toyota truck assembly operations, since it was now easier and cheaper to ship the complete vehicle directly from Japan. One effect of the action was to increase unemployment in the United States.

Early in 1981 the Japanese government, in an effort to stave off further agitation for restriction of Japanese motor vehicle imports into the United States, announced a policy of restricting exports of passenger automobiles to the United States by 7 to 8 percent for a year, with future action to be determined by the state of the American passenger car market. The Japanese automobile companies accepted the policy unenthusiastically, while in the United States the protectionists complained that the restrictions did not go far enough and the antiprotectionists objected to reducing the availability to American consumers of low-priced automobiles with high gasoline mileage. At the end of the year the restrictions became meaningless because the economic decline began to affect sales of imported as well as domestic cars.

The 1980s Arrive

The new decade began inauspiciously for the American automotive industry. Sales continued to sag through 1981, until at the beginning of 1982 about 350,000 workers were in either temporary or indefinite layoffs and over twenty plants were closed. The hoped-for revival of the economy—the main remedy for the industry's troubles—had so far failed to materialize. However, the industry was not simply waiting optimistically for conditions to improve. When that happy day arrived the automobile companies intended to be prepared to take advantage of it; they even hoped to help bring it about.

The prime requisite was to develop new models that would be competitive in both price and quality with what Japan and Western Europe had to offer, and to this end much was going on that the American public in general was unaware of. Under the combined pressure of sagging sales and the requirements imposed by the EPA, a substantial "downsizing" of American automobiles was in progress, and indeed had been for some years. It has been calculated that by the mid-1980s the average weight of American passenger cars would be under 3000 pounds, 600 pounds less than in 1979. This objective is being achieved not just by making cars smaller, but by using lighter materials—aluminum, plastic, and others—where that could be done without sacrificing essential strength, and by extensive use of computers in design to achieve the optimum shape and dimensions for the desired size. There was some feeling among observers of the industry that "downsizing" was not the best possible way to arrive at small cars comparable to what Japan and Germany were producing, but the American manufacturers were under some compulsion to move step by step, since none of them could afford to shut down entirely while they worked out completely new designs, as Henry Ford had done in 1927.

In 1980 less than half the passenger automobiles built in the United States had V-8 engines, compared with 80 percent two years before. The majority now were fours and sixes. Further refinements were in prospect: aerodynamic body designs to reduce air resistance, and computer controls in the power train to achieve maximum fuel efficiency.

The development and production of these new models called for extensive expenditure on plant and tooling. This was not simply for the kind of retooling that the industry was accustomed to for the annual model changeover, but for the comprehensive introduction of new techniques of manufacturing, specifically the application of robotics to a variety of production operations. The use of computer-controlled robots held out the prospect of achieving infinitely greater flexibility in scheduling work, including the ability to do something that was noticeably lacking when the crisis came in 1979: change models on the assembly line quickly in response to shifts in consumer taste. Since 1979 the American motor vehicle industry has spent $65 billion on remodeling facilities and redesigning products, this in the face of losses of $4.3 billion for the industry in 1980 alone. The industry was in fact taking a gigantic gamble, staking its solvency on the assumptions that the economy would in due course turn upward and that the new models would sell in large quantities.

More than technology was needed to restore the American motor vehicle industry to economic health. It was awkward that in a period of recession and sagging sales motor vehicle prices kept rising. The American producers were criticized for continuing to raise prices, but their critics overlooked the point that import car prices kept going up also. The basic cause was persistent high inflation. The manufacturers periodically tried to stimulate sales by offering cash rebates to buyers of new passenger cars, a form of price cutting, and had some limited success; Chrysler, indeed, showed encouraging signs of potential recovery by 1983. General Motors also tried to encourage buyers by offering financing at reduced interest rates through the General Motors Acceptance Corporation.

The level of interest rates was not only a deterrent to prospective purchasers of new cars, it was also a severe handicap to dealers because it greatly in-

Courtesy of the Motor Vehicle Manufacturers Association

Body Assembly. A factory of the early 1900s compared with a modern assembly line that shows extensive application of industrial robots.

creased their handling costs, and did so at a time when the dealers were already hard pressed by falling sales. Several thousand dealerships went out of business.

Finally, there were delicate problems of labor relations to be resolved. As the 1980s opened, wages and fringe benefits for workers in the American automotive industry were calculated at $20 an hour, about twice the average for American industry in general, and compared with an estimated $12 an hour for Japanese automobile workers. Similar wage differentials had existed in the past and were supportable because American production techniques were more efficient, but this advantage no longer existed. Manufacturing processes in the Japanese motor vehicle industry, and probably the German as well, had become superior in productivity, so that the high labor cost was now a handicap to the ability of the American producers to compete.

The leadership of the UAW was aware of the problem. With employment in the entire American automotive industry, including supplier firms, down from 2.4 million in 1978 to 1.8 million at the beginning of 1982, some changes in union policy were manifestly in order, and the union was prepared to make them, within limits. In the Chrysler crisis the UAW agreed to wage concessions and in return received representation on the Chrysler board of directors. The wage concessions were officially deferments of scheduled raises, but both parties must have realized that restoration of the increases lay in the indefinite future. Early in 1982 the UAW had discussions with General Motors, Ford, and American Motors in which the principal issues reflected the altered situation in the industry. The union was more interested in job security than in wage or benefit increases, and it proposed to General Motors that any savings in cost through wage or benefit reductions should be passed indirectly on to the consuming public in the form of lower prices. There was disagreement over the purchase by the American producers of components or even complete cars manufactured abroad, a practice termed "out-sourcing."

Agreement was reached with the Ford Motor Company first, then with General Motors and after that with American Motors. The details of the settlements differed, but the basic pattern showed the union on the defensive. It accepted a two-and-a-half year freeze of wage scales, postponement of scheduled cost-of-living increases, and elimination of a number of paid days off. In return the companies guaranteed incomes until retirement for workers with fifteen to twenty years seniority and made some concessions on plant closings. There was no commitment on "out-sourcing" unless it was considered that having to guarantee income to older workers would provide an incentive to keep work within the company. The agreement with General Motors was ratified by a narrow 52 percent majority.

CHAPTER THIRTEEN
The International Industry

The story of the American motor vehicle industry would be incomplete if it were confined to the United States. From its beginning the American industry has influenced and been influenced by automotive developments in the rest of the world. The early pioneers in the United States got many of their ideas from articles in journals like the *American Machinist* about European experiments with horseless carriages, with the curious exception of Percy Maxim, who was the best educated of the group and at least did know something about the Otto engine. European automobiles appeared on American streets in the 1890s, in small numbers but enough to show Americans what was being done across the Atlantic. Henry Ford became acquainted with the properties of vanadium and other alloy steels by studying European racing cars and used this knowledge to good advantage in the Model T.

With the rapid growth of the American motor vehicle industry after the turn of the century, American influence became stronger in Europe, especially in the area of techniques of production. The Cadillac demonstration of interchangeability in London in 1908 was a striking example; British observers frankly conceded that the feat could not be duplicated with British automobiles. British and French efforts to apply American production and marketing methods have been described in chapter 6. Before World War II they were only partially successful, but the basic lessons were learned for future use.

The effects of this reciprocal exchange of ideas and technologies are not quantifiable, but they were unquestionably mutually beneficial. The American companies received useful information on design and engineering. The design of the modern automobile, a vehicle built to be self-propelled, as distinguished from a buggy with a motor added, was first worked out in France in 1891 by Emile Constant Levassor, of Panhard and Levassor. In return, the Europeans learned the techniques of mass production and marketing that were first developed by American automobile manufacturers. In short, from the outset there was an international consciousness in automotive circles.

Seeking World Markets

The American automotive industry began early to export ideas and methods. As a matter of course, it also exported motor vehicles wherever it could find markets. With their enormous home market the United States automobile manufacturers were never as dependent on their export business as their counterparts in Europe and Japan, but exports came to account for about a tenth of their total sales, a large percentage which it would be hurtful to lose. Establishing subsidiaries and branch plants in other countries represented a logical way of bypassing tariff and other restrictions on American motor vehicles, although it was a recourse open only to the largest companies.

The beginning stages of this process were described in chapter 6. To recapitulate, most of the American motor vehicle manufacturers promptly established Canadian subsidiaries, a procedure that was mutually beneficial, because the Canadian market was attractive but not then large enough to support a purely indigenous motor vehicle industry. Ford was the first to move into Europe with an assembly plant in Manchester, England, in 1911, and another in Bordeaux, France, in 1913. The early growth of the British operation has been told in chapter 6. Ford subsequently extended its European activities to Germany, Denmark, Italy, Spain, and Sweden. In each case a new subsidiary was created. Andre Citroën offered to sell the Ford Motor Company a controlling interest in his company when he ran into difficulties in 1919, but the offer was refused, and Ford later built a new assembly plant near Paris. This decision might have been a mistake, because Ford then appeared in France as a "foreign" company and was subject to some discrimination. In the early 1930s the Ford Motor Company had a contract with the government of the Soviet Union whereby knocked-down Fords were assembled in two plants in Russia. This arrangement was short-lived, but automotive development in the U.S.S.R. was strongly influenced by Ford practice. Farther afield, by the end of the 1920s the Ford Motor Company had assembly plants in Argentina, Brazil, Mexico, South Africa, India, Malaya, Japan, and Australia.

When General Motors entered the European market in the 1920s it did so by acquiring control of the existing companies of Vauxhall in Britain and Opel in Germany, and so avoided to some extent the stigma of the outsider. However, when such opportunities did not exist, General Motors followed the Ford practice. Both companies, for instance, built assembly plants in Japan because in the 1920s there was simply no Japanese motor vehicle manufacturer of sufficient stature to offer an attractive investment. The point also needs to be made that Ford was not seen as a foreign company in the United Kingdom. Ford of Britain was largely autonomous and self-contained; it had British management and used British materials.

Ford and General Motors were the only American automobile companies to be involved in this kind of large-scale international activity before the end of World War II. They kept pace with each other in a steady expansion of their activities, entering new markets as they became promising. Both developed profitable markets in Latin America and to a lesser extent in Africa. General Motors entered Australia in 1931 by buying Holden, an Australian builder of automobile bodies, and developing it into a full-fledged motor vehicle manufacturing operation.

The entire American automotive industry saw its foreign trade suffer from the economic nationalism evoked by the Great Depression. Other countries moved to protect their domestic industries from United States competition, partly in reprisal for the restrictions on their trade imposed by the Smoot-Hawley Tariff of 1930. The totalitarian regimes of Germany and Italy had the most restrictive policies against both the importation of foreign motor vehicles and the operations of foreign companies within their borders, so that General Motors and Ford were subjected to discrimination in a variety of ways. Indeed, Ford was so harassed in Italy that it tried to reach an agreement to combine with Fiat, but Fiat's terms were unacceptable. Ford then turned to Isotta Fraschini in Milan, with a good deal of support from the local authorities, but negotiations for a merger were stopped by the Italian government. This situation lasted until the war broke out. Then the capacity of the General Motors and Ford installations became vitally important to the countries in which they were located and they were all turned willy-nilly to military production.

Worldwide Expansion

When World War II ended and industrial operations were restored to peacetime conditions, there was an explosive expansion of motor vehicle production throughout the world. In 1950 total world output was 10.5 million units; thirty years later it was 38.6 million, and this was a decline from the 42.5 million in 1978. In 1950 four fifths of the world's motor vehicles were made in the United States; in 1980 the American share was just over one fifth. Since United States production in 1980 was almost the same as it had been in 1950, just over eight million vehicles, after a peak of almost 13 million in 1978, this change represents expansion elsewhere, not decline in the United States. Western Europe in the 1950s and 1960s and Japan in the 1960s and 1970s developed the kind of mass market for automobiles that the United States and Canada had initiated a generation earlier, and other countries were trying to follow suit.

Thus during the years that followed World War II, certainly until the recession that began in 1980, the booming market for motor vehicles in the United States was accompanied by a still more booming market in the rest of the world. American producers were as eager as any others to take advantage of this situation.

General Motors and Ford extended their international operations, and at the end of the 1950s Chrysler joined them, without the same happy results. The competition was stiffer than it had been during the interwar period, when only the big American companies had the resources to establish foreign subsidiaries on any significant scale. By the 1970s Volkswagen was manufacturing or assembling motor vehicles in Brazil, Mexico, and South Africa; Fiat in Brazil and Argentina, as well as licensing production and giving technical assistance for the building of the Lada/Zhiguli automobile in the U.S.S.R.; Renault in Argentina and Spain; Peugeot-Citroën in Argentina, Chile, Iran, Spain, and Yugoslavia; Mitsubishi, Toyota, and Nissan in Australia and South Africa, with Nissan in Mexico and Toyota in the Philippines as well. In addition, nations that were seeking to develop their own motor vehicle industries, such as Argentina, Brazil, India, Mexico, and Spain, not only discouraged the importation of complete foreign-built vehicles but required that vehicles built or assembled within their borders should have prescribed proportions of domestically made parts and components. Finally, the creation of the European Economic Community strengthened the European automobile companies by giving them for the first time a market comparable to that enjoyed by their American rivals in the United States.

Under these conditions the American giants did very well. In 1980, outside the United States, the Ford Motor Company manufactured or assembled motor vehicles in Argentina, Australia, Belgium, Brazil, Canada, Denmark, Finland, Great Britain, Mexico, Singapore, South Africa, Spain, Sweden, and Venezuela. The Brazilian operation had been expanded by the purchase of Willys-Overland of Brazil in 1967, a step that removed one of the last vestiges of the Kaiser-Frazer venture into automobile manufacturing. General Motors was even more widespread. It had assembly or manufacturing plants in Argentina, Brazil, Chile, Mexico, and Venezuela in the Western Hemisphere; Belgium, Germany, Great Britain, Portugal, and Switzerland in Europe; Australia, New Zealand, South Africa, and Zaire; and in the Philippines and Malaysia along with an interest in Isuzu Motors Ltd. of Japan (see chart 13–1).

Chart 13-1 General Motors Overseas Operations, 1980

GENERAL MOTORS OVERSEAS OPERATIONS DIVISION
New York

GM Overseas Corporation

GM Overseas Distribution Corporation

LATIN AMERICA
G.M. Interamerica Corporation

Argentina	GM Argentina S.A.	●■
Brazil	GM do Brasil S.A.	●■
Chile	GM Chile S.A.	▲■
Mexico	GM de Mexico S.A.	●■
Uruguay	GM Uruguaya S.A.	▲■
Venezuela	GM de Venezuela S.A.	▲■

EUROPE

Austria	GM Austria GmbH	■
Belgium	GM Continental	▲■
Denmark	GM International A/S	■
Finland	Suomen GM OY.	○■
France	GM France	○
	GM Strasbourg S.A.	●
Germany	Adam Opel AG	■
	GM Deutschland GmbH	○
	GM GmbH	○
Great Britain	Vauxhall Motors Ltd.	●
	GM Ltd.	□
	GM Scotland Ltd.	○
Ireland	GM Ireland Ltd.	□
Luxembourg	GM Luxembourg S.A.	■
Netherlands	GM Continental S.A.	■
Norway	GM Norge A/S	▲■
Portugal	GM de Portugal Ltd.	▲■
Sweden	GM Nordiska AB	▲■
Switzerland	GM Suisse S.A.	▲■

ASIA

Iran	GM Iran Ltd. (40%)	●▲
Japan	GM Allison Japan Ltd. (60%)	▲■
	Isuzu Motors Ltd. (34.2%)	
Korea	GM Korea Co. Ltd. (50%)	
Malaysia	GM Malaysia SB	
Philippines	GM Philippines Mfg. Corp.	
	GM Philippines Inc. (60%)	
Thailand	GM Thailand Ltd.	
	Bangchan General Assembly Co. Ltd. (60%)	

AUSTRALASIA

Australia	GM Holden's Pty. Ltd.	●▲
New Zealand	GM New Zealand Ltd.	▲■

AFRICA

South Africa	GM South Africa (Pty) Ltd.	●▲
Zaire	GM Zaire S.A.R.L.	▲■

FUNCTIONS:

- ▲ Assembly
- ■ Importing
- ● Manufacturing of Complete Vehicles
- ○ Motor Component Manufacturing
- □ Manufacture of Terex Equipment

Source: Gerald T. Bloomfield, *The World Automotive Industry* (Newton Abbot, England: David and Charles, 1978); reproduced by courtesy of Gerald T. Bloomfield and David and Charles (Publishers) Ltd.
Note: The Terex Division, which manufactured off-highway earth-moving equipment, was sold in December 1980 to IBH Holding AG, of Germany.

This list does not include General Motors of Canada, where General Motors was the leading producer, with Ford in second place, just as in the United States. In Germany Opel was in second place, behind Volkswagen, with Ford fourth after Daimler-Benz. In Great Britain Ford was the second largest producer, narrowly behind ailing British Leyland (before the BMC-Leyland merger Ford was first). General Motors' Vauxhall was in fourth place in passenger car output, but its Bedford Truck Division was a strong third in the field of commercial vehicles. Neither Ford nor General Motors had any important position in either France or Italy. Both found discrimination against foreign firms too much to cope with, although General Motors did do some component manufacturing in France. Ford's difficulties in both countries before World War II have been recounted earlier in this chapter; the postwar situation proved no more favorable and finally in 1955 Ford SAF (Societé Anonyme Francaise) was sold to Simca for 15 percent of Simca stock. Three years later the Ford Motor Company sold its Simca holdings to Chrysler. There was a comparable situation in India, where governmental requirements regarding the proportion of Indian-built components that must be incorporated in vehicles assembled there caused both Ford and General Motors to locate their plants elsewhere. Ford had previously assembled cars in India but found the conditions too onerous and withdrew.

In the 1950s and 1960s Chrysler engaged in an ambitious program of expansion abroad. The company began to import Simca cars from France in 1957 and bought control of Simca in 1958. Seven years later Chrysler acquired a majority stock interest in the British Rootes Motors and took complete control two years later; Rootes was a combine that had begun as a sales organization and taken over a miscellany of vehicle manufacturers. It produced one popular model, the Hillman, and a well-known high-priced one, the Humber. Neither purchase added strength to the Chrysler organization. Both Simca and Rootes were in financial trouble, which made the Chrysler acquisition easier but also imposed an additional burden on Chrysler resources. In France Simca had to compete with three bigger rivals, Renault, Peugeot, and Citroën, while in Britain Rootes was overmatched by Ford of Britain, British Motor Corporation (BMC), a merger of Austin and Morris in 1952, and Leyland Motors. A year after the Chrysler purchase of Rootes, BMC and Leyland were merged, under some governmental pressure, as the British Leyland Motors Corporation, Ltd. (now BL), in a not especially happy attempt to create a giant British motor vehicle manufacturer that would be independent of American control. Governmental pressure also caused one of the two main Hillman assembly plants to be located near Paisley, Scotland, in a praiseworthy attempt to develop new industry in an area of high unemployment (a condition exacerbated by chronic work stoppages). Unfortunately for Rootes, and later Chrysler, the major suppliers of automotive parts and components are in the English Midlands, around Birmingham and Coventry, and three fifths of the United Kingdom market for motor vehicles is within a radius of fifty miles from London, so that the Hillman plant in Scotland had to cope with much longer hauls in each direction than its more favorably located competitors.

Chrysler's mounting financial troubles led to the sale of its European properties (in Spain as well as France and Great Britain) to Peugeot. This transaction gave Chrysler a 15 percent interest in Peugeot and $230 million in badly needed cash. There were also Chrysler subsidiaries in Australia and Japan. Both these were sold to Mitsubishi in 1980; Chrysler retained a 35 percent stock interest in the Australian company and received 15 percent of Mitsubishi's stock for Chrysler of Japan.

All of the Big Three companies had subsidiaries in the principal Latin American nations and held a respectable share of the Latin American market in spite of vigorous competition from both Europe and Japan, this share varying from country to country. In 1979 both General Motors and Chrysler withdrew from Argentina, and in the same year Chrysler's financial pressures led it to sell its assembly facilities in Colombia and Venezuela to General Motors.

In the 1970s connections with the Japanese automobile industry became attractive. Attempts to sell American automobiles in Japan did not go well. Part of the reason, perhaps the larger part, lay in restrictive Japanese policies that included high tariffs and elaborate requirements for inspection for safety and emission control that made all imported vehicles prohibitively expensive. In addition, American cars tended to be too big for Japanese use, given among other things a much higher price for gasoline than was the case in the United States.

The obvious way to deal with this situation was to associate with a Japanese automobile firm. The assembly operations that both General Motors and Ford had established in Japan in the 1920s would not suffice because they had long ceased to be important elements in the Japanese automotive industry. General Motors bought a 34 percent interest in Isuzu in 1971, and Ford and Chrysler established working relationships with Toyo Kogyo and Mitsubishi respectively. In fact Ford entered into a three-way relationship with Nissan and Toyo Kogyo in the early 1970s to form the Japanese Automatic Transmission Company, which used some Ford patents. Then in 1979 the Ford Motor Company acquired 25 percent of Toyo Kogyo's stock through a merger with Ford of Japan. None of these relationships was involved with selling American-built motor vehicles in Japan. Isuzu made the Luv pickup truck for Chevrolet and Toyo Kogyo the Courier pickup for Ford. Toyo Kogyo also made transaxles for Ford cars, while Mitsubishi built the Dodge Colt and the Plymouth Arrow, both compacts, for Chrysler as well as engines for the K-cars.

These were quite different relationships from the involvement of the American Big Three in other parts of the world. There they were major producers in the countries in which they operated. In Japan, however, Isuzu was a minor competitor in the Japanese automobile industry, with about 4.5 percent of the total Japanese output. Mitsubishi and Togo Kogyo each had about 10 percent, and the Mitsubishi motor vehicle operation was part of a much larger organization, but both were well behind Toyota and Nissan in automobile production. Ford and Chrysler were drawing on Japanese resources to bolster their position in the United States, rather than using their affiliations to establish themselves in Japan. As a matter of fact, what they were doing was symptomatic of the probable future course of the world automotive industry.

Supranational Industry

The international activities of the American automobile manufacturers display several patterns. The Ford pattern has consisted of planting subsidiaries in other countries under the Ford name. The General Motors pattern, imitated in Europe by Chrysler, has involved buying foreign motor vehicle companies as the means of doing business abroad. The ultimate results appear to have been about the same. Ford of Britain and Fordwerke in Germany have much the same relationship to the parent company as Vauxhall and Opel have to General Motors.

General Motors and the Ford Motor Company were among the earliest of the multinational organizations, and their example was followed by every major participant in the world automotive industry. The multinational company has become a familiar structure in modern business, so that adopting this form was a natural course for an industry with as strong an international character as the manufacturer and sale of motor vehicles. Yet in recent years there have been marked indications that the automotive industry has been moving beyond the conventional multinational form into something that is as yet vaguely defined but can best be described as supranational.

A preliminary example of this trend can be seen in the 1950s, when American Motors had its Metropolitan sports car built by the Austin Motor Company in Birmingham, England. At the time the Nissan Motor Company in Japan, in an attempt to catch up with Western automotive technology, received technical assistance from Austin and licensing to build and sell Austin cars in Japan. These relationships lapsed after a few years and none of the three companies held any stock interest in either of the others, but their association illustrated a kind of international intercompany cooperation other than the customary parent-subsidiary relationship of the conventional multinational.

At the heart of this new development was a trend to concentration that has characterized the automobile industry since at least the 1920s. The American industry came first, with its oligopoly well established by the end of the 1930s and made conclusive in the 1950s. The same pattern has appeared in every major motor vehicle producing nation except one. By the late 1970s British automobile manufacturing was concentrated in British Leyland, Ford, Talbot (Peugeot), and Vauxhall, with a few minor producers of whom the only important one was Rolls-Royce, which has its own specialized market. France had Renault and Peugeot-Citroën-Talbot (ex-Simca). Italy's motor vehicle production had been dominated by Fiat since its founding in 1899; the nearest competitor, Alfa Romeo, had about a fifth of Fiat's output. Fiat bought Lancia, a luxury car manufacturer, in 1969 and for some years had a strong minority stock interest in and gave financial support to Citroën.

The pattern was repeated in Germany where motor vehicle production was concentrated in five firms: Volkswagen, which in its rise to the top had picked up Audi, NSV-Auto Union, and Porsche; Opel; Daimler-Benz; Ford; and BMW. There were no others of any consequence. The exception is Japan. As of 1981 there were nine active competitors in the Japanese automobile industry—Toyota, Nissan, Honda, Toyo Kogyo (Mazda), Mitsubishi, Fuji Heavy Industries (Subaru), Daihatsu, Isuzu, and Suzuki, in that order. Toyota and Nissan between them had 57 percent of the total output, and the next three had another 31 percent. Whether competitive forces will lead to consolidation among this group remains a matter for conjecture. Japan was a very late arrival among major motor vehicle producers, and perhaps the trend to supranational organization could offset the tendency to oligopoly within a single country.

What was happening was that concentration was developing at the international level. Supranationalism derived from the same kind of competitive pressure as had produced oligopoly at the national level. Predictions by qualified observers of the automobile industry, including Giovanni Agnelli, the head of Fiat, and Gerald Meyers, former president of American Motors, agree that by the year 2000 there will be not more than ten or twelve motor vehicle manufacturers in the entire world, with the possible addition of a few specialized producers like Rolls-Royce. Agnelli in fact sees only six companies as certain to survive: Fiat, Ford, General Motors, Nissan, Toyota, and Peugeot. This list seems too limited. Renault and Volkswagen seem in healthy condition and it is inconceivable that the French and German governments would allow them to go out of business. Renault was nationalized after World War II and Volkswagen is 50 percent state-owned. British Leyland is also government-owned and will probably be kept alive; its failure would be an economic catastrophe for Britain.

Such a process of consolidation means that on the international level weaker companies must either consolidate with the stronger or vanish, just as has happened in most national automotive industries, and it must necessarily affect the structure of those industries, including the American. The growing relationship between Renault and American Motors might be regarded as a step in this direction. Each company had something to offer the other. American Motors needed the financial support that Renault could provide; Renault had an automobile (Le Car) aimed at the United States market and American Motors could give it a ready-made sales and service organization as well as facilities for eventually building the vehicle in the United States. In 1982 the association had reached a stage where Renault had close to a 50 percent stock holding in American Motors and was taking an increasing part in management. Renault's relationship with the Mack Truck Company was very similar. It included an agreement on vehicle sales as well as a stock interest. In a way Renault was doing what General Motors and Chrysler had done in Europe, with the difference that neither American company made its acquisitions in order to get an outlet for selling their existing models in Europe.

The Big Three had all been heavily involved in international operations, of course, but as the 1980s approached there were some new features in the nature of the involvement. Chrysler had to give up its European subsidiaries and some others, but it retained a relationship with Peugeot through the financial arrangements whereby Peugeot acquired Chrysler's European properties. Chrysler also had its interest in Mitsubishi of Japan, which made some Chrysler models and for a time marketed its own products in the United States through Chrysler dealers. These affiliations were not in any sense a merger. In fact Mitsubishi decided in 1981 to set up its own marketing system in the United States. Yet a Peugeot-Chrysler or Mitsubishi-Chrysler combination, or even an association of all three, cannot be ruled out as a future possibility. Early in 1981 Mitsubishi was contemplating joint production with Chrysler in the United States.

Such intercorporate relationships were becoming increasingly common under the pressures that operated on the world motor vehicle industry at the beginning of the 1980s. As the decade began General Motors was negotiating with Toyota for possible joint production, specifically for Toyota to operate a shut-down GM assembly plant in California. British Leyland had an agreement to assemble Hondas in the United Kingdom, to be sold under a BL name. Nissan had arranged with Alfa Romeo for joint production in a new assembly plant near Naples, Nissan to provide the basic design, body panels, and suspension, while Alfa Romeo contributed engines and transmissions. Nissan had also acquired a 35 percent interest in Motor Iberica, a major Spanish manufacturer of commercial vehicles. Six European companies (BL, Fiat, Peugeot, Renault, Volkswagen, and Volvo—an impressive collection) had formed a consortium to share long-term research. Where it could be achieved, cooperation was certainly preferable to competition in a period of economic decline, especially when construction of a new automobile assembly plant meant an expenditure of not less than a billion dollars. Given the massive investment required, it was most likely that the incentive to cooperate would continue even after economic conditions improved. The cooperation, it should be noted, did not require corporate merger or even mutual stock interest, although those had a tendency to come after the cooperation had gone into effect.

There was another facet to this growth of internationalization. Mention has been made of how Chrysler and Ford bought parts from their Japanese affiliates, and how Chrysler used Volkswagen engines in some of its small car models. This practice of "out-sourcing" has become commonplace among motor vehicle producers. For them it is essentially a matter of getting their materials and supplies at the lowest cost, and it is by no means limited to American firms. As one example, the Nissan Motor Company purchased some $13 million worth of materials in the United States in 1978 for use in the assembly of Datsun cars in Japan, including catalytic converters, sealed beam headlights, spark relay valves, and upholstery, and these purchases did not include items installed after Datsuns arrived in the United States, such as air conditioners, stereo radios, roof racks for station wagons, and molding and trim.

When the Ford Escort was put on the market in 1980, it was advertised as a "world car." In part this term meant that the vehicle had been designed so that it could be assembled and used in every part of the world, but more emphasis was put on the fact that its design had utilized the talents of engineers from several countries and its materials and components were the best that could be procured from all over the globe. Whatever the validity of these particular claims, the concept of the "world car" definitely foreshadows the motor vehicle of the future and the future course of the motor vehicle industry. The UAW may disapprove of "out-sourcing," and automotive unions elsewhere undoubtedly share this attitude, but union objections to the practice seem futile. The modern automobile and the means of constructing it utilize both increasingly sophisticated technologies and a wider assortment of materials than ever before. No one country, not even the United States, can provide all the

Table 13–2

World Motor Vehicle Production

Year	U.S.	Britain	Canada	France	*Germany	Italy	Japan	Other	Total
1920	2,227,349	N.A.	94,144	40,000	N.A.	21,080	N.A.	N.A.	2,382,573
1930	3,362,820	236,528	153,372	230,000	71,100	46,400	458	32,759	4,133,437
1938	2,508,467	444,877	166,086	227,220	342,169	70,777	24,388	212,339	3,977,303
1950	8,005,859	783,673	387,726	357,552	306,034	127,847	31,597	577,526	10,577,813
1955	9,204,049	1,237,068	452,114	725,061	908,702	268,766	68,932	877,998	13,742,690
1960	7,905,117	1,810,700	397,739	1,369,210	2,055,127	664,633	481,551	1,712,801	16,376,878
1965	11,137,830	2,177,261	846,609	1,641,696	2,976,477	1,175,548	1,875,614	2,710,998	24,542,033
1970	8,283,949	2,098,498	1,159,504	2,750,086	3,842,247	1,854,232	5,289,147	4,388,279	29,665,962
1975	8,986,605	1,648,399	1,424,006	2,861,305	3,186,208	1,458,629	6,941,571	6,753,964	33,262,697
1980	8,009,841	1,312,914	1,374,329	3,378,433	3,878,415	1,611,856	11,042,884	8,033,899	38,642,571

*Figures from 1950 on are for West Germany only.

Source: World Motor Vehicle Data, 1981 (Detroit: Motor Vehicle Manufacturers Association of the United States, Inc., 1981) and *A Guide to the Motor Industry of Japan* (Tokyo: Japan Motor Industrial Federation, 1965).

technical skills or supply all the materials that a motor vehicle manufacturer now needs in order to compete effectively in a market that has come to transcend national boundaries completely. Automobile companies will have to pool their resources on an international scale.

The current situation is comparable to the growth period of the American automobile industry during the development of the mass market in the 1920s. At that time there were numerous small companies making motor vehicles, most of them with local or at best regional markets. Few survived. The companies that survived did so mainly through combinations and mergers that gave them the ability to engage in manufacturing and marketing on a national scale. The Ford Motor Company was the conspicuous exception, achieving national stature entirely on its own. As automobile ownership and use have grown in other parts of the world, the same forces have come to operate on a global scale. Table 13–2 shows how world motor vehicle production changed over a sixty-year period.

CHAPTER FOURTEEN
Summary and Conclusion

As the United States entered the decade of the 1980s the future of its motor vehicle industry was uncertain. It was fairly easy, in fact, to find the opinion expressed that the industry had no future, but this opinion stemmed either from wishful thinking, from the anti-automobile and general antitechnology body of opinion that had emerged in some quarters during the 1960s and 1970s, or from simple ignorance. The American automobile industry was neither dead nor dying; it was undeniably facing serious problems, but the odds were strongly in favor of its survival and substantial recovery.

Whatever emerged in this situation would be new and represent a distinctive phase in the history of the American automobile industry, certainly not a return to the era when, like Caesar, it could be said to "bestride the narrow world like a Colossus." Its previous phases present an intriguing and on the whole impressive record. At the beginning, when motor vehicle manufacture started, the United States was already an industrial giant, but was somewhat slow to take up this new device. Until the early years of the twentieth century American automotive technology lagged behind European, and a strong case can still be made that most of the innovations in the vehicle itself have continued to be European in origin.

The Era of Growth

Once an American motor vehicle industry got established, however, it rapidly moved into a position of world leadership by concentrating on the techniques of production that would change the motor car from a novelty available only to the wealthy to an item accessible to middle and eventually to low income people. The Americans were not the only ones, and perhaps not even the first,

177

to see this possibility. Two French firms, DeDion and Renault, experimented with low-priced gasoline-powered vehicles around the turn of the century, but the Americans were indisputably the first to turn the prospect into reality. They had an advantage in having a continental-sized market and a society with a generally higher standard of living than existed elsewhere. The evidence is quite convincing that the Europeans who tried to reach a mass market for automobiles in the early part of the twentieth century were blocked by inadequate purchasing power. Even as late as the 1930s Germany could plan for a "People's Car" only under government sponsorship. Nevertheless, even if the opportunity was more favorable in the United States, it was still necessary for someone to see it and be willing to accept the risks involved in exploiting it.

The American motor vehicle manufacturers gave to the world not only the techniques for mass production of a complex piece of machinery, but also for the mass marketing that was a necessary concomitant and for the managerial organization required to control the giant enterprises that had to emerge, mass production on a small scale being a contradiction in terms. It has even been argued that the industrial world unwittingly moved into an inescapable impasse; the assembly lines made products available to masses of people on a scale and at a price-level unprecedented in all history, but once the assembly lines start to roll, the economic and social cost of stopping them becomes insupportable. This aspect of mass production was dramatically brought to public attention in recent years when both British Leyland and Chrysler were faced with bankruptcy and their respective governments had to step in to avert the economic disaster that would have ensued.

This problem was not a consideration when Ford, Durant, Sloan, and Chrysler were giving the United States its long domination of world motor vehicle manufacturing. Then and afterward motor vehicle manufacturing has been regarded in the United States and elsewhere as a major economic asset, and it was well after mid-century before there was any serious question about the desirability of the products. There was concern about the traffic congestion created by growing numbers of automobiles and still more concern about the mounting human and economic toll of highway accidents, but it was assumed that these problems could be solved by improved systems of traffic control, better designed and better built roads and streets, and more rigorous qualifications and training for drivers. Against these difficulties was the overmastering fact that the automobile offered cheap and convenient transportation, providing freedom of movement for ordinary people on a scale never before attained. To quantify the achievement, by 1929 there were enough passenger automobiles in the United States to carry the country's entire population at once. During rush hours in large cities and on summer Sunday afternoons, many motorists must have felt that this was actually being done.

The rise of the American automobile industry to its position of supremacy required more than technological skill and a favorable market situation. These could not have produced this result by themselves; a high degree of entrepreneurial boldness and managerial talent was also necessary. It was a high risk industry and still is, but for those who were willing to take the risks and could provide the needed organizational and managerial talent, the achievements and the rewards were great. Henry Ford and Billy Durant had entrepreneurial boldness. Neither showed any great administrative ability, but in the formative years of the Ford Motor Company Henry Ford had an outstanding business manager in James S. Couzens and other conspicuously able assistants in Knudsen, Wills, Sorensen, and Flanders. Durant had equivalent talent at his disposal in Nash, Chrysler, and Sloan, but conspicuously failed to use it. Chrysler was also an entrepreneur willing to take risks and he had expert financial management in B. F. Hutchinson, treasurer of the Chrysler Corporation. Alfred P. Sloan was a great industrial statesman, who provided a model of organization and management for large-scale enterprise. Roy D. Chapin was a brilliant business leader, while John N. Willys, who succeeded as an entrepreneur, lacked Sloan's ability to organize a large enterprise.

The decline of United States domination of the world automotive industry does not necessarily imply a lessening of managerial skill. It was not a decline in the productivity of the American industry but rather an inevitable catching up by the rest of the world. With the formation of the European Common Market in the 1950s European motor vehicle manufacturers for the first time enjoyed a market area comparable in size to what the Americans had enjoyed from the beginning, and Western Europe attained the levels of automobile production, ownership, and use that the United States and Canada had reached thirty years earlier. Japan arrived at this stage still later, stimulated by rising living standards, the construction of a modern highway system, and successful penetration of export markets. Moreover, the maturing of the United States automobile industry meant that its managerial problems became those of keeping established concerns going rather than building new enterprises, a less spectacular if no less difficult operation and one that called for somewhat different kinds of managerial talent.

There have been great automotive executives in the years since World War II: George Romney, Ernest Breech, and "Engine Charlie" Wilson will do as examples, perhaps along with Lee Iacocca, the former Ford president who took on the task of saving the Chrysler Corporation from extinction. Yet it is

Table 14–1

Motor Vehicle Production in the United States, 1900–80

	Passenger Cars	Trucks and Buses	Total
1900	4,192	N.A.	4,192
1901	7,000	N.A.	7,000
1902	9,000	N.A.	9,000
1903	11,235	N.A.	11,235
1904	22,130	700	22,235
1905	24,250	750	25,000
1906	33,200	800	34,000
1907	43,000	1,000	44,000
1908	63,500	1,500	65,000
1909	123,990	3,297	127,287
1910	181,000	6,000	187,000
1911	199,319	10,681	210,000
1912	356,000	22,000	378,000
1913	461,500	23,500	485,000
1914	548,139	24,900	573,039
1915	895,930	74,000	969,930
1916	1,525,578	92,130	1,617,708
1917	1,745,792	128,157	1,873,949
1918	943,436	227,250	1,170,686
1919	1,651,625	224,731	1,876,356
1920	1,905,560	321,789	2,227,349
1921	1,468,067	148,052	1,616,119
1922	2,274,185	269,991	2,544,176
1923	3,624,717	409,295	4,034,012
1924	3,185,881	416,659	3,602,540
1925	3,735,171	530,659	4,265,830
1926	3,692,317	608,617	4,300,934
1927	2,936,533	464,793	3,401,326
1928	3,775,417	583,342	4,358,759
1929	4,455,178	881,909	5,337,087
1930	2,787,456	575,364	3,362,820
1931	1,948,964	432,262	2,280,426
1932	1,103,557	228,803	1,331,860
1933	1,560,599	329,218	1,889,817
1934	2,160,865	576,205	2,737,070

Table 14–1

Motor Vehicle Production in the United States, 1900–80

	Passenger Cars	Trucks and Buses	Total
1935	3,273,874	697,367	3,362,820
1936	3,679,242	782,220	4,461,462
1937	3,929,203	891,016	4,820,219
1938	2,019,566	488,841	2,508,407
1939	2,888,512	700,377	3,588,889
1940	3,717,385	745,901	4,840,502
1941	3,779,682	1,060,820	4,840,502
1942	222,862	818,662	1,041,524
1943	139	699,689	699,828
1944	610	737,524	738,134
1945	69,532	655,683	725,215
1946	2,148,699	940,866	3,089,565
1947	3,558,178	1,239,443	4,797,621
1948	3,909,270	1,376,274	5,285,544
1949	5,119,466	1,134,185	6,273,651
1950	6,665,863	1,337,193	8,003,056
1951	5,338,435	1,426,828	6,765,263
1952	4,320,794	1,218,165	5,285,544
1953	6,116,948	1,206,266	7,323,314
1954	5,558,897	1,042,174	6,601,071
1955	7,950,377	1,253,672	9,204,049
1956	5,806,756	1,112,002	6,918,758
1957	6,120,029	1,100,402	7,220,431
1958	4,247,427	873,842	5,121,269
1959	5,599,492	1,124,096	6,723,588
1960	6,703,108	1,202,011	7,905,119
1961	5,522,019	1,130,919	6,652,938
1962	6,943,334	1,253,977	8,197,311
1963	7,644,377	1,464,399	9,108,776
1964	7,745,492	1,562,368	9,307,860
1965	9,335,227	1,802,603	11,137,830
1966	8,604,712	1,791,586	10,396,298
1967	7,142,659	1,611,077	9,023,736
1968	8,848,620	1,971,790	10,820,410
1969	8,224,392	1,981,519	10,205,911

Table 14–1

Motor Vehicle Production in the United States, 1900–80

	Passenger Cars	Trucks and Buses	Total
1970	6,550,128	1,733,821	8,283,949
1971	8,583,653	2,088,001	10,671,654
1972	8,828,205	2,482,503	11,310,708
1973	9,667,152	3,014,361	12,681,513
1974	7,324,504	2,746,538	10,071,042
1975	6,716,951	2,269,562	8,986,513
1976	8,497,893	2,999,703	11,487,596
1977	9,213,654	3,489,128	12,702,782
1978	9,176,635	3,722,567	12,899,202
1979	8,433,662	3,046,331	11,479,993
1980	6,375,506	1,634,335	8,009,841

Source: Motor Vehicle Manufacturers Association of the United States, Inc.

impossible to avoid the feeling that something has been lost since the days of Henry Ford and Alfred P. Sloan. The zest of the Ford Motor Company's rebirth appears to have faded, although there has been no reversion to the chaos of the elder Henry Ford's later years. The Chrysler Corporation has suffered from unwise and overambitious expansion as well as from misjudgments in design and the introduction of new models. General Motors, the leading power in the industry, has been inept and insensitive in its public relations.

Emerging Problems

One can sympathize with the plight of the leaders of the American automobile industry in the years since 1960. They were facing novel conditions for which their training and experience had not prepared them. They had made their careers in the industry that had been termed "capitalism's favorite child"; now it and its products were under vociferous criticism, charged with responsibility for atmospheric pollution, the decline of inter- and intracity public transportation, traffic congestion, the decay of central cities, and failure to promote highway safety or conservation of energy. The critics were a minority and they had no visible effect on the purchase and use of motor vehicles, but they were vocal and influential enough to secure a considerable body of restrictive legislation, something that automobile executives were unaccustomed to. In addition, government agencies at all levels were trying to promote the revival and expansion of mass transportation, principally rail, with the avowed purpose of reducing the use of motor vehicles. Most of these efforts were concerned with urban transportation, in the hope of reducing traffic on city streets and promoting the recovery of central city areas, but there also was a strong movement to restore intercity rail passenger traffic.

Along with these problems came the petroleum crisis. It was not only that oil prices rose and that Americans turned to smaller cars than they had previously preferred; the motor vehicle industry along with the rest of the nation had to face the alarming fact that the United States had become dependent on foreign sources for its all-important supply of oil. It is not at all surprising that executives, whose main preoccupations had hitherto been with production, sales, and labor relations, and whose basic indoctrination had been short-term profit maximization, should have been bewildered by the problems they were now called upon to solve, or that they should have made some mistakes in responding to them.

Yet Detroit's response to this new situation was more effective than has generally been recognized. The point needs to be reiterated that the American motor vehicle manufacturers did not ignore small cars. They had experimented with them shortly after World War II and found little public interest. In the ensuing thirty years small foreign cars and domestic compacts made their way onto the market in respectable numbers, but without appreciably dislodging the larger vehicles that American buyers seemed to prefer. A large proportion of the purchasers of small passenger automobiles bought them as second cars, with the family's primary reliance continuing to be a high-powered eight-cylinder model. Thus United States automobile management had ample grounds for continuing to "think big." They had what appeared to be adequate reason for believing that the change to smaller cars could be gradual, and the great size of the Big Three companies undoubtedly made for a considerable amount of organizational inertia.

By contrast, the European and Japanese competitors who appeared on the American scene were oriented toward small motor vehicles. In their countries petroleum has to be imported (the development of North Sea oil has been very recent and benefits only a few countries) and is taxed considerably more highly than in the United States. The cars themselves are also taxed more heavily, so that passenger automobiles intended for more than an exclusive luxury market have had to be designed for maximum economy. When these companies began to compete in the United States motor vehicle market, they were smaller and more adaptable than the long-established American producers, and they, at any rate the most successful of them, were very much "on the make" where their American rivals tended to be complacent, a state of mind that their long domination of the world automotive scene was calculated to induce.

The complacency was severely shaken by the dramatic upheaval in the market for passenger automobiles that occurred in 1979 and the prolonged downswing in the economy that ensued. It has generally been overlooked that the American automobile firms were not the only ones to suffer from the change in consumer choices. European firms that had put their hopes on mid-sized passenger cars (British Leyland, Peugeot, Mercedes-Benz) were hard hit also. Indeed, if the problem had simply been to switch production from large to small cars, American automotive management was quite competent to do so quickly and efficiently. The suddenness of the change hurt, but by the end of 1980 the Big Three were prepared to meet the competition in the small car field. Had the economy revived as it was expected to at that time, they would have been in good shape to take advantage of the upswing.

Allowing for the fact that the slump in the economy was longer and deeper than anything the United States had experienced since the Great Depression of the 1930s, this was a situation that the leaders of the automobile industry understood. They may have been slow to react, but once they realized that action was required, they responded. They redesigned their product lines and they reexamined their sales techniques. In 1982 Chrysler was even tampering with the near-sacrosanct exclusive dealer franchise system by encouraging dealers in other makes to sell Chrysler products as well. Because of the prolonged recession results were slow to materialize, but there was one encouraging indication in the fact that in the otherwise gloomy year of 1981 sales of American-made pickup trucks rose and regained some of the ground that had been lost to the Japanese.

The Prospect

The outlook of the United States automobile industry for the 1980s and beyond disclosed promising features. The recession at the beginning of the decade adversely affected sales of new cars, but like its predecessor of fifty years before, it had a minor impact on the ownership and use of motor vehicles. Nor did the increased emphasis on mass transportation appear to pose a threat to the automobile. Urban rail transit systems proved reasonably popular and Amtrak, the federally-supported rail passenger service, showed a steady increase in patronage, but the effect upon the volume of traffic on the highways was negligible. Surveys of new rail rapid transit systems have been quite uniform in showing that their patrons have largely been people who previously rode buses. There is an irreducible minimum of patrons of public transportation, composed of those people who because of age, infirmity, or economic status are unable to own or drive automobiles.

For the majority, however, there is the incontestable fact that no form of public transportation, existing or in prospect, can compete with the private automobile in economy or convenience. Public transportation can replace travel by car only if it can offer the same sort of flexibility in schedule and door-to-door convenience and do it at lower cost. It is significant that the most acceptable method to date of reducing automobile usage for commuting has been through car and van pooling.

The allegation that the United States has entered a "postautomotive" era is unconvincing, and the rest of the world certainly has not. Americans show no disposition to give up their cars and would undoubtedly do so only in response to a drastic economic change or under a degree of compulsion unacceptable in American society as it is now constituted. Yet the motor vehicle itself and the conditions under which it will be used will certainly change, and these are matters which of necessity will be of profound concern to the industry. Motor vehicles will continue to be closely regulated for exhaust emission, safety, and fuel economy, and there is a strong possibility that large cities might be driven to impose restrictions on automobile use at peak hours and in congested areas. This would not constitute an innovation. Ancient Rome had severe traffic congestion and tried to relieve it by allowing wheeled vehicles to enter the city only at night. A more recent example was the "diamond lane" experiment in Los Angeles, whereby one freeway lane was restricted to vehicles carrying three people or more. It was a promising idea, but it was imposed so arbitrarily that it aroused intense public antagonism and had to be abandoned, although the system still operates on a separate bus lane on the San Bernardino Freeway. That seems to have been acceptable because the bus lane was specially built to be reserved and had not been usable for ordinary traffic. Nationwide, the diversion of highway tax revenues to support mass transportation has been accompanied by a deterioration in the country's highway network, and this may eventually affect motor vehicle usage.

At longer range the industry must plan for the motor vehicle of the future. It is certain that there will be changes, but uncertain just what they will be. Some prospects such as air-cushion vehicles and fuel-cell power plants can be disregarded as being too far in the future for practical consideration. More immediate possibilities, such as electric and steam power, also seem out of the running. In spite of intensive recent experimentation with the electric car by General Motors, there is no evidence that the limitations of the battery are about to be overcome, although this is a field where a technological breakthrough is always possible. William Lear, manufacturer of the Learjet and other aircraft, tried to develop improved steam automobiles as a remedy for atmospheric pollution, but he had to give up because he was unable to keep the manufacturing cost at a level that would make the vehicle reasonably competitive, and the same difficulty has stopped other promoters of steam cars. Other ideas have been publicized, but they have all so far faced the difficulty that it is one thing to devise a novel technology but quite another to adapt it to mass production and everyday use.

For the predictable future most motor vehicles will continue to be powered by some form of the internal combustion engine: the conventional gasoline or diesel piston engine or perhaps a gas turbine, which is also an internal combustion engine. Changes in fuels are a likely prospect, because the world's supply of petroleum is finite. There is more to be found, but it is in locations where getting the oil will be very costly, so that the price of conventional automotive fuels is bound to rise. Some vehicles are already equipped to burn propane, but problems of safety have so far made it impractical for ordinary passenger cars. There has been some experimentation and much talk about gasohol, a mixture of gasoline and alcohol, which so far has been handicapped by high cost and limited production facilities, plus the fact that the alcohol is made from grain, and using the grain for this purpose depletes the world's food supply. There has also been serious consideration of "synthetic" fuels, which are not synthetic at all but are derived from coal, shale rock, and tar sands. All three are plentiful in North America, but the processes for extracting oil are very expensive and present serious environmental problems.

To sum up, in the 1980s the United States motor vehicle industry had reached a stage at which the ability to produce and sell that had given it its world leadership was no longer sufficient to maintain its position. Its management must now make allowance for political factors, regulating and perhaps restricting the production and use of motor vehicles, for possible change in social acceptance of the automobile, although any such change would probably develop very slowly, and for environmental concerns. The industry must also try to anticipate the direction that automotive technology will take in the design and production of vehicles. Computerization and robotization can be taken for granted; they are already here.

This situation does not apply to the automotive industry alone. It is something that all American industry has to face. The interrelationships between business and government have become increasingly complex, and may be expected to remain so. The place of industry in American society and what is expected of large business organizations have been subtly changing, not necessarily for the worse, although criticism of industry and technology has been more vociferous than it used to be. This is not the anticapitalist criticism of the Marxists, which has never found any appreciable following in the United States and which approves of industry and technology as long as they are state-owned and controlled. It is an emotional, nihilistic attitude that chooses to blame science, technology, and industry for what it sees as the ills of modern life. It is not really a novel attitude. C. P. Snow in his famous essay, *The Two Cultures and the Scientific Revolution* (1959) pointed out that this kind of hostility to industrialism existed among what he termed the "literary intellectuals" since the beginning of the Industrial Revolution; he saw it as resentment of something that these critics do not understand. His explanation remains valid.

These new and unfamiliar conditions pose as great a challenge to the American motor vehicle industry as it faced when it undertook to change the horseless carriage from a rich man's toy to an article of general use. In its period of growth the industry found leaders of impressive stature. They took great risks and at times they made great mistakes, but together they produced an economic revolution and transformed American society. The industry needs to find the same quality of leadership to deal with the problems that lie ahead for it—the same quality but not necessarily the same qualities, because the problems are of a different character and considerably more complex than those that the industry faced in its years of growth, indeed through the first two thirds of the twentieth century.

It is probably unfair to compare the present generation of automotive management with the founders of the industry, because pioneering has a glamour that cannot be duplicated, and humanity seems always ready to believe that there was a past Golden Age when "in those days—the giants were on earth." Present-day motor vehicle executives have a quite different range of problems to deal with than did their predecessors; in addition, their companies have become so big that the individual is ordinarily overshadowed by the organization. Yet with all due allowance for these changed circumstances, the leadership of the United States automobile industry since about 1960 has given an appearance of mediocrity. There has been a noticeable absence of outstanding figures, and management in general has responded slowly and reluctantly to the new issues that confronted it: pollution, safety, the energy crisis, import competition. The patent lack of innovation may be ascribed to the inertia of large organizations that do not have vigorous leadership. It is noticeable that American Motors, the smallest of the United States automobile manufacturers, took the lead in introducing compacts. To repeat what has already been said, the management of the automobile industry could not possibly have foreseen the abrupt change in consumer choices that occurred in the spring of 1979, and it was moving toward a greater emphasis on small cars, under the pressure of import competition and government mandated standards of fuel economy. Although the 1979 crisis could not have been averted, more foresighted leadership might have reduced its impact by taking a long-range view of the probable inevitable increases in the cost of automotive fuels. In summary, the management of the American motor vehicle industry between the late 1940s and the beginning of the 1980s was not as bad as it is alleged to have been, but it could definitely have been better than it was.

The American motor vehicle industry has a great past. It has a future for as far ahead as it is possible to judge, but whether its future will match what has gone before depends on whether it can produce the kind of bold and imaginative leadership that made it great in the first place. The motor vehicle has an established place in American life, but to keep that place requires its manufacturers to be alert and responsive not just to economic trends but to political problems, social and cultural influences, environmental consideration, and technological developments. This is a formidable but not impossible task. If it can be accomplished, the American automobile industry may again come to be looked on as "quintessentially American."

BIBLIOGRAPHICAL ESSAY

The literature on the American motor vehicle industry is extensive and of widely varied quality. There are works by automobile buffs and by antique car enthusiasts (the two are not quite synonymous), public relations blurbs, and books by dedicated and uncritical admirers of the automobile and by equally dedicated and uncritical foes. They all have some historical value as long as their limitations are recognized and understood. Surprisingly, in view of the important effects that the industry has had on the economy and on society, the number of serious scholarly studies is remarkably small.

Among the few comprehensive historical studies the most recent is James M. Laux et al., *The Automobile Revolution* (1982). It is a worldwide study, originally published in France, so that the coverage of the American automotive industry, while sound, is necessarily limited. One of my books, *The American Automobile* (1965), carries the story into the early 1960s. Merrill Denison, *The Power to Go* (1956), is a little earlier. It is mixed in quality, strongest on the history of commercial vehicles. *Automobiles of America* (1968), published by the Automobile (now Motor Vehicle) Manufacturers Association, is a very valuable compendium of facts.

The motor vehicle industry in the United States will reach its centennial during the 1990s. A complete history of the industry, done by qualified scholars (it would have to be a cooperative operation) and with full support from the individual companies, would be an appropriate observance.

Chapter 1
Prelude

The development of motorized road vehicles appears in most of the standard histories of engineering and technology, notably Charles Singer et al., *A History of Technology*, vol. 5 (1958), T. K. Derry and Trevor I. Williams, *A Short History of Technology*

(1960), and Melvin Kranzberg and Carroll Pursell, eds., *Technology in Western Civilization,* 2 vols. (1967). Eugen Diesel, Gustav Goldbeck, and Friedrich Schildberger, *From Engines to Autos* (1960), describe the inventions of the Otto four-cycle engine, the Daimler and Benz cars, and the diesel engine. The focus of historical attention has naturally been the gasoline powered vehicle. Steam cars have received some attention, the best work on the subject being C. St. C. B. Davison, *History of Steam Road Vehicles* (1953), a product of the Science Museum in South Kensington, London. On the American side, Charles C. McLaughlin, "The Stanley Steamer: An Experiment in Unsuccessful Innovation," in *Explorations in Entrepreneurial History,* vol. 7 (1956), is a penetrating study of the best-known of American steam automobiles. For some reason the history of the electric automobile in the United States has been virtually ignored by scholars. A. T. Willson, *The First Hundred Years: Baker Raulang* (1953), is a company history of a firm that made electric cars in Cleveland, Ohio; otherwise there are only scattered references. A good historical study would be very timely in view of the strong interest there is in the possibility of reviving electric power for motor vehicles.

Chapters 2 and 3
The Pioneering Years

For the early days of the automobile industry James J. Flink, *America Adopts the Automobile, 1895–1910,* is the indispensable authority. It is a brilliant exposition of the coming of the motor vehicle to the United States, the founding of the industry, and the steps whereby the automobile made its place in American society, including the establishment of service facilities, the formation of automobile clubs, the problems of legislative controls, and the kind of people who bought cars at the beginning.

This period has been well covered both by scholars and by the antique car enthusiasts—the latter have unearthed much factual information that would otherwise have remained buried. There are several substantial works that take the history of the industry from its beginning until the 1930s: E. D. Kennedy, *The Automobile Industry* (1941)—he calls the industry "capitalism's favorite child"; C. B. Glasscock, *The Gasoline Age* (1937); and my *American Automobile Manufacturers: The First Forty Years* (1959). A recent study of the industry's initial years is George S. May, *A Most Unique Machine: The Michigan Origins of the American Automobile Industry* (1975). It is a thorough, detailed work that does much to explain why Michigan became the center of the industry. May has also written *R. E. Olds: Auto Industry Pioneer* (1977), which provides insights on this important automotive pioneer that explains why he became a "might-have-been." Another view of Olds is in Glenn A. Niemeyer, *The Automotive Career of Ransom E. Olds* (1965), the first scholarly work to examine the place of Olds in the history of the automotive industry. Hiram Percy Maxim, *Horseless Carriage Days* (1937), is a delightful autobiographical account of the beginning of the automobile industry in New England. Charles B. King, *A Golden Anniversary, 1895–1945* (1946), is a brief autobiography of another pioneer, and Winton's career is summarized in William G. Keener, "Ohio's Pioneer Auto Maker: Alexander Winton," *Museum Echoes* 28 (1955). *The Pope Manufacturing Company: An Industrial Achievement* (1907), published by the company just as it was going under, is the only reasonably complete account of the Pope enterprise. A new study of the company would be useful, as would full-length biographies of both Pope and Winton.

Even more valuable would be a biography of Henry M. Leland by an author with training in both business history and the history of technology. *Master of Precision: Henry M. Leland* (1966), by Ottilie M. (Mrs. Wilfred L.) Leland, his daughter-in-law, and Minnie D. Millbrook, has the advantage of full access to family papers, but Leland should have a biographer outside his immediate family. His contributions to the growth of the American motor vehicle industry have never been fully appreciated.

Chapter 4
Mass Production

The best general accounts of the development of mass production are Christy Borth, *Masters of Mass Production* (1950), Roger Burlingame, *Backgrounds of Power* (1949), and Siegfried Giedion, *Mechanization Takes Command* (1969). They are definitive for the period covered in this chapter; however, they were all written just before the introduction of automation into the automobile industry, and of course well before robotics. Those stories have still to be told.

Henry Ford and the Ford Motor Company have been written about exhaustively. The authoritative work is the massive company-sponsored study supervised by the great American historian Allan Nevins. The first two volumes cover the period of the Ford rise and ascendancy: Allan Nevins, *Ford: the Times, the Man, the Company* (1954), and Allan Nevins and Frank E. Hill, *Ford: Expansion and Challenge, 1915–1932* (1957). An excellent short biography is Roger Burlingame, *Henry Ford: A Great Life in Brief* (1955). Keith Sward, *The Legend of Henry Ford* (1948), should be read by anyone interested in the Ford story. It effectively counters the idealization of Henry Ford that his admirers had created. Anne Jardim, *The First Henry Ford: A Study in Personality and Business Leadership* (1970), is an attempt at a psychological approach that is not quite convincing.

John K. Galbraith, *The Liberal Hour* (1960), offers a persuasive argument that Ford was very good at taking credit for other people's achievements and that his company's spectacular rise was largely due to the business skill of James S. Couzens. Reynold M. Wik, *Henry Ford and Grass Roots America* (1972), is especially illuminating on the effect of the Model T and the Fordson tractor on farm life and on the admiration that Henry Ford aroused among farmers. David L. Lewis, *The Public Image of Henry Ford*

(1976), shows the facts and legends that grew up around him. No other individual in the automotive industry throughout the world has attracted such universal notice or become such a figure of legend.

Charles E. Sorensen, *My Forty Years with Ford* (1956), unwittingly makes it clear why he was called "Cast-iron Charlie," but he lets us see the Ford Motor Company from the inside and has useful insights on the development of the Model T and the introduction of the moving assembly line. A reinterpretation of the Five Dollar Day and the work of the Ford Sociological Department is presented in Stephen Mayer III, *The Five Dollar Day: Labor Management and Social Control in the Ford Motor Company, 1906–1921* (1981). A somewhat different point of view appears in R. L. Bruckberger, *Image of America* (1959), where the Five Dollar Day is hailed as a beneficial and far-reaching social revolution.

The most complete account of the Selden Patent case is William L. Greenleaf, *Monopoly on Wheels* (1961), which is part of the Nevins project on Ford. I have taken a more favorable view of Selden and the ALAM in *American Automobile Manufacturers*. The classic contemporary description of the introduction of the moving assembly line by Horace Arnold and Fay Faurote, *Ford Methods and the Ford Shops*, was reissued in 1973. It remains the best account of the impression made on the engineering profession by this innovation.

Chapter 5
Industrial Organization

Two books by Alfred D. Chandler, Jr., are fundamental to this subject, especially the Sloan organization of General Motors: *Strategy and Structure: Chapters in the History of the Business Enterprise* (1963) and *Giant Enterprise: Ford, General Motors, and The Automobile Industry* (1966). These should be supplemented by Paul F. Douglas, *Six Upon the World* (1954), and Peter F. Drucker, *The Concept of the Corporation* (1946), each providing its own analysis of the significance of the General Motors organization.

The last history of General Motors was Arthur Pound, *The Turning Wheel* (1934), a good book written to observe the company's twenty-fifth anniversary. The long lapse since then has been partially, perhaps largely, due to the company's sensitivity to anti-trust suits, which makes it reluctant to make any of its records available to scholars. An up-to-date history would be an important work. Studebaker has two histories: Stephen Longstreet, *A Century on Wheels: The Story of Studebaker* (1952), a centennial volume, and Kathleen A. Smallzried and Dorothy J. Roberts, *More Than You Promise* (1942), which concentrates on the Studebaker family. Both display an unfounded optimism and tend to gloss over the company's disaster in the early 1930s.

Biographies of the leading figures in the organization of the motor vehicle industry are surprisingly scarce. Durant has only recently come into his own in two fine books: Lawrence R. Gustin, *Billy Durant: Creator of General Motors* (1973), and Bernard A. Weisberger, *The Dream Maker: William C. Durant Founder of General Motors* (1979). There is no biography of Sloan, and there certainly ought to be. He has two autobiographies: *Adventures of a White Collar Man*, in collaboration with Boyden Sparks (1941), and *My Years with General Motors* (1964). The latter has an illuminating account of Sloan's reorganization of the company but is otherwise disappointing.

There are no biographies of Benjamin Briscoe or John N. Willys, nor is there any history of United States Motor, Briscoe's attempt to rival Durant. Since this organization became Maxwell and eventually Chrysler, it deserves more recognition. In the history of business—indeed, in all history—there are just as important lessons to be learned from the failures as from the successes.

Chapter 6
The Coming of Mass Consumption

Much of the information in this chapter comes from books already listed, but there are also two very valuable contemporary works: Ralph C. Epstein, *The Automobile Industry* (1928), and Lawrence H. Seltzer, *Financial History of the American Automobile Industry* (1928). Even an important event like the rise of Chrysler has to be studied in general histories of the automotive industry. Walter Chrysler has an autobiography written in collaboration with Boyden Sparks, *Life of an American Workman* (1937), but he would appear to deserve a good biography. The history of the Chrysler Corporation has still to be written; when and if it is done, it should include Maxwell and the other predecessor companies.

The story of the independents has also been overlooked by historians. There are, as previously mentioned, two Studebaker histories, but they could be improved on. For the Hudson Motor Car Company there is only J. C. Long, *Roy D. Chapin* (1945), an official biography of good quality. There is nothing on Nash, Packard, or Willys-Overland, although they would all be attractive subjects for study. The White Motor Company, as the major independent producer of commercial vehicles, offers a potentially profitable field for research, as do Mack, for many years almost a synonym for "heavy truck," and such firms as Marmon and Graham-Paige.

In the area of marketing, the emergence and growth of the problems of dealer relations are well covered in Stewart Macaulay, *Law and the Balance of Power: The Automobile Manufacturers and Their Dealers* (1966), and B. P. Pashigian, *The Distribution of Automobiles: An Economic Analysis of the Franchise System* (1961). Dealer complaints in the 1930s led to an investigation of the automobile industry by the Federal Trade Commission, published in 1939 under the title *Report on the Motor Vehicle Industry*. It is a gold mine of factual data, unfortunately written in pedantic governmentese. Almost every paragraph begins "It is said that—," as if the writer or writers were unwilling to be committed to a positive statement, even when they were recounting well-established facts.

There is a biography of Kettering, *Professional Amateur: The Biography of Charles F. Kettering* (1957), written by one of his close associates, Thomas A. Boyd. An excellent modern scholarly study is Stuart W. Leslie, *Boss Kettering: Wizard of General Motors* (1983).

Chapters 7 and 8
Depression and War

The history of the New Deal has been written about extensively. Every description of the state of the economy has of necessity included the motor vehicle industry, which was by this time in effect the main determinant of the nation's economic condition, and the rise of organized labor, including the United Automobile Workers. Much of this literature has been and continues to be strongly partisan, but it is possible to get a reasonably accurate picture of the situation.

For the motor vehicle industry itself the third volume of the Nevins and Hill series, *Ford: Decline and Rebirth, 1933–1962* (1962), gives a good description of the state of the industry as a whole as well as a detailed account of what happened to the Ford Motor Company. Sidney Fine, *The Automobile Under the Blue Eagle* (1963) and *Sit-Down: The General Motors Strike in 1936–1937* (1969), does remarkably well in untangling the complexities of New Deal labor policy, intraunion rivalries, and the rise of the UAW. Eli Chinoy, *Automobile Workers and the American Dream* (1955), is an original approach to the problems and attitudes of assembly-line workers. There are also Frank Cormier and William J. Eaton, *Reuther* (1970), and Robert MacDonald, *Collective Bargaining in the Automobile Industry* (1963), both of them informative.

Much of the information on the automotive industry in World War II comes from *Freedom's Arsenal,* published by the Automobile Manufacturers Association in 1950. It is not really a history, but a compilation of documents, speeches, and factual data illustrating the work of the Automotive Council on War Production. The Ford contribution is told in the Nevins and Hill volume just referred to and in Sorensen's autobiography. Part of the General Motors story is told in a company publication, *History of the Eastern Aircraft Division* (1944).

Other information comes from histories of the aircraft industry. Particularly recommended are Irving B. Holley, Jr., *Buying Aircraft: Material Procurement of the Army Air Forces: The United States Army in World War II* (1964) and *Ideas and Weapons* (1953). The war production problem was the final part of William S. Knudsen's long career. He has one biography, Norman Beasley, *Knudsen* (1947). He could well have another in the light of all the material that has been forthcoming since then, and a scholarly study of the automotive industry's part in military production should now be feasible.

Chapter 9
The Triumph of Bigness

For the quarter century after World War II there are two excellent studies of the American automobile industry, both by economists. Charles E. Edwards, *The Dynamics of the United States Automobile Industry* (1965), is particularly informative on the American Motors and Studebaker-Packard mergers, although he saw their prospects in a somewhat more favorable light than they actually warranted. Lawrence J. White, *The Automobile Industry Since 1945* (1971), is comprehensive and perceptive. The author suggests breaking up the Big Three into ten independent companies as a means of encouraging freer entry into the industry—this was before the crisis of the early 1980s. The topic of entry is also the theme of Harold C. Vatter, "Closure of Entry in the American Automobile Industry," in *Oxford Economic Papers* (1952). It is particularly valuable as an analysis of the Kaiser-Frazer venture.

The rehabilitation of the Ford Motor Company is described in detail by Nevins and Hill in their third volume, and also by Booton Herndon, *Ford: An Unconventional Biography of the Men and Their Times* (1967). This book is principally a biography of Henry Ford II, but it also describes Henry, Sr., and Edsel, along with a number of the men who helped Henry II to rebuild the company, including the "Whiz Kids."

Chapter 10
The Rise of the Small Car

The history of foreign car competition in the United States market for motor vehicles has still to be written and probably cannot be written for some time to come, since the process is still ongoing. The one comprehensive survey is in my *Nissan Datsun: A History of Nissan Motor Corporation in U.S.A., 1960–1980* (1982), a twentieth anniversary commemoration which was written, at the company's request, to relate the growth of Nissan in the United States to the context of the overall development of the import car business. There are two histories of European companies: Walter H. Nelson, *Small Wonder: The Amazing Story of the Volkswagen (1961)*, and Michael Sedgwick, *Fiat* (1974). Both are useful as far as they go, but much has happened to the Volkswagen since 1960. Toyota has a twentieth anniversary booklet, *Toyota: The First Twenty*

Years in the U.S.A. (1977), but it is very much a slick-paper, public relations production, of limited value as history.

There has been less on the history of American-built small cars. Trade publications and business periodicals remain the principal sources of information and analysis on this subject. Edwards's *Dynamics of the United States Automobile Industry* (1965), is the last systematic study of American Motors, although since the book was published the company has changed markedly. George Romney's contributions to the motor vehicle industry in general and American Motors in particular, most of all his pioneering with compact cars, make him an obvious candidate for a good biography, but none has so far appeared.

Chapter 11
The Government and the Automobile Industry

The growth of governmental controls in the motor vehicle industry is likewise too recent a development to have generated very much in the way of historical study. The long-term issues of dealer relations have been very well analyzed in the works already referred to, Macaulay, *Law and the Balance of Power* and Pashigian, *The Distribution of Automobiles.* There seems little to add in this area, unless some indications of possible relaxation on the exclusive franchise system should prove to be harbingers of a major change. For the regulations regarding pollution, safety, and energy, information has to be drawn from newspapers, periodicals, government reports, and so on.

Two annual publications are especially useful for this purpose: *Motor Vehicle Facts and Figures,* put out by the Motor Vehicle Manufacturers Association, and *Ward's Automotive Yearbook,* published by Ward's Communications, Detroit. There is at least one substantial book to be written on this subject, and the time is getting ripe for doing it.

Chapter 12
The Industry in Turmoil

This is also a topic for which details are still scattered through newspapers, periodicals, trade journals, and other references. There are two books with a bearing on it. One is J. Patrick Wright, *On a Clear Day You Can See General Motors* (1979). This is the story of John DeLorean, a one-time G.M. executive who finally left to become a management consultant and tried to produce a high-priced automobile in Northern Ireland. This venture hit the recession of the early 1980s and failed. DeLorean is very unflattering about the management of General Motors. The other is William J. Abernathy, *The Productivity Dilemma: Roadblock to Innovation in the Automobile Industry* (1975), which is a dispassionate, scholarly study of the complexities of introducing innovations into a mass production operation. Reading it will generate more understanding of and sympathy for the alleged shortcomings with which American motor vehicle management has been charged.

In addition, there is now work being done on the economic, social, and cultural effects of the motor vehicle that suggests more questioning of the automobile's desirability than there used to be. James J. Flink, *The Car Culture* (1979), is a fine study that sees a lessening of "automobility." Emma Rothschild, *Paradise Lost: Decline of the Auto-Industrial Age* (1973), is an obituary of the motor vehicle industry that seems somewhat premature.

There is also interesting work being done on the influence of the automobile in specific situations, particularly urban life. One outstanding example is Mark S. Foster, *From Streetcar to Superhighway* (1981). It demolishes the notion held in some quarters that the motor vehicle was an unwelcome intruder on the streets of American cities and that it drove out a superior form of transportation.

A penetrating analysis of the motor vehicle industry's problems in the 1970s is William Tucker, "The Wreck of the Auto Industry," *Harper's Magazine,* October 1980, pp. 45–60.

Chapter 13
The International Industry

The international aspect of the American motor vehicle industry has received some substantive treatment. *The Automobile Revolution,* cited at the beginning of this bibliographical essay, has some description of the foreign operations of the American manufacturers. Even better is Gerald T. Bloomfield, *The World Automotive Industry* (1978), which has the unique feature of having been written by an eminent geographer, so that it offers a perspective not found in strictly historical works. *World Motor Vehicle Data,* published annually by the Motor Vehicle Manufacturers Association of the United States, is a complete collection of facts.

The Nevins project on the Ford Motor Company produced a volume on Ford's foreign operations, Myra Wilkins and Frank E. Hill, *American Business Abroad: Ford on Six Continents* (1964). It has the high quality of the rest of the series. In his *My Years with General Motors,* Alfred P. Sloan explains the reasons for the purchase of Vauxhall and Opel, but other than that there is no history of General Motors' foreign operations anymore than there is of its domestic operations. The Chrysler history is equally blank; its European ventures may well be something the Chrysler Corporation would prefer to forget. It is still much too early for a history of American Motors' association with Renault, but it will make an interesting story in due time.

The emergence of what I have chosen to call "supranationalism" is much too recent for historical study. Whether the world motor vehicle industry actually will develop farther in this direction or not is still speculative, but in either case there will be an important topic for historical research.

Chapter 14
Conclusion

The opinions expressed in this chapter are entirely my own. To assist in formulating them I have considered the ideas of others whose knowledge and judgment I respect, and I have used such factual data as is available about the condition and prospects of the United States motor vehicle industry as it faces the 1980s and after. These references have largely been listed already.

On the outlook for the industry several articles have proved helpful: James A. Mateyka and Leonard Sherman, "The American Automobile: Facing up to Its Consumer," and T. Arthur Shields, "The Automotive Industry: A New Crossroads," *Outlook,* Summer 1980; and Kathleen K. Wiegner, "Down But Very Far From Out," *Forbes,* 18 September 1978. The 1981 edition of *Motor Vehicle Facts and Figures* has a detailed description of steps that the industry took to meet its crisis.

SELECTED BIBLIOGRAPHY

Abernathy, William J. *The Productivity Dilemma: Roadblock to Innovation in the Automobile Industry.* Baltimore: Johns Hopkins University Press, 1978.

Arnold, Horace, and Faurote, Fay. *Ford Methods and the Ford Shops.* 1915. Reprint. New York; Arno Press, 1973.

Automobile Manufacturers Association. *Automobiles of America.* Detroit: Wayne State University Press, 1968.

AMA. *Freedom's Arsenal.* Detroit: AMA, 1950.

Beasley, Norman. *Kundsen: A Biography.* New York: McGraw-Hill Book Co., 1945.

Bloomfield, Gerald T. *The World Automotive Industry.* Newton Abbott, England: David and Charles, 1978.

Borth, Christy. *Masters of Mass Production.* Indianapolis: Bobbs-Merrill Co., 1945.

Boyd, Thomas A. *Professional Amateur: The Biography of Charles F. Kettering.* New York: Dutton, 1957.

Bruckberger, R. L. *Image of America.* New York: Viking Press, 1959.

Burlingame, Roger. *Backgrounds of Power.* New York: Charles Scribner's Sons, 1949.

Chandler, Alfred D., Jr. *Giant Enterprise: Ford General Motors, and the Automobile Industry.* New York: Harcourt Brace and World, 1964.

————. *Strategy and Structure: Chapters in the History of the Industrial Enterprise.* Cambridge, Mass.: MIT Press, 1962.

Chinoy, Gilbert. *Automobile Workers and the American Dream.* Garden City, N.Y.: Doubleday and Co., 1955.

Chrysler, Walter, with Boyden Sparks. *Life of an American Workman.* Philadelphia: Curtiss Publishing Co., 1938.

Cormier, Frank and Eaton, William J. *Reuther.* Englewood Cliffs, N.J.: Prentice-Hall, 1970.

Davison, C. St. C. B. *History of Steam Road Vehicles.* London: Science Museum, 1953.

Denison, Merrill. *The Power to Go.* Garden City, N.Y.: Doubleday and Co., 1956.

Diesel, Eugen, Goldbeck, Gustav, and Schildberger, Friedrich. *From Engines to Autos.* Chicago: Henry Regnery and Co., 1960.

Douglass, Paul F. *Six Upon the World*. Boston: Little, Brown and Co., 1954.

Drucker, Peter F. *The Concept of the Corporation*. New York: John Day., 1946.

Edwards, Charles E. *Dynamics of the United States Automobile Industry*. Columbia, S.C.: University of South Carolina Press, 1965.

Epstein, Ralph C. *The Automobile Industry*. Chicago: A. W. Shaw Co., 1928.

Federal Trade Commission. *Report on the Motor Vehicle Industry*. Washington, D.C.: Government Printing Office, 1939.

Fine, Sidney. *The Automobile Under the Blue Eagle*. Ann Arbor: University of Michigan Press, 1963.

———. *Sit-Down: The General Motors Strike in 1936–1937*, Ann Arbor: University of Michigan Press, 1969.

Flink, James J. *America Adopts the Automobile*. Cambridge, Mass.: MIT Press, 1970.

———. *The Car Culture*. Cambridge, Mass.: MIT Press, 1975.

Foster, Mark S. *From Streetcar to Superhighway*. Philadelphia: Temple University Press, 1981.

Galbraith, John K. *The Liberal Hour*. Boston: Houghton Mifflin, 1960.

Giedion, Siegfried. *Mechanization Takes Command*. New York: Oxford University Press, 1948.

Glasscock, C. B. *The Gasoline Age*. Indianapolis: Bobbs-Merrill Co., 1937.

Greenleaf, William C. *Monopoly on Wheels*. Detroit: Wayne University Press, 1961.

Gustin, Lawrence R. *Billy Durant: Creator of General Motors*. Grand Rapids, Mich.: Wm. B. Eerdmans Publishing Co.

Herndon, Booton, *Ford: An Unconventional Biography of the Men and Their Times*. New York: Weybright and Talley, 1969.

Holley, Irving B., Jr. *Buying Aircraft: Material Procurement for the Army Air Forces: The United States Army in World War II*. Special Studies, no. 7. Washington, D.C.: Government Printing Office, 1964.

Jardim, Anne. *The First Henry Ford: A Study in Personality and Business Leadership*. Cambridge, Mass.: MIT Press, 1970.

Kennedy, E. D. *The Automobile Industry*. New York: Reynal and Hitchcock, 1941.

Laux, James M., Bardou, Jean-Pierre, Chanaron, Jean-Jacques, and Fridenson, Patrick. *The Automobile Revolution: The Impact of an Industry*. Translated by James M. Laux. Chapel Hill: University of North Carolina Press, 1982.

Leland, Ottilie M., and Millbrook, M. D. *Master of Precision: Henry M. Leland*. Detroit: Wayne State University Press, 1966.

Leslie, Stuart W., *Boss Kettering: Wizard of General Motors*. New York: Columbia University Press, 1983.

Lewis, David L. *The Public Image of Henry Ford*. Detroit: Wayne State University Press, 1976.

Longstreet, Stephen D. *A Century on Wheels: The Story of Studebaker*. New York: Henry Holt and Co., 1952.

Macaulay, Stewart. *Law and the Balance of Power: The Automobile Manufacturers and Their Dealers*. New York: Russell Sage Foundation, 1966.

MacDonald, Robert. *Collective Bargaining in the Automobile Industry*. New Haven: Yale University Press, 1963.

Maxim, Hiram Percy. *Horseless Carriage Days.* New York: Harper, 1937.

May, George S. *A Most Unique Machine: The Michigan Origins of the American Automobile Industry.* Grand Rapids, Mich.: Wm. B. Eerdmans Publishing Co., 1975.

―――. *R. E. Olds: Auto Industry Pioneer.* Grand Rapids, Mich.: Wm. B. Eerdmans Publishing Co., 1977.

McLaughlin, Charles C. "The Stanley Steamer: A Study in Unsuccessful Innovation." *Explorations in Entrepreneurial History* 7 (October 1954).

Meyer, Stephen III. *The Five Dollar Day: Labor Management and Social Control in the Ford Motor Company, 1908–1921.* Albany: State University of New York Press, 1981.

Nevins, Allan, and Hill, Frank E. *Ford: The Times, the Man, the Company.* New York: Charles Scribner's Sons, 1954.

―――. *Ford: Expansion and Challenge, 1915–1932.* New York: Charles Scribner's Sons, 1957.

―――. *Ford: Decline and Rebirth, 1933–1962.* New York: Charles Scribner's Sons, 1962.

Niemeyer, Glenn E. *The Automotive Career of Ransom E. Olds.* East Lansing: Michigan State University Press, 1963.

Pashigian, B. P. *The Distribution of Automobiles: An Economic Analysis of the Franchise System.* Cambridge, Mass.: MIT Press, 1961.

Pound, Arthur. *The Turning Wheel: The Story of General Motors Through Twenty-Five Years, 1908–1933.* Garden City, N.Y.: Doubleday, Doran, 1934.

Rae, John B. *The American Automobile: A Brief History.* Chicago: University of Chicago Press, 1965.

―――. *American Automobile Manufacturers: The First Forty Years.* Philadelphia: Chilton Company, 1959.

―――. *Nissan/Datsun: A History of Nissan Motor Corporation in U.S.A., 1960–1980.* New York: McGraw-Hill Book, 1982.

―――. *The Road and the Car in American Life.* Cambridge, Mass.: MIT Press, 1971.

Rothschild, Emma. *Paradise Lost: The Decline of the Auto-Industrial Age.* New York: Random House, 1973.

Sedgwick, Michael. *Fiat.* New York: Arco, 1974.

Seltzer, Lawrence H. *A Financial History of the American Automobile Industry.* Boston: Houghton Mifflin, 1928.

Sloan, Alfred P., Jr., with Boyden Sparks. *Adventures of a White Collar Man.* New York 1941.

―――. *My Years with General Motors.* Garden City, N.Y.: Doubleday, 1964.

Sorensen, Charles E. *My Forty Years with Ford.* New York: Rinehart, 1948.

Sward, Keith. *The Legend of Henry Ford.* New York: Rinehart, 1948.

Vatter, Harold G. "Closure of Entry in the American Automobile Industry." *Oxford Economic Papers,* n.s. 4 (October 1952).

Weisberger, Bernard A. *The Dream Maker: William C. Durant, Founder of General Motors.* Boston: Little, Brown and Co., 1979.

White, Lawrence J. *The Automobile Industry Since 1945.* Cambridge, Mass.: Harvard University Press, 1971.

Wik, Reynold M. *Henry Ford and Grass Roots America.* Ann Arbor: University of Michigan Press, 1972.

Wilkins, Myra, and Hill, Frank E. *American Business Abroad: Ford on Six Continents.* Detroit: Wayne State University Press, 1964.

White, J. Patrick. *On a Clear Day You Can See General Motors.* Chicago: Wright Enterprises, 1979.

203

ABOUT THE AUTHOR

Born in Glasgow, Scotland, in 1911, John Bell Rae emigrated with his parents to Providence, Rhode Island, in 1923. He received his undergraduate and graduate degrees from Brown University and subsequently went from a faculty appointment at Massachusetts Institute of Technology to become professor of history at Harvey Mudd College in 1959. John Rae began his research in the history of technology and specifically a lifelong interest in automotive history while he was associated with the Research Center for Entrepreneurial History at Harvard from 1953 to 1959. His principal publications related to automotive history are *American Automobile Manufacturers: The First Forty Years* (1959); *The American Automobile* (1968); *Climb to Greatness: The American Aircraft Industry, 1920–1960; Henry Ford: A Great Life Observed* (1969); *The Road and the Car in American Life* (1971); *Nissan/Datsun: A History of Nissan Motor Corporation in the U.S.A., 1950–1980* (1982).